RD LOAN

Literary Theory at Work: Three Texts

Literary Theory at Work: Three Texts

edited by Douglas Tallack

for
The University of Nottingham Critical Theory Group

B T Batsford Ltd. *London*

© Douglas Tallack 1987

First published 1987
Reprinted 1991

Typeset by Progress Typesetting Ltd
and printed in Great Britain by
Billing & Son Ltd, Worcester
Published by B. T. Batsford Ltd
4 Fitzhardinge Street, London W1H OAH

British Library Cataloguing in Publication Data

Literary theory at work: three texts.
    1. Criticism—Case studies 2. English literature—History and criticism I.
    Tallack, Douglas II. University of Nottingham. *Critical Theory Group*
    820'.9   PN81

ISBN 0–7134–5139–4
ISBN 0–7134–5140–8 Pbk

14/10/91

Contents

→ actually refer to
the passage we are
doing !

Contributors

The contributors are part of the Critical Theory Group at the University of Nottingham. This group of staff and postgraduates from a number of Arts departments first met in the late seventies in order to keep up to date with developments in criticism. The Critical Theory Group now teaches an M.A. course and provides supervision for research degrees, as well as running a programme of seminars and guest lectures. Amongst its recent activities have been commissions at two conferences of the National Association for the Teaching of English and a special issue of *Renaissance and Modern Studies*.

Diana Knight teaches courses on the nineteenth-century novel and narrative theory in the French Department. She is writing a book on Roland Barthes.

Bernard McGuirk is in the Hispanic Studies department. He teaches and does research in Latin American literature, modern French poetry and critical theory.

Steve Giles is in the German department, where he teaches modern literature, thought and politics. He is researching into Marxism and culture in the early years of the Weimar Republic.

Anne Jones is writing a Ph.D. on critical theory and the Spanish American short story in the Hispanic Studies department. She has taught at Nottingham and Southampton Universities, Trent Polytechnic, and the British Institute, Seville.

Roger Poole teaches courses on modern literature and Freud in the English Studies department. He is writing a book on Modernism.

David Murray is in the American Studies department. He teaches and does research in modern American poetry and North American Indian texts.

Elaine Millard teaches English and Communication Studies at Bilborough Sixth Form College and has recently completed an M.A. in Critical Theory.

Douglas Tallack teaches intellectual and cultural history and social theory in the American Studies department. He is writing a book on twentieth-century American thought and culture.

Steve Smith is a postgraduate in Critical Theory. He is writing a Ph.D. on contemporary Marxist and post-structuralist theory and teaches part-time in the departments of French and Hispanic Studies.

Introduction
Douglas Tallack

Literary Theory at Work is addressed to those students and teachers who want critical theory to give them a grasp upon a literary text. This pragmatic aim does not, however, dilute theory and all the contributors would insist that theory is most illuminating and most radical, even most subversive, when dealing with a literary text. Moreover, existing forms of practical criticism and various literature-and-life approaches may be theoretically full of holes but have still to be rigorously contested where they continue to have influence: in the routine teaching, study and examination of literary texts.

Judging from publications, conferences and occasional newspaper reports, too many students and teachers of literature are now aware of developments in criticism for literature and theory to be kept apart. Consequently, it is important for this collection to address a widely acknowledged but perhaps misunderstood problem: the division in literary studies which leaves many teachers, in secondary and in higher education, stranded between two camps. On the one hand, a stubborn traditionalism ensures a regular supply of students for literature courses but, too often, reinforces the very climate of anti-intellectualism which threatens the humanities and social sciences. On the other hand, a theoretical avant-garde is perceived as so busy with its own battles that application to texts is barely on the agenda or is shunned as a sign of the institutionalizing of theory. For their part, students – and not just those in higher education – experience the often alarming gap between the seminar room and pure theory at first hand but usually without access to the debate and have, somehow, to make adjustments. It is in an attempt to break down this divide that these essays offer practical answers to the question, Can theory be integrated into the standard pattern of literature teaching and study?

Challenging the traditional ways of reading texts can only have benefits, not least in that it might encourage their advocates to argue a case, instead of assuming it to be patently obvious that criticism begins with the author or the autonomous text or a social and historical context. The critical tradition could even re-emerge as a good deal more interesting and less monolithic than it sometimes appears. Challenging theory by judging it in terms of its pay-off also brings benefits – as each essay in this collection seeks to demonstrate – but it also risks distortion. Difficulty is not common sense (or nonsense) in disguise. Still, the (very slight) risks of institutionalizing theory are worth taking if the oppositions which critical theory directly questions are not to be reinstated by that between theory and practice. Although – to take the most extreme instance – it is often claimed that deconstruction cannot be taught, texts *can* be deconstructed and it is only by doing so that we can scrutinize the relationship between the assumed generality of theory and the specificity of criticism. Similarly, if it is objected that a systematic trying-out of theory could become so engrossing that the politics of theory and literature teaching are marginalized, then it can be argued that these questions will become more engrossing and more mind-numbing the longer theory stays out of the ruck of reading texts in seminar rooms.

In this connection it is worth recalling that the opposition between theory and application is not of the making of the theorists represented in this collection. Contributors draw significantly upon practical applications of theories in the work of Genette, Todorov, Millett, Barthes, Bakhtin, Lukács, and Macherey, while *reading* (literature in some cases) is hardly peripheral to the work of Freud and Derrida, and even Lacan on one famous occasion. Behind the title, *Literary Theory at Work*, is William James's claim that theory is less 'a solution . . . than . . . a program for more work'. If some of the theoretical positions adopted in this book sit uneasily with an unabashed pragmatism, it is at least fair to assume that no theory and no interest in theory arises in a vacuum in the first place.

For these reasons *Literary Theory at Work* is openly written to a format: nine essays (each applying a particular theory) and three literary texts, allowing for three readings of each text. In more ways than one, it is a *text-book*. Theoretical starting points are not assumed or footnoted but are set out in the first section of each essay and returned to in the third section after the application. Space inevitably precludes a full account of a theoretical position but contributors have consistently made use of easily available further reading, in particular: the New Accents series; two or three of Jonathan Culler's very clear accounts of structuralism and its aftermath; and surveys, especially Terry Eagleton's *Literary Theory: An Introduction*, and the companion volume to this one, Ann Jefferson and David Robey's *Modern Literary Theory: A Comparative Introduction*. However, where the work of, say, Barthes, Lacan and Derrida will take only so much concentrated explanation, it is the extension into a detailed application in section two of each essay which offers the best opportunity to grapple with difficult theoretical arguments. Wherever possible, applications maintain a pedagogical angle (as articles written for an academic journal need not) by signposting the stages of a theoretically informed reading of a text. This tactic is also important in so far as it out-argues the inevitable objection that a reading could have been arrived at without the theory. It is important to emphasize that no reading is theory-free.

Theory and practice intersect in different ways, of course. Some contributors question institutional/pedagogical expectations. For instance, the essays by Knight, McGuirk, Smith and Tallack distance themselves from standard notions of explicating a text. Some contributors, notably Giles and Murray, see no point in joining existing critical debates about a text but, instead, offer ways in which we can engage with it. In contrast, Millard, Jones and Tallack find it necessary for their different purposes to work against and/or within prior readings. There are also important variations in the concluding sections of the essays. McGuirk, Giles and Poole consider how applying the theory exposes it to further *theoretical* questioning (rather than simple evaluation), while the introduction of a literary-historical perspective in Murray's conclusion broadens the scope of an otherwise concentrated application.

The straightforward format of each essay extends to the overall organization of the book. However, putting theory on the line in individual essays written by members of a teaching and research group at one institution has some interesting spin-offs, particularly when the collection is considered as a whole. Each essay has been written and is presented in close proximity not simply to two other, and perhaps competing, readings of the same literary text but also a number of conflicting and/or complementary theories. The implicit and explicit cross-references convey some sense of the crowded arena in which contemporary criticism is written, and this could not have been achieved in a book written by a single author in which different approaches are tried out. Commitment to a theory would suffer in the attempt to provide a balanced overview, and it may be preferable to opt for commitment, as in Terry Eagleton's *Re-Reading Literature* series. Amongst books dealing solely with theories the same problem occurs. It is quite possible to read through the latest survey, Raman Selden's *A Reader's Guide to Contemporary Literary Theory* (1985), or even the New Accents series, and come away with the impression of literary theory as a unified, if very agitated body of thought in which individual theories coexist in the eclectic global institution satirized by David Lodge in *Small World*. At the literary conference near the end of that novel a panel, consisting of a structuralist, a marxist, a deconstructionist, a reader-response theorist and a liberal humanist, is thrown into confusion when a speaker from the floor asks each one 'What follows if everybody agrees with you?'. When the essays in this collection were tried out in seminars and circulated amongst the contributors a question of this sort did not arise, not because it did not occur to anyone but because the practice of criticism made it theoretically impossible to take such an unobstructed view from the floor. There were helpful local agreements on what would be attempted in a feminist reading of *St Mawr*, or a deconstruction of *In the Cage*, and suggestions were made as to what an Althusserian reading of *Heart of Darkness* would look like. Such advice from contributors and from other members of the wider Critical Theory Group at Nottingham has found its way into the essays and improved them. But practical advice on application was accompanied by serious, even irreconcilable, differences of principle. These manifested themselves not in splendid isolation from criticism, as is often assumed, but in the process of doing it.

This introduction is certainly not a voice from the floor, but the relationship between the essays – for example the three on *St Mawr* – warrants further comment before it is left to the reader. The essays by Poole, Millard and Giles are undoubtedly readings of the same text and, by being collected in the same book, they coexist and perhaps will strike some readers as equally convincing. But if I baldly summarize the principles at stake in each essay (drawing closely on the contributors' own statements), I can at least ask the simple question which draws theory and criticism together: Do choices need to be made between readings and, if so, on what grounds?

For Roger Poole, there are 'events' in an author's mind that are independent of relations of production and political and historical circumstances. To write on Lawrence, in particular, and indirectly on Modernism is to insist on the truth of this position. Moreover, it is the reason why a psychoanalytical reading that brings together Freud and Lacan comes closest to explaining how *St Mawr* came to be this way and not another way.

Steve Giles's reading could not be more different. From Lukács' standpoint, the presuppositions which *St Mawr* works with can certainly be characterized as broadly psychological – and that is what is wrong with the text. *St Mawr* concentrates on the psychological and interpersonal, instead of the socio-economic. Yet it is by taking full account of the form and style of the text that the socio-economic base can be identified, and Lawrence, *St Mawr* and Modernism located historically.

It is precisely Elaine Millard's point that the disagreements between the other two readings of *St Mawr* ignore gender differences. It is particularly significant that simply to make this case stick in an application, she has to appropriate a methodology from Barthes's *S/Z* and modify it so as to unsettle structures of reading. 'Reading as a woman' questions explanatory models of history (Giles) and the psyche (Poole).

It is equally interesting to speculate why readings applying the theories of Genette, Bakhtin, and Althusser and Macherey to *Heart of Darkness* should not collide in the way that the readings of *St Mawr* do. Or, to ask whether a 'sexual politics' reading of *In the Cage* differs from structuralist and post-structuralist readings of the same text for reasons that identify it closely with the other explicitly feminist reading in the collection. This cautious attempt to fill the gaps between the essays suggests the value of preserving more of the approach work and even the 'stutters' of literary theory that are left in the seminar room in the wake of the authoritative reading which gets into print.

Although the critical issues raised by this collection are far-reaching, decisions about the contents were practical. We included theories and texts which we have worked with and which work in seminars. We learned, especially, from trying out some of the approaches through a commission at the Nottingham conference of the National Association for the Teaching of English. As we point out in the article based on that conference and upon which we have drawn for this book (*English in Education*, Summer 1986), the remarkable degree of interest in, and knowledge about, the theories we presented at NATE indicates that teachers in higher education are merely fuelling their own preconceptions by restricting critical theory to selected students in their own institutions.

The nine theories we eventually included are broadly representative of contemporary critical theory. They also represent some of the key theoretical debates, for example between structuralism and post-structuralism and between an earlier and later marxist criticism. Approaches that we could not cover in a separate essay are, to some degree, incorporated in other ways. For instance, the principle, if not the methods, of reader-response theory is built into Millard's essay. We chose theories before literary texts but applied no consistent rationale for matching them. It seemed an interesting test to see what an approach derived from Kate Millett could make of a Henry James text, rather than one by D. H. Lawrence. In the case of a psychoanalytical approach, *St Mawr* was so obvious it seemed worth trying again, with the help of Lacan as well as Freud.

For reasons stated in the opening paragraphs, we chose authors with a recognized status. While critical theory challenges the notion of 'literature', and the canon is at least being questioned in a range of theoretical studies as well as in publishing ventures, the texts of such as Conrad, James and Lawrence are there to be read, and may have to be read. All three appear on English (and American) literature syllabuses in secondary and higher education, including the Open University's course on the novel. James and Conrad are part of F. R. Leavis's 'Great Tradition' and Lawrence was, in effect, later added to it in a separate book. The three texts chosen were written within thirty years of each other and count as Modernist texts. As it happens, in some of the essays Modernism connects directly with theoretical debates, both between figures represented in this book and between them and traditional critics of literature. Having said all this it would be easy to find at least as many justifications for a completely different trio of authors, to say nothing of choices drawn from other genres. One justification is of particular importance to the use of the collection, however, and that is the availability of the literary texts in paperback editions. *Heart of Darkness, In the Cage* and *St Mawr* are short enough to read or re-read alongside this collection but long enough to have relevance to the novels which are the focus of most theory and criticism of fiction.

In the introduction to *Modern Literary Theory*, Ann Jefferson and David Robey seem to anticipate the need for the practical focus provided by *Literary Theory at Work*:

> We have been stressing the connections between literary theory and critical practice, and although we shall keep this connection particularly in mind in the rest of the book, we must make it clear that it is not a matter we have pursued in great detail in our discussion of individual theories.

The two collections do complement each other. Ironically, though, the detailed attention given here to literary texts questions the conclusion reached by Jefferson and Robey:

> The machinery of theory cannot be wheeled on as a substitute for criticism, which alone is capable of picking up the nuances and the particular idiom of the work of a given writer. With the current debate about the status and value of literary theory, it is perhaps worth stressing that we are not suggesting that theory should ever replace criticism.

Further comment is left to the nine essays that follow.

1 Structuralism I: Narratology
Joseph Conrad, *Heart of Darkness*

Diana Knight

I

Gérard Genette's *Narrative Discourse* (1972) is both a classic text of French structuralism and the central point of reference for all studies in the literary domain of narratology.[1] Structuralism introduced into the study of literature a set of concepts and a new vocabulary by which its object – perhaps narrative or a genre in general, perhaps a specific literary work – would be first decomposed and then recomposed into an abstract model intended to show up how it worked. This involved a crucial shift of interest away from the interpretation of individual texts, for the structuralist was interested less in what a text means than in how it means, that is to say in how the literary system makes particular literary meanings possible in the first place.

The wider context was an enthusiastic belief that all cultural practices were similarly open to analysis of their underlying methods and ideological values. Indeed the philosophical and political implications of the structuralist ethos were developed into a polemical stance:

> Structuralism scandalized the literary Establishment with its neglect of the individual, its clinical approach to the mysteries of literature, and its clear incompatibility with common sense. The fact that structuralism offends common sense has always been a point in its favour. Common sense holds that things generally have only one meaning and that this meaning is usually obvious, inscribed on the faces of the objects we encounter. The world is pretty much as we perceive it, and our way of perceiving it is the natural, self-evident one. . . . Thinkers who have argued that the apparent meaning is not necessarily the real one have usually been met with scorn: Copernicus was followed by Marx, who claimed that the true significance of social

processes went on 'behind the backs' of individual agents, and after Marx Freud argued that the real meanings of our words and actions were quite imperceptible to the conscious mind. Structuralism is the modern inheritor of the belief that reality, and our experience of it, are discontinuous with each other; as such, it threatens the ideological security of those who wish the world to be within their control, to carry its singular meaning on its face and to yield it up to them in the unblemished mirror of their language. . . . it exposes the shocking truth that even our most intimate experience is the effect of a structure.[2]

Not only was the notion of lived experience under attack, but it was no longer possible to take language itself as its unproblematic vehicle. By siding with Ferdinand de Saussure in the long debate over the 'origins' of language, structuralism found in this turn-of-the-century linguist the ready-made tools with which to take apart the tautologous rhetoric of an anti-intellectual world-view.[3] If it is true that language is a purely arbitrary system, and that the meaning of a given word in use depends upon a shifting system of implicit differences – from other sounds and from other concepts also circulating in the system – then the notion of naturally founded, self-contained meanings is at best a naive illusion and at worst a dangerous deceit. The coining of barbaric and slightly ridiculous neologisms, so often attacked by irritated detractors of structuralism, draws deliberate attention to this central theoretical issue. For accusations of over-use of 'jargon' necessarily depend upon normalizing notions of what constitutes 'clear' language. This policing of the linguistic terrain was famously denounced by Roland Barthes as a politically motivated defence of class-bound speech patterns. These may have become naturalized as the obvious way to speak or write, but they are actually no more natural or jargon-free than any other. Barthes's claim to 'prefer jargon to clichés' serves as a reminder that tampering with language is an important part of the attempt to undermine received views of the world, and to unmask literature as an artificial system of ideologically determined meanings.[4]

Though Genette's narratology may seem a harmless enough activity, it is certainly a product of the polemical context sketched so far. Genette focuses his structuralist attack on what he had called, in 1966, the falsely naive question 'why narrative?':

If we agree, following convention, to confine ourselves to the domain of literary expression, we will define narrative without difficulty as the representation of an event or sequence of events, real or fictitious, by means of language and, more particularly, by means of written language. This positive (and current) definition has the merit of being simple and self-evident; its principal drawback may be precisely that it confines itself and confines us to self-evidence, that it conceals from us what specifically, in the very being of narrative, constitutes a problem and a difficulty, by effacing as it were the frontiers of its operation, the conditions of its existence. To define narrative positively is to give credence, perhaps dangerously, to the idea or feeling that narrative *goes without saying*, that nothing is more natural than to tell a story or to put together a set of actions in a myth, a tale, an epic, or a novel.[5]

In *Narrative Discourse*, Genette sets out to interfere with the unthinking consumption of literary story telling. To do this he develops his own version of the linguistic model so important to structuralism. His basic idea is that narrative action – to be derived like every other aspect of the system from the words on the page – could usefully be considered as the expansion of a verb: Ulysses returns to Ithaca, Marlow follows Kurtz up the Congo, etc. He therefore formulates the relations between events and their telling via categories derived from the grammar of the verb, namely *tense* (narrative time: order, pace and frequency), *mood* (forms and degrees of representation: dramatic or narrative mode, direct or indirect speech reporting, focalization), and *voice* (active or passive relation of the narrating subject with his own story: levels of embedded narration, absence or presence of narrator in narrated story world). Though Genette suggests that his adaptation of the grammar of the verb is largely metaphorical, to take it literally is to operate a 'making strange' effect whereby the recalcitrant self evidence of narrative is undermined. Narrative is necessarily verbal, both through its linguistic representation of the actions or states that constitute its subject matter, and through the very act of narration that founds it as narrative in the first place. Like Molière's Monsieur Jourdain who is amazed to discover that he speaks in prose, all narrators, whatever the sophistication of their narrative, have necessary if implicit recourse to verbal choices. These choices are perhaps analogous, in degree of consciousness, to those facing someone speaking or writing in a foreign language – which past tense here? does that take the subjunctive? isn't that an active verb in French? The fact that various areas of the verb function differently in different languages serves to underline that no verbal choice, and hence no narrative one, ever 'goes without saying'.

The importance of *Narrative Discourse* depends on Genette's decision to bring together a potentially arid 'system' and one of the most sophisticated and challenging novels in the French canon: Marcel Proust's *A la recherche du temps perdu*. The choice of object-text was a provocative gamble – the point being that Genette produces a brilliant reading of Proust not despite but because of his narratological approach. What Genette wants to demonstrate is that Proust's singular and extraordinary text is made possible by its unique exploitation of the perfectly ordinary features of narrative upon which every fictional writer is obliged to draw. Yet neither in theory nor in practice does Genette seek to undermine the 'genius' flavour of Proust's work: 'The specificity of Proustian narrative taken as a whole is *irreducible*, and any extrapolation would be a mistake in method; the *Recherche* illustrates only itself. But, on the other hand, that specificity is not *undecomposable*' (pp. 22–3). At the same time Genette confronts head-on the problem of the relationship between his project of building a general system of narrative possibilities, and his more specific critical account of an individual work. *Narrative Discourse* is born of the clash between criticism and theory, and will make no attempt to subordinate one to the other:

> I must therefore recognize that by seeking the specific I find the universal, and that by wishing to put theory at the service of criticism I put criticism, against my will, at the service of theory. This is the paradox of every poetics, and doubtless of every other activity of knowledge as well: always torn between these two unavoidable commonplaces – that there are no objects except particular ones and no science except of the general – but always finding comfort and something like attraction in this other, slightly less widespread truth, that the general is at the heart of the particular, and therefore (contrary to the common preconception) the knowable is at the heart of the mysterious. (p. 23)

Genette's *tour de force* in combining the general and the particular in his essay justifies this rather dizzying claim that the mystery of literature is a knowable category, and that complex narrative strategies may well be its very secret.

Since practice is clearly an integral part of Genette's theory, I have chosen to illustrate its impact with a brief extract from his reading of Proust (pp. 41–3). Genette is comparing the chronological order of the narration of events with that of the supposed real story. The chosen passage concerns the confused reaction to the Dreyfus Affair of the character Swann, who is Jewish. Genette focuses upon the enormous and rapid leaps forwards and backwards (from an initial point) in the narrator's account and discussion of Swann's behaviour. A typical example of Proust's convoluted and image-ridden prose is staked out by Genette with letters of the alphabet from (A) to (O), with each letter identifying a temporal shift. From his point of entry into the represented story time – 1898 – Genette finds that his fifteen shifts move between nine different chronological positions, ranging back to the 1870 war and forward to the 1914–18 war. The combination and hierarchical subordination of temporal positions are illustrated by Genette by means of an algebraic formula:

$$A4[B3][C5-D6(E3)F6(G3)(H1)(I7<J3><K8(L2<M9>)>)N6]O4.$$

To follow through Genette's analysis is to become very aware of the astonishing zigzagging in time at the microcosmic level of Proust's novel, even at points where the main story-line unfolds in a more or less linear manner:

> Besides, even if he approved of all the attempts to secure a fresh trial, he did not wish to be mixed up in any way in the antimilitarist campaign. He wore, (G) a thing he had never done previously, the decoration (H) he had won as a young militiaman, in 70, (I) and added a codicil to his will asking that, (J) contrary to his previous dispositions, (K) he might be buried with the military honours due to his rank as Chevalier of the Legion of Honour. A request which assembled around the church of Combray a whole squadron of (L) those troopers over whose fate Françoise used to weep in days gone by, when she envisaged (M) the prospect of a war. (N) In short, Swann refused to sign Bloch's circular. (pp. 41–2)

Despite all the critical ink spilled over Proust's philosophy of time and memory, this basic yet rather extraordinary feature of the narrative organization of time seems simply not to have been noticed. To read Proust after Genette is necessarily to read with a constant awareness of the novel's narrative 'game with time', a game which, according to Genette, perhaps subsumes its better-known themes of time.[6]

The potentially discordant clash between systems and aesthetic appeal is foregrounded by Genette himself. For example, in his chapter on frequency he analyses a very 'written' descriptive passage in which the narrator describes in poetic detail the changing light effects – according to season, weather, and degree of remaining daylight – as the family returns home from its regular afternoon walks. To demonstrate the 'complete iterative system' Genette produces a diagram (p. 137), 'which reveals, under the apparently even continuity of the text, a more complex and more entangled hierarchical structure'. He then immediately digresses to take on the likely accusation that a model cannot account for the 'beauty' of this page of Proust. Such, he says, is not his intention, since he has placed himself not at the surface level of the words on the page, 'but at the level of "immanent" temporal structures that give the text its skeleton and its foundation' (p. 137). Here, as throughout his analysis of *A la recherche*, Genette claims to have uncovered the system of selections and relationships which implicitly govern the text's polished surface. Finally, he rounds off his description of this typically structuralist manoeuvre by refusing the charge that his schematic diagram has destroyed the complexity of Proust's text: 'If the object of analysis is indeed to illuminate the conditions of existence – of production – of the text, it is not done, as people often say, by reducing the complex to the simple, but on the contrary by revealing the hidden complexities that are the *secret* of the simplicity' (pp. 137–8). The 'beauty' of Proust's writing, which may either have left the reader suitably awestruck or been put down to the hidden mysteries of artistic creation, is again and again shown by Genette to be at least partly the result of sophisticated handling of the most basic tools of narrative.

II

Narratology was chosen for this first essay because it is an easy enough branch of literary theory to understand, and because it is a theory that actually asks to be put into practice. The best way for a newcomer to see the point of Genette's method is to try it out for herself on a challenging literary text. *Heart of Darkness* may well seem a text that cries out for exegesis, and certainly one that was never meant to be reduced to the nuts and bolts of its narrative components. Yet how and from what position is a student supposed to join in the game of competing critical readings of this well-worn yet wilfully obscure text – synthesize all the existing ones, choose between them, or produce a truly original one of her own? Better, surely, to suspect that the sense of obscurity and taboo is a literary construct. Better, like Genette seeking the knowable at the heart of Proust's masterpiece, to defer interpretation, to apply without complexes a narrative grid, and to see whether it will lead to the heart of the text's own foregrounded darkness.

I have chosen to concentrate on one section of *Heart of Darkness*: Marlow's visit to the Intended.[7] This is the scene that F.R. Leavis, irritated by Conrad's insistence on 'making a virtue out of not knowing what he means', memorably describes as 'another bad patch'.[8] I hope to show that the straining for significance so apparent in this scene depends on exploitation of the narrative system, and not only on the 'adjectival insistence' of which Leavis complains. Conrad's own gloss on the final scene indicates that its function in the work as a whole is to summarize the story and to raise it to a loftier plane: 'the interview of the man and the girl locks in – as it were – the whole 30,000 words of narrative description into one suggestive view of a whole phase of life, and makes of that story something quite on another plane than an anecdote of a man who went mad in the Centre of Africa'.[9] It is likely, therefore, that the scene will qualify as what Genette calls a *syllepsis* – one artificially set up to represent a wider set of meanings, and which acts as a magnetic pole for supplementary information and incidents through its integration of various 'digressions . . . retrospections, anticipations, iterative and descriptive parentheses' (p. 111). In his attempt to inject a summarizing significance Conrad uses narrative devices related to each of Genette's verbal categories. I shall discuss them in the order: voice, tense, mood.

Should the final fling at fixing a full (if unnameable) meaning be attributed to Conrad or Marlow? Leavis appears to make no distinction whatsoever between Marlow and the unnamed narrator of *Heart of Darkness*, nor between these two and Conrad, its real-life author. Yet the closing lines of *Heart of Darkness*, by returning to the opening setting of the *Nellie* on the Thames, draw attention to what is probably the most crucial element in the construction of Conrad's text – the embedding of Marlow's narrative. In his discussion of *narrative levels* Genette takes as a typical example of embedding the case (as here) where the narrator of a second narrative is already a character in the first. In Genette's model the first narrator of *Heart of Darkness* is by definition both *extra-diegetic* and *homo-diegetic*, while Marlow as narrator is both *intra-diegetic* and *auto-diegetic*. By *diegesis* Genette means not the story itself but the spatial-temporal universe to which that story belongs. Where there are two diegeses, Genette reserves the term for the first one encountered (whether or not it is the more important of the two), and names the embedded diegesis (here Marlow's narrative), a *meta-diegesis*. *Meta-* is being used in the sense of 'proceeds from', so that if one of the characters in Marlow's narrative were to produce a further story of her own, this meta-diegetic narrator would produce a *meta-meta-diegesis*. This extra level exists in fragmentary form through the harlequin Russian's story of his relations with Kurtz, and through Kurtz's infamous 'report for publication'. However, although Marlow does quote directly from both, his more normal tendency as narrator is to absorb other people's stories into his own (producing an ambiguous level which Genette would call a *pseudo-meta-diegesis*). The *extra/intra* distinction concerns the level at which the narrator is located as narrator of his story, while *homo/hetero* defines whether or not the narrator participates in his own story. Thus the first narrator is extra-diegetic because he is neither the object of anyone else's narration nor, as narrator, temporally and spatially on the same plane as the story he tells. But since he acts at the diegetic level as one of the group that hears and reacts to Marlow's story, he is homo-diegetic (in fact there are no hetero-diegetic narrators in Conrad's text). It follows that Marlow is both intra- and homo-diegetic, since his action in the first-level story is to tell a story about himself to his four intra-diegetic narratees. Further, since he is a central character in that story (as opposed to some oblique witness), he qualifies for the refined description: auto-diegetic.[10]

Genette provocatively describes his neologisms as a technology which will seem 'barbaric to the lovers of belles lettres' (p. 263). He gaily assigns them to some future rubbish tip of obsolete poetic terms, once they have served their purpose of drawing attention to previously unnoticed features of the narrative system. Yet many of his terms have gradually filtered into standard critical language. If

I have laboured the definitions pertaining to voice it is because they do surely add clarity to the description of a text like *Heart of Darkness*, and to identification of its problem areas. What matters, of course, about these possible variations of narrative level and stance is the way Conrad chooses to exploit them.

Both the diegetic and the meta-diegetic narrative are introduced as one of a class. The extra-diegetic narrator appears to be a writer who has told stories before ('as I have already said somewhere' (p. 27)), while Marlow's yarns are described as being typical of Marlow in being untypical of the general run of seamen's stories. This allows the extra-diegetic narrator to set up an expectation of mystery through the much-glossed metaphor of the nut and the haze, and through the warning: 'one of Marlow's inconclusive experiences' (p. 32). As homo-diegetic narrators both the first narrator and Marlow straddle two narrative levels. In the case of Marlow, however, this straddling allows his very act of narration to become an object of interest at least as important as the story he tells. The first narrator's close attention to Marlow's disembodied voice, the occasional glimpses of his Buddha-like pose (into which he is frozen by the closing lines of the text), raise Marlow's attempt to verbalize and understand his experience into the major theme of *Heart of Darkness*:

> 'I did not see the man in the name any more than you do. Do you see him? Do you see the story? Do you see anything? It seems to me I am trying to tell you a dream' ....
>
> 'Of course in this you fellows see more than I could then. You see me, whom you know...'
>
> It had become so pitch dark that we listeners could hardly see one another. For a long time already he, sitting apart, had been no more to us than a voice. There was not a word from anybody. The others might have been asleep, but I was awake, I listened, I listened on the watch for the sentence, for the word, that would give me the clue to the faint uneasiness inspired by this narrative that seemed to shape itself without human lips in the heavy night-air of the river. (pp. 57–8)

The thematic and symbolic resonances of the entire work depend absolutely on the interplay of the two narrative levels, underlined so graphically at this early stage of the story, and worked at to its very end. Meaning pours out of the implicit parallel between the two physical settings. The once-colonized Thames, the becalmed boat with its reassuring pilot figure in the bows, the faltering voice in the oppressive darkness – all feed into and are invaded in their turn by the shadowy inner tale of Marlow's quest for the voice of Kurtz. 'Do you see the story?' With understanding and truth so specifically linked to instances of literal vision and to effects of light and darkness, the advice to the reader is clear. A reading of the visit to the Intended depends unavoidably on the overflow of meaning from the narrative frame, of which exchanges with the narratees serve to remind us: 'Curiosity? Yes...' (p. 115); 'Do you understand?' (p. 118). Above all the account of the visit will be seen to be invaded (both lexically and figuratively) by the motif of darkness set up in the title, developed on both narrative levels, and held together by the final words of the text: 'into the heart of an immense darkness' (p. 121).

Although narration is subsequent to the events recounted in both diegeses, it is again only through the intra-diegetic Marlow that the possibilities of retrospection are exploited. The extra-diegetic narrator does not take up the possibility of telling us what he thinks about Marlow's tale with the benefit of hindsight, whereas Marlow often introduces distinctions between his thoughts 'then' and 'now': 'I don't defend myself. I had no clear perception of what it was I really wanted. Perhaps it was an impulse of unconscious loyalty, or the fulfilment of one of these ironic necessities that lurk in the facts of human existence. I don't know. I can't tell. But I went' (p. 116). More crucially, to speak from a position of full knowledge of the ending allows a narrator to range over the entire chronological stretch of his narrative, so that Marlow's metaphysical-sounding comment: 'the mind of man is capable of anything – because everything is in it, all the past as well as all the future' (p. 69), is also a description of his epistemological potential as a retrospective narrator. Genette uses the term *anachrony* to describe any disturbance of linear chronology (as in his analysis of Swann's thoughts on the Dreyfus Affair, discussed above), classing infringements of narrative order under *prolepsis* – events referred to or anticipated before their proper moment; and *analepsis* – retrospective recalls (*repetitive analepses*), or the filling-in of previously ellipsed events at a later moment of the narrative (*completing analepses*).

Since it relates the final episode in the story of Marlow's involvement with Kurtz, it is not surprising that the account of the visit to the Intended contains nothing that could strictly speaking be called prolepsis. However, the whole scene itself is the object of several proleptic allusions earlier in the text, and the ironic appellation, the 'Intended', often occurs before her official entry into it. The major advance notices obviously serve to influence our reading of the scene: 'That is why I have remained loyal to Kurtz to the last, and even beyond, when a long time after I heard once more, not his own voice, but the echo of his magnificent eloquence thrown to me from a soul as translucently pure as a cliff of crystal' (p. 113). Most striking, perhaps, is the very first reference to 'the girl' during the massive proleptic digression set off by Marlow's account of the killing of the cannibal helmsman:

> 'Voices, voices – even the girl herself – now –'
> He was silent for a long time.
>   'I laid the ghost of his gifts at last with a lie', he began, suddenly.
> 'Girl! What? Did I mention a girl? Oh, she is out of it – completely. They – the women I mean – are out of it – should be out of it. We must help them to stay in that beautiful world of their own, lest ours gets worse. Oh, she had to be out of it. You should have heard the disinterred body of Mr Kurtz saying, "My Intended" '. (p. 84)

Up to this point in the story prolepsis has been used in a fairly straightforward way to arouse curiosity about Kurtz. But recounting the helmsman's death (which has such specific analogies with Kurtz's death – the pilot-house setting, the play with the shutter, the glimpse of some sombre truth at the very moment of death) incites Marlow to lay all his narrative cards on the table. A spectacular disturbance of narrative order (pp. 84–7) ranges back beyond the starting point of the story to Kurtz's education, and forward through stacks of ivory, through extracts from his pamphlet (including its P.S.), through midnight dances and unspeakable rites, right up to the chronological end-point of his narrative – the visit to the Intended. From the moment of the death of the helmsman it is apparent that prolepsis is being used to add significance rather than suspense.

The attempt to hold together two or more moments of time is a typical feature of Marlow's narrative. His opening evocation of the Thames 1900 years ago, which on rereading can be seen to allude proleptically to the murkier elements of the tale to come, allows him to hold together the Roman and Belgian conquests through the mediation of the Thames as the place of narration (which, like the time of narration, is unknown in the case of the extra-diegetic narrator). Above all he strives to draw parallels between the three death scenes – death of the helmsman and of Kurtz, death of Kurtz and his own near demise, the details of which are so strikingly ellipsed in his narrative. But if the lack of details is given a realistic motivation ('a period of time which I remember mistily' (p. 113)), the strategic placing of this 'wrestle with death' immediately after Kurtz's burial, and the melodramatic, analeptic commentary to which it gives rise, suggest that the point of the ellipsis is to permit a displacement of Marlow's own missed opportunity for final pronouncements – a displacement in favour of his vicarious experience of the extremity and summing-up of Kurtz: 'No! It is his extremity that I seem to have lived through' (p. 113). But since Kurtz's last moment has already been curiously linked (proleptically) with that of the cannibal helmsman, whose last moments had also left Marlow with the sense of a profound bond of familiarity ('the intimate profundity of that look . . . remains to this day in my memory' (p. 88)), it is clear that Marlow (or Conrad through the instrument of Marlow's memory and psychology), is working very hard indeed to *hold together* these different moments of his story – to the extent of overdetermining the links between the three men. The method, from the first death scene on, is one of a gradual subsuming of the emotions and significances attaching to previous episodes.

The reason for my own return to these earlier moments of the text is twofold. First, it is easy to see that this rather obsessive technique reaches its apotheosis in the final scene of the meta-diegesis. Second, by the time the reader arrives at the apocalyptic recalls of Kurtz that invade and eventually swamp this scene, Kurtz's last days, his last discoursing, and most especially his last words have already accumulated all the weight of these previous meanings. The much-maligned fiancée[11] is clearly Conrad's chosen *device* for summing up and freezing into one climactic scene all the ironies and unspeakable significances that have been snowballing along the meta-diegetic axis of Marlow's narrative.

The first repetitive analepsis is introduced into the narrative as a vision that comes unexpectedly to Marlow as he enters the building where the Intended lives: 'I had a vision of him on the stretcher, opening his mouth voraciously, as if to devour all the earth with all its mankind' (p. 116). Recalling Tony Tanner's

happy description of Kurtz as a metaphorical cannibal of whom it
is not entirely ruled out that he is a literal one,[12] this is a significant
starting point for the elaboration of a vision around Marlow's first
view of Kurtz (framed and brought into range of vision by his
binoculars), a vision which becomes vivid enough to enter the
house with him, and to call up metonymically details that were
spread over several pages describing the events at the Inner
Station: 'the stretcher, the phantom-bearers, the wild crowd of
obedient worshippers, the gloom of the forests, the glitter of the
reach between the murky bends, the beat of the drum, regular and
muffled like the beating of a heart' (p. 116). The 'memory'
assumes an increasingly hallucinatory quality, taking in the sound
of his words, filling in details omitted from the original account
(completing analepsis), until vision and sound are counterpointed
as Kurtz both seems to stare out of the glass door panel and to
repeat once more his whispered cry.

From then on repetitive analepses gather around the Intended
herself. The first, a typical example of Marlow holding together
two temporal moments, is set off by his perception that, for the
girl, Kurtz 'had died only yesterday. And, by Jove! the impression
was so powerful that for me, too, he seemed to have died only
yesterday – nay, this very minute. I saw her and him in the same
instant of time – his death and her sorrow – I saw her sorrow in the
very moment of his death' (pp. 117–18). Second, it is the sound of
the girl's voice that seems to summon up 'the ripple of the river,
the soughing of the trees swayed by the wind, the murmurs of the
crowds, the faint ring of incomprehensible words cried from afar,
the whisper of a voice speaking from beyond the threshold of an
eternal darkness' (p. 119). Third, it is the girl's action of stretching
out her black-clad arms 'across the fading and narrow sheen of the
window', as if to clasp the retreating figure of the Kurtz that
nobody 'will see . . . again, never, never, never' (p. 120), that
sparks off yet another ironic recall, and leads Marlow to produce a
combined prolepsis and analepsis (an anticipation of a future recall
of this moment and of one further in the past), by likening the
girl's gesture to that of the bare brown arms of the native woman,
originally 'stretched tragically . . . over the sombre and glittering
river' (p. 109), after the retreating Kurtz:

Never see him! I saw him clearly enough then. I shall see this eloquent
phantom as long as I live, and I shall see her, too, a tragic and familiar

Shade, resembling in this gesture another one, tragic also, and bedecked with powerless charms, stretching bare brown arms over the glitter of the infernal stream, the stream of darkness. (p. 120)

Finally, as the conversation turns dangerously to the subject of Kurtz's last words, the latter invade the scene to such an extent that they are no longer motivated by memory or nervous imagination – the dusk simply whispers them all on its own: 'The horror! The horror!' (p. 121).

The choice of homo-diegetic narration implies a restriction of narrative viewpoint to the perceptions of the narrator himself. But Marlow's retrospective position gives him the choice of either exploiting his omniscience as he narrates, or artificially restricting himself to the knowledge available to him at the moment of his participation in events. The latter has certain narrative advantages: the arousal of curiosity (remarks of the 'who was this Kurtz?' sort), the build-up of suspense (the pages leading up to the attack on the steamer), or the creation of irony ('perhaps he was just simply a fine fellow who stuck to his work for its own sake' (p. 64)). Yet as he tells his story, Marlow takes advantage of the benefits of hindsight to inject superior knowledge gained at a later point in order to add layers of interpretation to earlier events: 'Since I had peeped over the edge myself, I understand better the meaning of his stare, that could not see the flame of the candle, but was wide enough to embrace the whole universe, piercing enough to penetrate all the hearts that beat in the darkness' (pp. 112–13). Does Marlow cheat, however? Is this retrospective understanding not already built into the initial presentation of the scene with its spectacular interpretation of Kurtz's final experience? 'It was as though a veil had been rent. I saw on that ivory face the expression of sombre pride, of ruthless power, of craven terror – of an intense and hopeless despair. Did he live his life again in every detail of desire, temptation, and surrender during that supreme moment of complete knowledge?' (p. 111). It is clear from this crucial example that interpretation is inserted into the straight reporting of the episode through the use of hypothesis, and especially through the use of the modal phrase 'as though'. Similarly, Kurtz's presence and his words are actually conjured up in the last scene by a whole series of modal locutions: '*as if* to devour all the earth', 'the vision *seemed* to enter the house with me' (p. 116), 'he *seemed* to have died only yesterday' (p. 117), 'my strained ears *seemed* to hear distinctly', '*as though* I had blundered into a place of cruel and absurd mysteries' (p. 118).[13] If anything these phrases, which are accompanied by verbs of direct perception – 'I *noticed* she was not very young' (p. 117), 'I could *see* the glitter of her eyes' (p. 119), 'I *heard* a light sigh' (p. 121) – emphasize the restricted focalization at the same time as offering the possibility of transgressing it. It is this transgression that Genette christens *paralepsis* – the inclusion of more information than is strictly accessible to the perceiver's visual or aural viewpoint. He suggests that the use of modal locutions – *perhaps, undoubtedly, as if, seem, appear* – might be classed as 'unavowed paralepsis', the point being that they allow the narrator to say hypothetically what he could not assert without stepping outside focalization through one character. I should like to examine more closely the role of paralepsis in Marlow's account of his visit to the Intended, for I believe that it is a key figure in Conrad's narrative system. Not only is it employed for the injection of melodramatic significances, but also for the incorporation of symbolism, of a metaphorical level of meaning that actually feeds off literal perceptions.

Genette's discussion of paralepsis belongs to his wider analysis of *focalization*, itself a sub-category of *perspective*. His transposition of grammatical mood to the representation and regulation of *narrative* information depends on a pictorial analogy: 'as the view I have of a picture depends for precision on the distance separating me from it, and for breadth on my position with respect to whatever partial obstruction is more or less blocking it' (p. 162). Now the decision to visit the Intended is taken on the basis of Marlow's impression of her from a photograph. This gives rise to a self-conscious allusion to the problems of representation, and invites us to pay attention to Marlow's own manipulation of light and pose in his presentation of the girl: 'I know that the sunlight can be made to lie, too, yet one felt that no manipulation of light and pose could have conveyed the delicate shade of truthfulness upon those features' (p. 115). When the girl makes her first appearance through a high door and comes floating forward towards Marlow in the dusk, it is very much as if she had stepped out of her portrait. The frame narrows in to become the ashy halo of hair that surrounds her eyes and their expression, with the whole portrait set against a backcloth of gathering gloom.

Marlow's final pictorial description of her freezes her into another pose, that of a 'tragic gesture' of stretching out her arms as if after a retreating figure, framed for the reader 'across the fading and narrow sheen of the window' (p. 120).

Even before the appearance of the Intended in mourning, the funereal atmosphere imparted to the description of the empty drawing-room could be regarded as a form of paralepsis. It is after all a year since Kurtz's death, and the Marlow who calls on the girl has no reason to anticipate the extent of her grief, has not yet had his perception that for her Kurtz had died only yesterday. The symbolism is typically injected through modal phrases:

> I had to wait in a lofty drawing-room with three long windows from floor to ceiling that were *like three luminous and bedraped columns*. The bent gilt legs and backs of the furniture shone in indistinct curves. The tall marble fireplace *had a cold and monumental whiteness*. A grand piano stood massively in the corner; with dark gleams on the flat surfaces *like a sombre and polished sarcophagus*. (p. 117)

The description of the girl that follows is very marginally anchored in direct observation of the falling dusk and the fact that she is not 'girlish'. Marlow carefully imbues what might have seemed literal light effects with metaphorical significance, and so builds into his perception of the girl the purity and 'delicate shade of truthfulness' already read into her photograph:

> The room *seemed* to have grown darker, *as if* all the sad light of the cloudy evening had taken refuge on her forehead. This fair hair, this pale visage, this pure brow, *seemed* surrounded by an ashy halo from which the dark eyes looked out at me....She carried her sorrowful head *as though* she were proud of that sorrow, *as though* she would say, I – I alone know how to mourn for him as he deserves. (p. 117)

Then, as Marlow shakes hands with her: 'such a look of awful desolation came upon her face that I *perceived* she was one of those creatures that are not the playthings of Time' (p. 117). This may be presented as an act of straight perception, yet the capitalization of 'Time' indicates the infiltration of an abstract noun which, like the 'complete knowledge' and 'glimpsed truth' attributed to the dying Kurtz (pp. 111 and 113), strictly belongs to a different level of perception, and constitutes another instance of paralepsis. Consider too, in the 'last words' passage, Marlow's combination of a verb of direct perception with an adjective heavy with wider significance: 'I *saw* on that *ivory* face' (p. 111). This tension between the literal and the metaphorical runs right through the handling of visual light effects in the Intended scene, to consecrate the girl as an embodiment of truth, to be preserved at all costs from the invading and triumphant darkness:

> But with every word spoken the room was growing darker, and only her forehead, smooth and white, remained illumined by the unextinguishable light of belief and love. (p. 118)

> bowing my head before the faith that was in her, before that great and saving illusion that shone with an unearthly glow in the darkness, in the triumphant darkness. (p. 119)

> She stood up; her fair hair seemed to catch all the remaining light in a glimmer of gold. (p. 119)

By the end of Marlow's narrative, darkness has assumed a wholly metaphorical sense: 'I could not tell her. It would have been too dark – too dark altogether...' (p. 121). The extra-diegetic narrator returns briefly to round off the diegesis, and in seven lines of text exactly repeats Marlow's narrative strategy. First Marlow is frozen into 'the pose of a meditating Buddha', then the director's comment on the state of the tide causes the narrator to look up at the river and the sky. The final description is clearly focalized as what the narrator sees when he takes his eyes off Marlow, but already modals and metaphor return in a final instance of paralepsis:

> *I raised my head.* The offing was barred by a *black* bank of clouds, and the tranquil waterway leading to the uttermost ends of the earth flowed *sombre* under an *overcast* sky – *seemed* to lead into the *heart of an immense darkness.* (p. 121)

My own analysis has come full circle, and it has become apparent that significance is built into *Heart of Darkness* on both its horizontal and vertical axes. On the one hand significance straddles the two diegetic levels, through analogy and through the literal/figurative play-off by which it becomes impossible to process descriptions of light, darkness, hearts, etc., without slipping into a metaphorical reading. This amounts perhaps to a version of what Genette calls *metalepsis*, the transgression of diegetic levels, especially given the problem of whether to locate the title of the work (so often alluded to on both levels), inside or

outside the narrative itself. On the other hand, significance
snowballs along the horizontal line of the metadiegesis, gathering
strength as it rolls, largely through the use of repetitive analepses
which eventually cling to the figure of the Intended. Finally, the
obsessive modal locutions impose the extravagant insights and
speculations of the Marlow who admits that, on his return to
Brussels, it was his 'imagination that wanted soothing' (p. 114).

In fact, my narratological analysis of the final scene has left me
wanting to explore the whole text as an adventure of Marlow's
imagination. Although this might suggest a step into critical
exegesis, the reading would remain within the parameters of the
verbal category of mood. In particular I would restore its literal
grammatical sense, even though Genette himself rather strangely
suggests that this is not appropriate: 'since the function of
narrative is not to give an order, express a wish, state a condition,
etc.' (p. 161). But the *status* of the events recounted is surely a
crucial aspect of narrative representation, and there is no reason to
suppose (with Genette) that narrative mood is always indicative.
This seems especially important in the case of a narrator who
constantly evokes forms of unreality – dreams, nightmares,
phantoms and visions – and whose final lie to the Intended
reaffirms for the reader repressed truths and repressed knowledge.
Further, to follow the adventure of Marlow's imagination would
raise more centrally the question of metalepsis, in that imaginative
leaps might well seem to consign Conrad and the reader, as well as
Marlow and the extra-diegetic narrator, to Kurtz's black and
muddy hole. For this connection was surely in Conrad's mind
when he described Kurtz's lack of 'restraint' in the very terms
earlier applied to his own adventure as an imaginative artist: 'In
that interior world where [the artist's] thought and his emotions go
seeking for the experience of imagined adventures, there are no
policemen, no law, no pressure of circumstances or dread of
opinion to keep him in bounds'.[14]

III

'It is less easy after Greimas and Genette to hear the cut and thrust
of the rapiers in line three, or feel that you know just what it feels
like to be a scarecrow after reading *The Hollow Men*'.[15] *Heart of
Darkness*, source of the original Hollow Man and his papier-
mâché rivals, might well seem a suitable test-case for Terry

Eagleton's claim. Yet my analysis, quite contrary to expectation, seems to have led me to suggest that Conrad did indeed want his reader to end up feeling like a Hollow Person. To describe a text in detail is inevitably to make discoveries about it, and once one starts discovering one is already interpreting to some extent. At the same time, narratology is certainly more teachable than the intuitive production of the 'perceptive' and 'thoughtful' comments that so often, as Eagleton suggests, amount to aesthetic value judgements on stylistic effects. Moreover, its detailed description of narrative stance, focalization, and time structures suggests a new sort of close reading exercise. If, as all the contributors to this volume would surely agree, it is desirable to unsettle the boundaries and definition of literature, narratology avoids the possible danger of losing touch altogether with literature as an object of study. For the desired demystification is achieved not by philosophical or theoretical decree, but by the precise and disciplined description of the mechanics of a single, sophisticated text.

Further reading

An excellent introduction to Genette is Stephen Bann's review article: 'Genette' (*London Review of Books*, 2–16 October 1980, p. 17). Apart from *Narrative Discourse*, the only volume of Genette in translation is *Figures of Literary Discourse*, trs. Alan Sheridan (Oxford, Blackwell, 1982), which contains important articles of structuralist theory and criticism. *Nouveau discours du recit* (Paris, Seuil, 1983), is a section-by-section review of *Narrative Discourse* in the light of ten years of work in the same field. It contains a very useful bibliography, updating that of *Narrative Discourse* itself. Genette has inspired various full-length studies of and in narratology – for works in English see: Shlomith Rimmon-Kenan, *Narrative Fiction: Contemporary Poetics* (London, Methuen, 1983); Seymour Chatman, *Story and Discourse: Narrative Structure in Fiction and Film* (Ithaca, Cornell U.P., 1978); Gerald Prince, *Narratology: the Form and Functioning of Narrative* (Berlin, Mouton, 1982); Christine Brooke-Rose, *A Rhetoric of the Unreal: Studies in Narrative and Structure, especially of the Fantastic* (Cambridge, CUP, 1981). Two important translated works from other traditions are Boris Uspensky, *A Poetics of Composition: the Structure of the Artistic Text and a Typology of a Compositional Form*, trs. Valentina Zavarin and Susan Wittig (Berkeley, University of California Press, 1973), and F.K. Stanzel, *A Theory of Narrative* (Cambridge, CUP, 1984 (1979)). Jean Verrier's 'Temporal structuring in the novel' (*Renaissance and Modern Studies*, 27,

1983, pp. 30–46), is a discussion of the suitability of Genette for teaching narrative at secondary school level. Finally, for wider reading on Saussure and French structuralism, see the suggestions in Ann Jefferson and David Robey, eds., *Modern Literary Theory: A Comparative Introduction* (London, Batsford, rev. ed., 1986), pp. 119–21.

2 Structuralism II: Character Theory
Henry James, *In the Cage*

Bernard McGuirk

I

At the time of writing, not only structuralist theory but also commentary upon it is in a late stage of development – not to say 'old hat'. Thus, in 1985, Raman Selden can write:

> Structuralism has attracted some literary critics because it promises to introduce a certain rigour and objectivity into the delicate realm of literature. This rigour is achieved at a cost. By subordinating *parole* to *langue* the structuralist neglects the specificity of actual texts, and treats them as if they were like the patterns of iron filings produced by an invisible force.... Their approach is necessarily static and ahistorical. They are interested therefore in neither the moment of the text's production (its historical context, its formal links with past writing, etc.) nor the moment of its reception (the interpretations imposed on it subsequent to its production).[1]

It is a somewhat forbidding challenge, therefore, to resist the blasé assumption that the lessons, nay, the dangers, of structuralism have been long ago and easily digested and to pursue the supposedly more challenging alternatives of either post-structuralist and/or Marxist literary analysis. Yet for many students and teachers of literature (for many critics and writers) some of the claims of structuralism still come as thunderbolts, still pose problems and still throw down challenges to established modes of thinking about literature which, quite simply, will not 'go away' and, as such, constitute a suitable starting point for most contemporary discussion of critical theory.

Since this chapter is to deal with a Henry James narrative, one could do worse than allow the discussion of character to begin with his own oft-cited view of its nature, relationally (i.e. *structurally*) defined:

What is character but the determination of incident?
What is incident but the illustration of character?
What is either a picture or a novel that is *not* of character?
What else do we seek in it and find in it?[2]

It would be easier to illustrate the thinking underlying James's famous rhetorical formulation were a closely defined alternative view to be at hand. The problem is, however, despite assumptions as to a so-called 'realist' notion of character, that no clear-cut definition of such exists. Philosophically, an extreme mimeticist claim that a literary character constitutes a mere (or pure) reflection of a person has generally been regarded as untenable. It is none the less the underlying assumption governing both untutored and – too often – 'tutoring' conceptions of character(ization). To take an example from the 'school' experience of English Literature, perhaps the most common task of the 'O' level candidate has been to attempt a 'character study' of Macbeth, or Desdemona, or David Copperfield, as if those names evoked a real person to be described, analysed, criticized or even morally appraised. No amount of debunking of this approach (e.g. L.C. Knights's 'How many children had Lady Macbeth?') has yet weaned the student of literature, at least in the Anglo-Saxon tradition, away from a belief *in*, albeit in the absence of a definition *of*, the 'realist' notion of character. It is against the background of such an assumption that James's interrogatives may best be situated.

By underlining the *relational* opposition of character and incident in the James quotation, it has been my intention both to prepare an outline of the structuralist position and to draw immediate attention to its artificiality. In confining the realm of character definition to those 'words on the page' which, at the same time, delimit the action of a given narrative, the extreme structuralist position excludes consideration both of the individual and the collective in psychoanalytical or political terms. In short, to use a favourite structuralist label, character is to be understood wholly in terms of *spheres of action*. As such, it will readily be noticed, the character/incident conflation in James's definition, baldly stated and broadly understood, may be deemed a structuralist position. What then is the attraction of such an oversimplification?

First, as with most areas of structuralist enterprise, the

character/incident inseparability promises rescue from the seeming chaos of approaching character with a 'view to isolating moral, psychological or political norms or departures from normality. As such, the structuralist view of character constitutes one of many narratological devices, a momentary, analytical and unapologetically artificial or stylized theory of how literary characterization works or functions. And 'function' is the operative word. Beginning with the formalist, Propp, and developing through the more rigorously structuralist work of Greimas and Todorov, character theory has concentrated on the action, or verbal (sometimes adjectival) predicate attached to a fictional (sometimes named) subject.[3] It is as if the activity which we associate with characterization in literature were reducible to a simple sentence or, more complexly, a sequence of simple sentences – e.g.

> Adam is born.
> Adam is alone (lonely).
> Eve is born.
> Adam desires Eve.
> Eve desires fruit.
> etc.

To be convincing, a structuralist theory of character must be all-embracing, must be able to account for, even to predict, *all* narratives, however complex. Not surprisingly, however, it was, in the first instance, the more primitive, archaic or traditional narrative forms which served to illustrate most early structural character theory.

Rather than describing, or identifying, a simple series of subjects and predicates, however, formalist and structuralist character theory has examined ever more complex narratives with a view to eliciting recurrent patterns of functional sequences, providing for links between isolated actions and even chains of predictability for narrative development(s). As such, it is the *diegetical*[4] patterning of fictional discourse rather than any psychologizing which determines structuralist discussion of character. It is hardly surprising, therefore, as Jonathan Culler has pointed out, that 'character is the major aspect of the novel to which structuralism has paid least attention and has been least successful in treating'. For, as Culler goes on to suggest, 'stress on the interpersonal and conventional systems which traverse the individual, which make him a space in which forces and events meet rather than an individuated essence, leads to a rejection of a prevalent conception of character in the novel'.[5] In defence of such theories, however, it is worth underlining the obvious: namely, that however much we might disagree with the above 'transcendence' of the individual by the sign or conventional system of signs *socially*, it is somewhat harder to refute the structuralist view of character as that which amounts to a series of signs on a page *fictionally*. For this reason, not least, it is worth considering the work of several theorists who construe character-(ization) as nothing more or less than narrative function(s).[6]

☆ ☆ ☆

What follows is but a summary of summaries, for numerous writers on critical theory, notably Jonathan Culler, have outlined the development of structuralist notions of character, usually beginning with the contribution of Vladimir Propp's 'theory of the roles or functions that characters may assume' (*SP*, p. 232). A useful, and very succinct, prelude to any discussion of character as function, however, is to be found in the short section on 'Actions' under the heading 'Towards a structural status of characters' in Roland Barthes's seminal 1966 essay 'Introduction to the Structural Analysis of Narratives'.[7] Here, Barthes reminds us that in Aristotelian poetics 'the notion of character is secondary, entirely subsidiary to the notion of action' (*IMT*, p. 104). Furthermore, and this is the point I should wish to emphasize – 'it must not be forgotten that classical tragedy as yet knows only "actors" not "characters" ' (*IMT*, p. 104 n. 1). The shift in meaning from *persona* as 'a voice from behind a mask' to *person* as 'being' is a relatively modern, arguably Romantic, development. Rather than the subjectivity subsequently attributable to actOR, or the specific reification of an actION, formalist and structuralist theory will focus on a different linguistic function, namely, on the participial actANT, a form which 'partakes of the nature of a verb and an adjective' and underpins those notions which construe character as 'describing action'.[8]

Such a linguistic nicety may be useful in approaching Propp's isolation of seven folk-tale roles (villain/helper/donor/sought-for-person and her father/dispatcher/hero/false hero) and A.J. Greimas's consequent actantial paradigm:

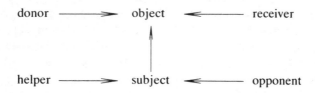

Inevitably, such a skeletal model has been subjected to all manner of criticisms and both Barthes and Culler recognize, respectively, refinements and possible objections. For Barthes, in 1966, at least, the attraction of an all-embracing explanatory model may have led him to restrict his reservations to questions of the grammatical subject, i.e. 'the *personal* (*je/tu* first person/second person), or the *apersonal* (*il*, third person), singular, dual or plural instance of the action' (*IMT*, p. 109). But, of course, for Barthes, these subjectivities are explicable only in terms of discourse, i.e. relationally, not mimetically, or with reference to the external world of lived experience. Culler's major objection is the non-equivalence of the sender–receiver relation to the others in the model. But to these and other objections I shall return in application of theory to text.

Meanwhile, I would draw attention to an even more funda-mentalist structuralist practice, namely that of Tzvetan Todorov, who reduces the Greimas paradigm to its supposed motor functions: desire, communication and participation.[9] It may be readily observed that this constitutes a return to the initial *linguistic* base of the conjunction of a subject with a predicate, infinitely more abstract and 'value-free' than ever was the hero/villain reduction of Propp.

It is in the nature of much structuralist abstraction that different theorists depart from and return to a fundamentally *linguistically* derived proposition. Thus, even the later Barthes, in *S/Z* (1970), suggests that, in reading, we operate a so-called 'semic' code by which a series or network of actions come to rest or be associated with a proper name – 'to read is to struggle to name'.[10] And this perhaps brings us full circle inasmuch as it admits the inevitability of a reader's propensity to 'naturalize' linguistic structures into associations with 'lived' experience, with recognizable psycho-logies – in effect, with individual subjects.

The circular nature of this theoretical discussion of structuralist character analysis is virtually mirrored in Roland Barthes' own shifting preoccupations. Concerned initially with anti-realist, polemical abstractions, he comes, in *S/Z*, admittedly via much complex grappling with the implication of abstract structuralist networks, to the very *readerly* perspective of 'struggle' with a text. The struggle that is about to take place occurs within another network of sorts – *In the Cage*.

II

The James story opens with a display of precisely those narrative features which a structuralist theory would construe as a classic actantial model. Within the tightly restricted 'sphere' proposed by the title, an initial source of action is expressed in the impersonal verb of the text's opening: 'It had occurred . . .'. Thereafter, the first paragraph constitutes a detailed listing of functions, each designed to supplement that isolated point in a modern communications network known simply as 'telegraphist'. Even here, at the outset and in a binary relation, 'her' function is given only by reference to 'the other telegraphist'. The 'young person spending, in framed and wired confinement, the life of a guinea-pig or a magpie' (1, 9)[11] is introduced between hyphens, as an aside. A 'struggle to name' her, to echo Barthes, ensues, beginning with that absence of personal identity mirrored in the reaction of others: 'she should know a great many persons without their recognizing the acquaintance' (1, 9). Subsequently, the struggle will be to 'see any one . . . who could add something to the poor identity of her function' (1, 9).

The anonymity of the mere telegraphist's function from which escape is sought is, however, concealed by the apparent specificity of the description of a *particular* place of work:

> This transparent screen fenced out or fenced in, according to the side of the narrow counter on which the human lot was cast, the duskiest corner of a shop pervaded not a little, in winter, by the poison of perpetual gas, and at all times by the presence of hams, cheese, dried fish, soap, varnish, paraffin, and other solids and fluids that she came to know perfectly by their smells without consenting to know them by their names. (1, 9)

Surely here, the traditional critic might argue, is the emergence of individual character, a glimmer of individual, subjective consciousness, refusing involvement with the banal (unnamable) reality surrounding her. Two points are to be made, however, by the structuralist. First, the role and significance of what Barthes has called the 'reality effect'.

The temptation to construct a 'realistic' character from within a 'realistic', detailed description is strong. But does the above description actually denote specific elements in the real world? Listen to Barthes on the matter:

> Semiotically, the 'concrete detail' is constituted by the *direct* collusion of a referent and a signifier; the signified is expelled from the sign, and along with it, of course, there is eliminated the possibility of developing a *form of the signified*, that is, the narrative structure itself. (Realist literature is, to be sure, narrative, but that is because its realism is only fragmentary, erratic, restricted to 'details', and because the most realistic narrative imaginable unfolds in an unrealistic manner.) This is what might be called the *referential illusion*. The truth behind this illusion is this: eliminated from the realist utterance as a signified of denotation, the 'real' slips back in as a signified of connotation; for at the very moment when these details are supposed to denote reality directly, all that they do, tacitly, is signify it. Flaubert's barometer, Michelet's little door, say, in the last analysis, only this: *we are the real*. It is the category of the 'real', and not its various contents, which is being signified; in other words, the very absence of the signified, to the advantage of the referent, standing alone, becomes the true signifier of realism. An 'effet de réel' (a reality effect) is produced, which is the basis of that unavowed 'vraisemblance' which forms the aesthetic of all the standard works of modernity.[12]

The difficult concepts in this, one of Barthes' most important contributions to structuralist theory, repay careful re-reading. Yet, once it has been realized that the 'reality effect' hinges on the difference between denotation and connotation, it becomes apparent that, for our purposes here, characterization is as much a part of Barthes' 'unavowed "vraisemblance" ' as description itself. It is therefore instructive to return to the above extract with the 'illusion' of realist characterization in mind. What 'slips back' with the 'real', in our example from the opening paragraph of *In the Cage*, is the notion of an individual('s) reaction to it. Concomitantly, it is the *category* of characterization, and not its various contents, which is being signified. Further, saying '*I am the real* (because of my reaction to reality)' is only an additional feature of the *referential illusion* – one arising out of the presence, here, of Barthes' *apersonal* grammatical subject (recall *IMT*, p. 109) as a 'singular instance of the action'.

The second point a structuralist would adduce concerns overlapping or plural 'spheres of action'. That 'sphere' labelled 'telegraphy', pointedly enough, is separated only by a 'transparent screen' from the 'grocery'. And hence arises the actantial binary of she/Mr Mudge. The interdependence (the 'engagement') of the two is 'so unreservedly, so irredeemably recognized' as to trigger a series of quasi-geometrical narrative functions in the second and third paragraphs of Chapter I. The second 'sphere of action', and one intricately linked with that of telegraphic communications, is the horizontal/vertical interplay of social relations, the 'class'-system and, specifically, the action of social climbing. The terms of the contract binding female with male are displayed directionally. 'Mr Mudge's removal to a higher sphere', since their engagement, ironically, permits the illusion of *her* temporary (except on Sundays) liberation from the horizontal plane where previously, daily, 'he had moved to and fro before her as on the small sanded floor of their contracted future' (1, 10). Though the text pluralizes actantial spheres, for instance, with an echo of the title's cage in 'the small sanded floor' or, by extension, with the cockpit or bullring of inseparable adversaries contracted in conflict, the illusion of liberation forms part of the female principle's struggle towards individual identity. This is expressed, in the first instance, by an assault on temporal continuity: 'She was conscious now of the improvement of not having to take her present and her future at once. They were about as much as she could manage when taken separate' (1, 10). The struggle, here again, involves 'name'. In the present, 'she' is as yet 'unnamed'. Insufficient as that *an*onymous state may be, it is preferred to the future imposition of another's name, the assumption, in marriage, of the wifely *ep*onymous 'Mrs Mudge'. Where 'he' and 'she' might come together is not so much delineated as *blurred*: rendered *unclear* in the conjunction of her female('s') supplementing of his male ('Mr') status and, hence, MR/SMUDGE.

The many ciphers of upward and downward social mobility of Chapter I, which ends on the cataloguing of the falling and, in one case (hers alone) 'rebounding', of 'incredulous ladies, suddenly bereaved' (1, 11), is inseparable from the play of names. Ann

Jefferson, dealing with the transition from the *bourgeois*, realist novel to the *nouveau roman*, cites Robbe-Grillet's view that 'the redundancy of fictional character is determined by social changes in the world in which we live':

> The character novel belongs well and truly to the past, it typifies a certain era: when the individual was at his height.
> Perhaps it is not a sign of progress, but . . . for us the fate of the world is no longer related to the rise and fall of a few men or a few families....To have a name was doubtless very important in the days of the Balzacian bourgeoisie. A character was all the more important as it was also a weapon in any confrontation, it represented the hope of success, it was a means of wielding power. It meant something to have a face in a universe where personality was both the means and the end of all endeavour.[13]

My long deliberation on the functions of the first chapter of *In the Cage* has used structural analysis to situate James's text as ripe for the application of actant theory. In the five spheres of critical action which follow, I shall seek to illustrate from the text the major areas of structuralist 'character' theory.

✩ ✩ ✩

cages, networks, webs, fabrics . . .

> She was so boxed up with her young men, and anything like a margin so absent, that it needed more art than she should ever possess to pretend . . . an approach to a relation of elegant privacy. (7, 29)

> Some one had only sometimes to put in a penny for a stamp, and the whole thing was upon her. (2, 12)

Enclosure and confinement are thus expressed in terms of a box or machine, with the possibility, even, of the frame within frame of infinite regression or *mise en abyme*:[14]

> . . . the sounder . . . being the innermost cell of captivity, a cage within a cage, fenced off from the rest by a frame of ground glass. (3, 15)

The struggle to emerge from sealed-off inaction is, however, a reflex response to that message-*receiving* (input), conveyed here in terms of a minimal economic factor ('a penny'). Thereafter, all action consists of message-*sending*, conducted within the socio-economic rules both of the initial input and of a dominant social group, 'the class that wired everything, even their expensive feelings' (4, 18).

The constant process of 'wiring', from within confinement, constructs a 'cage'. But the network is many-layered, and ever more expansive. From the post office, the 'web of revelation . . . was woven' (11, 42) with a view to escaping from 'the want of margin in the cage' (11, 39) to 'simply the margin of the universe' (11, 40). The promise of revelation, in release, is sometimes expressed Romantically (I shall return to this in the 'Intertexts' section):

> The moonbeams and silver threads presented at moments all the vision of what poor *she* might have made of happiness. (5, 23)

Yet the very italicization which most stresses personal identity is followed up within a few lines by another which underlines 'her' unfulfilled wish for essentiality:

> She quivered on occasion into the perception of this and that one whom she would, at all events, have just simply liked to *be*. (5, 23)

Her own role, as a mere relational point within a system of characterization is, I would argue, a corollary of one of the basic Saussurian claims, 'dans la langue il n'y a que des différences, sans termes positifs'. I retain the French here because of the ambiguity of 'terme', both termi*nology* and termi*nation*. For, in the very next paragraph of James's text, the actant theory is subjected to a classic *mise en abyme*:

> . . . and she read into the immensity of their intercourse stories and meanings without end. (5, 23)

'Her' own role is without end, projected from an absent centre, a mere *parole* from the *langue* of 'literary characterization'.

The 'immensity' of 'meanings without end' is the final fabric woven by the text, namely that of the social relations and class system proposed in relation to Chapter 1. The 'Cage' of society, in this text, is constituted by the horizontal/vertical interplay of 'wired' communications and the 'objective' of social climbing. The grid outlined here is but a sample of the multiple criss-cross references of *In the Cage*, the lines of which will be explored more fully in the sections which follow:

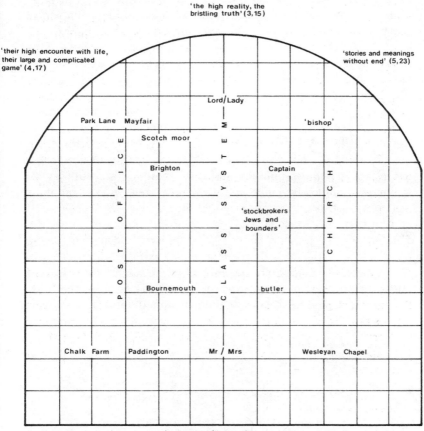

'the high reality, the bristling truth' (3,15)

'their high encounter with life, their large and complicated game' (4,17)

'stories and meanings without end' (5,23)

Lord/Lady · Park Lane · Mayfair · Scotch moor · 'bishop' · Brighton · Captain · 'stockbrokers Jews and bounders' · Bournemouth · butler · Chalk Farm · Paddington · Mr / Mrs · Wesleyan Chapel

'reality... could never be the escape, the rise' (26,96)

intertexts

. . . there was often half an hour during which she could pull out . . . a book – a book from the place where she borrowed novels, very greasy, in fine print and all about fine folks, at a ha'penny a day. (2, 11)

That was the hour at which, if the ha'penny novels were not all wrong, he probably came home for the night. (12, 45)

Even that abstraction 'intertextuality' – a structuralist common-place – has a price. And so this section, as the last, arises from a minimal economic factor ('a ha'penny'). In order to 'read into the immensity of their intercourse stories and meanings without end'

(5, 23) it may well seem, at first sight, necessary to keep 'the page clear. On the clearness, therefore, what she did retain stood sharply out; she nipped and caught it, turned it over and interwove it' (5, 24). 'Our young critic' (8, 31), however, as structuralist theory would argue for *any* reader, cannot begin *tabula rasa*, let alone subjectively. For 'she' is the sum of her reading practice. The action of her text, therefore, 'would be a scene better than many in her ha'penny novels' (11, 42), the 'economy class' above which her 'reading' struggles to rise, 'to beat every novel in the shop' (12, 43). A story constructed, confected, concocted from message-sending, none the less divulges the receipt of a message made up of all-too-familiar lines or 'wires', the outlines of Romance, endlessly, inescapably interwoven in yet another 'sphere of action', that 'cage' called literary genre. And again, I end on network. In the criss-cross of intertextuality it is only the *synchronic*, the horizontal level of relations which 'our young critic' can manipulate in her telegraphist's wiring role. Access to the vertical, the diachronic system of lineage, aristocratic descent and even the precipitate upward social mobility of 'bounders' (24, 88) is ever denied to the organizing, unnamed actant.

☆ ☆ ☆

systems: names, no names, non-names

   . . . the betrothed of Mr Mudge . . . (7, 28)

> steamers . . . conveyed them, close-packed items in terrific totals of enjoyment, to the Isle of Wight and the Dorset coast. (18, 64)

In the absence of named identity, systems flourish, both in singular and plural 'instances of the action'.

First, the singular instance. Even in the early attempt at self-insertion into a role within the sender–receiver function, the betrothed telegraphist fails to pin down by name the lady 'she would have just simply liked to *be*'. The first telegram 'had no signature' (3, 14); the second 'Cissy'; the third 'Mary'. 'There had once been one . . . who, without winking, sent off five over five different signatures' (3, 14). There is simply no clue, no access to that most specific of reality effects, the name. And the fluctuation of names renders unstable the whole system of definition, let alone any attempt at self-identification. Consequently, even the name of 'her' Captain is the Everard but never *concrete* detail – for 'that was doubtless not *his* true name either' (3, 16).

> He was sometimes Everard, as he had been at the Hôtel Brighton, and
> he was sometimes Captain Everard. He was sometimes Philip with his
> surname and sometimes Philip without it. In some directions he was
> merely Phil, in others he was merely Captain. There were relations in
> which he was none of these things, but a quite different person – 'the
> Count'. There were several friends for whom he was William. There
> were several for whom, in allusion perhaps to his complexion, he was
> 'the Pink 'Un'. Once, once only by good luck, he had, coinciding
> comically, quite miraculously, with another person also near to her,
> been 'Mudge'. (4, 20–1)

This 'miracle', this bringing down of the Captain to the level of her
betrothed, might even be explained by a 'once only' (by good luck)
slip, an impropriety, an excess of zeal in the desire to interfere
with, to be involved with, the sender–receiver relations at a level
other than the merely horizontal, for 'sometimes she put in too
much – too much of her own sense' (3, 14). This longing for
involvement in another network is inseparable from the 'struggle
to name' – 'she would have given anything to have been able to
allude to one of his friends by name' (11, 40).

Ironically, such heavy attachment to naming ill prepares the
telegraphist for confronting personal identity. Once out of the
impersonal communications system she flounders, at once seeking
a message-sending substitute:

> The hall *was* free, and the electric light played over the gilded and
> lettered board that showed the names and numbers of the occupants of
> the different floors. What she wanted looked straight at her – Captain
> Everard was on the third. (12, 44)

Name-play and name-plate are equally safe, equally textual,
equally distant from a realist notion of the transparent, unmediated character-depiction of the sign. Thus, in her actantial
dependence on the signature(s) of Captain Everard, the telegraphist moves *out of the cage* at her peril. In order that her continued
function – and therefore her propriety – can be assured, she 'would
just give him a few days more to come back to her on a proper
impersonal basis' (22, 79). To move out of the interdependence of
the message-sender/message-receiver system is to risk oblivion, or
relegation to an inferior sphere of action, 'the effect of becoming
so cheap, that there were long stretches in which inspiration,
divination and interest, quite dropped' (2, 12), 'for she had no
interest in the spurious or the shabby, and no mercy at all for the

poor' (5, 23). Thus, integrity (i.e. *non*-cheapness) is maintained
only *in the cage*:

> It was wonderfully innocent now, his oblivion of all but his danger.
> Anything else that had ever passed between them was utterly out of it.
> Well, she had wanted him to be impersonal! (22, 81)

Having 'most unspeakably . . . put to the test . . . the possibility of
her having for him a personal identity' (4, 20), the final – and only
– message received by the telegraphist is that speakability (and
writeability) exclude all possibility of a personal identity. A text
knows no characters – only spheres of action. The speakability, the
utterance of actantiality, is crucial:

> 'Oh!' said the girl, knowing at this the deepest thrill she had ever felt. It
> came to her there, with her eyes on his face, that she held the whole
> thing in her hand, held it as she held her pencil, which might have
> broken at that instant in her tightened grip. This made her feel like the
> very fountain of fate, but the emotion was such a flood that she had to
> press it back with all her force . . . 'You can't give us anything a little
> nearer?' . . . . 'We've got to recover it.' She was as struck with the
> beauty of this plural pronoun as she had judged he might be with that
> of her own. (22/23, 83)

The orgasmic nature of the language here is inseparable from the
'union' of plural pronouns ('And the two shall be one') which was
earlier, outside the cage, in the park, in fear, inconceivable. Only
now safely encaged (and engaged) is the deeply thrilled telegraphist able to come together, in a marriage of pronouns, with her
Everard captain.

And so, to end this section, to the 'plural instances of the
action':

> It was a striking part of the business, for example, that it was much
> more the women, on the whole, who were after the men than the men
> who were after the women. (5, 24)

While upward mobility out of the cage is excluded, sideways shifts
into parallel spheres of action are contemplatable. The most
important and obvious such sphere in James's text is the
arrangement of flowers. At first glance, this system also appears to
offer upward mobility, though what is divulged, again, is yet
another intricate entrapment of message-sending and receiving:

'Should *I* see them? – I mean if I *were* to give everything up for you.'
Mrs Jordan at this became most arch. 'I'd send you to all the
bachelors!'
. . . . 'Do *they* have their flowers?'
. . . . 'You should see Lord Rye's.'
'His flowers?'
'Yes, and his letters. He writes me pages on pages – with the most
adorable little drawings and plans. You should see his diagrams!' (7,
30)

Here I end on overlapping networks, the 'mixtures of bachelors
and flowers' (8, 33) which constitute Mrs Jordan's *roulette*: 'They
simply *give* me the table – all the rest, all the other effects, come
afterwards.' (6, 26) The sphere of flower arrangement also permits
the illusion of control of a system, the illusion of a system with a
subject at the centre but, ultimately, a cameo of absent authorship
– in this case, 'The Death of the Centre', 'The Death of
Character'.[15]

☆ ☆ ☆

. . . over Jordan

'I am not wherever I am the plaything of my thought'[16] is a
Lacanian proposition borne out by the activities of both Mrs
Jordan and the telegraphist, who had 'a play of refinement and
subtlety greater, she flattered herself, than any of which she could
be made the subject' (5, 22). In short, subjectivity is incompatible
with play, as has been shown both in the play of names and the
play of spheres. Just as the realization of the 'beauty of the plural
pronoun' *propagates* in the telegraphist a knowledge 'that she
could almost play with him and with her new-born joy' (23, 83), so
with Mrs Jordan, 'in whom she recognized an equal' (2, 12), the
telegraphist may enter the 'speakability' of an actant relationship:
'the thing they could now oftenest say to each other was that they
knew what they meant' (6, 26). Yet this 'meaning' derives
exclusively from their 'equality', their horizontality, the guarantee
that 'each profusely curtained for the other the limits of low
horizons' (24, 87). In their conversational 'fencing' with each
other, they are entirely mutual foils. 'Reality, for the poor things
they both were...could never be the escape, the rise' (26, 96).
Thus, in mutual awareness that an end of their actant status (their
*un*reality) would imply an end to the story, and to their existence,

they cling to their final encounter, remain 'together, as if it would be indeed their last chance' (26, 97). Which, as the story ends here, it was. And if a final reminder of the primacy of *diegesis*, 'the spatial/temporal universe to which that story belongs',[17] is needed, it may be observed that the span of their relationship, the time-span of the text, is the London-social 'season' (2, 13). As textual 'debutantes' they come out but fail to rise; in the *horizontal* network of a 'caging' text, they are married – and married off!

☆ ☆ ☆

ducks and Drakes

> She quite thrilled herself with thinking what . . . a bad girl would do.
> . . . 'Come, therefore; buy me!' There was a point indeed at which
> such flights had to drop again – the point of an unreadiness to name,
> when it came to that, the purchasing medium. (11, 42)

Play is game and game, in this text, is often 'gaming'. In 'their high encounter with life, their large and complicated game' (4, 17), the actants are the playthings of a system of numbers. In conversation with Mr Mudge, the telegraphist 'tantalizes' his Wesleyan 'propriety' by shifting attention from a concern for low-society issues to high-society activities:

> 'Talk of the numbers of the poor! What *I* can vouch for is the numbers
> of the rich! . . . 'And where do they come from?' her companion
> candidly inquired. She had to think a moment; then she found
> something. 'From the "spring meetings". They bet tremendously.' (10,
> 36–7)

Each protagonist is caught up in the sphere of activity ('unreadily') named *gambling*. At the most obvious level, Everard ('*the Pink 'Un*') plays ducks and drakes with both numbers and names, with horses and with people. Yet it is not only his fate, his marriage, that is decided by his 'debts' (27, 98):

> Mr Drake loomed, in a swift image, before her; such a figure as she
> had seen in open doorways of houses . . . majestic, middle-aged, erect,
> flanked on either side by a footman and taking the name of a visitor.
> Mr Drake then verily *was* a person who opened the door! (26, 94)

Despite the 'verily *was*', Mr Drake's role is not so much a person's as a function. Not only does Drake permit Mrs Jordan to duck beneath the normal barrier of entry into 'society', to cross the Jordan of social aspiration, but also it is he who is attributed with the 'settlement' of the telegraphist's marriage to Mr Mudge. As the door of one cage opens to let her pass into another, it occurs to her 'that it was strange such a matter should be at last settled for her by Mr Drake' (27, 102). What is at stake is again the directional function of horizontal facilitating. The gamble of social aspiration, the gaming and playing of the spheres of action in which the girl in the network has been involved, are now at an end. Mr Drake's textual function of 'opening doors', of maintaining the *social* order, is an internal parallel to the most unreadily named entity of all – that 'I' – that extra-diegetic narrator who, in an all but imperceptible intrusion at the outset, promises the very abolition of character-mimesis and the embodiment of actant-diegesis which is *In the Cage*:

> This was rapidly to give it a place in an order of feelings on which I shall presently touch. (4, 19)

III

criss-cross reference

The final network of this discussion will be constituted by the interwoven lines of complementary or contrary enquiry developed by other essays in the volume. Just as I accept that there is no one, exclusive practice called structuralism, but rather an infinite network of structuralisms, or structuralist activities, so I argue, in this analysis of *In the Cage*, that views of structuralism such as Raman Selden's as 'necessarily static and ahistorical' involving 'rigour . . . achieved at any cost' are hopelessly restrictive and misleading. It is too easy to focus attention merely on the systems and functions that structuralists have, indeed, painstakingly elaborated. As Diana Knight argues in her application of Gérard Genette's method to *Heart of Darkness*, structuralism in practice – which is what this volume is about – is based on a salutary 'handling of the most basic tools of narrative' (D.K., p. 14 above). In the process, as Jonathan Culler claimed in *Structuralist Poetics* in 1973, structuralist activity continues today to make it 'possible to see new virtues in other criticism and to organize it in new ways' (*SP*, p. x). For many developments in contemporary criticism, structuralist practice has provided the concepts and, equally consistently, has subverted any claim that 'structuralism is dead! Long live post-structuralism/or Marxism/or Psychoanalysis/or

Feminism'. It is questionable whether it is even possible, let alone desirable, to attempt to separate structuralist criticism from several of the approaches exemplified in this collection.

Far from applying to *In the Cage* those 'neat catalogues of structuralism', which Anne Jones suspects of aspiring to 'critical mastery' (A.J., p. 71 below), and, in the process, excluding a sexual political reading – this study of characterization, by exploiting a deliberately plural and open-ended series of structuralist strategies, ought to complement much of her reading. For not only may an actant theory of character-functions tie together male supremacy with exploited femininity, it may also do so in the context of other, overlapping networks of social class, of money functions, or of the vested political interests at work in the text. 'Liberation' is combated by more than just one network of relations. In this sense, structuralism need not be ahistorical. For I hope to have avoided the danger, in setting the text against itself and by juxtaposing quotations from *In the Cage* either in pattern or in conflict, of merely pointing to paradigms or paradoxes. It is rather the *use* of such models that Marxist, Feminist or Deconstructive readings, say, are invited to employ. Structuralist practice may be seen, and used, as a multiple enabling device, as plural as the ideologies of its users. Is not the Barthes of *Mythologies* and *S/Z* engaged in an exposure of the *structured* nature of ideologies? Equally, Macherey, Kristeva and Derrida, in turn, have absorbed the lessons of structuralism to render more generalizable, more predictive, even, the themes and implications underlying their respective critical *praxes*.

Bearing in mind that, as Douglas Tallack points out, 'Derrida . . . . draws attention to the way that deconstruction "inhabits" even the structuralist model of language inspired by Saussure' (D.T., p. 161 below), it may seem an all-too-obvious deconstructive reversal to claim that the same structuralist model itself 'inhabits' deconstruction. Thus the 'undecidability' and 'dissemination' of meaning and 'inter-textuality' which pervade Douglas Tallack's reading of *In the Cage* are equally at work throughout the present essay. Derrida's notion of 'différance', of course, is structuralist 'différence' (relationality) *at work*. What is at issue, in politicizing structuralist practice, is precisely a matter of 'strategy' and 'risk', as Derrida points out. The (free-)play of metaphors, of names and of numbers, in a deconstructive reading of *In the Cage*, is but a step further than structuralist *inter*-play. Concomitantly, class as a *'differential* concept' (D.T., p. 212n below), the frame as *mise en abyme*, and the 'labyrinths' of a shifting 'center' as endless, overlapping networks of structural spheres of action, all 'inhabit' both structuralist and post-structuralist readings. Inseparably. All readings are inextricably enmeshed – *In the Cage*.

Further reading

Jonathan Culler's suggestion that 'character is the major aspect of the novel to which structuralism has paid least attention and has been least successful in treating', which I mentioned in my introductory remarks, should now be more readily situated. For once actant theory has been accepted, 'characterization' as an expression of individual subjectivity ceases to apply. It is thus in the broader context of structuralist theory that this essay has worked as, for instance, in my extension of Barthes' 'reality effect' from description to include character depiction. Much of the Further Reading from Diana Knight's opening chapter, then, is relevant here.

Apart from the Culler, Jefferson, Barthes and Greimas references discussed in my text and given in footnotes, the following items are worthy of mention. Still the best point of entry into Formalist/Structuralist analysis of character functions is Vladimir Propp's *The Morphology of the Folktale* (Austin, Texas UP, 1968), first published in Russian in 1928. Tzvetan Todorov's 'Narrative-men', chapter 5 of *The Poetics of Prose* (Oxford, Blackwell, 1977), is a useful if heavily slanted application to *The Arabian Nights* of the notion that character is but action. The principal device of 'embedding' one action within another is a relevant corollary to actant theory. This Todorov essay is markedly more structuralist in its application, however, than Todorov's mediocre 'The structural analysis of literature: the tales of Henry James' in *Structuralism: an Introduction*, ed. David Robey (Oxford, Clarendon, 1973), pp. 73–103. Overlong and rambling, this study is more concerned with genre than character, positing the view that James's mystery stories involve a syntagmatic progression towards an *absence* of secret. Barthes' hermeneutic code definition in *S/Z* is a far more concise and effective rendering of the central thesis.

Shlomith Rimmon-Kenan in *Narrative Fiction: Contemporary Poetics* (London, Methuen, 1983), includes discussion of character in Chapter 3, 'Story: characters', and Chapter 5, 'Text: characterization'. As in so much of her writing, she summarizes usefully the work of other theorists, beginning here from the assumption that 'Character is dead' and discussing the work of Barthes, of Forster ('flat' and 'round' characters) and of Seymour Chatman. She admits, in part, her debt to Chatman who, in 'On the Formalist-Structuralist theory of character' (*Journal of Literary Semantics*, I, 1972, pp. 57–79), and in *Story and Discourse* (Ithaca, New York, Cornell UP, 1978) sees such character theory as reductive, yet struggles to find an alternative, lapsing into an over-complicated discussion of so-called 'paradigms of traits' which seem no less structured than actant theory itself.

Finally, three short but important meditations on character, only the first of which is structuralist in orientation: Philippe Hamon, 'Pour un statut sémiologique du personnage' (*Littérature*, 6, 1972, pp. 86–110); Hélène Cixous, 'The character of character' (*New Literary History*, 5, pp. 383–402); and Marcia M. Eaton, 'On being a character' (*British Journal of Aesthetics*, 16, 1976, pp. 24–31).

3 Marxism and Form
D.H. Lawrence, *St Mawr*

Steve Giles

I

Introduction

There has been an increasing tendency in recent years for Marxist
critics in Britain to distance themselves from the concerns of
traditional aesthetics. Terry Eagleton's *Literary Theory: An
Introduction* presents a devastating attack on the very concepts of
Literature and Literary Studies, while Tony Bennett is sceptical of
virtually the entire tradition of Marxist criticism, whose attempt to
theorize the universal and eternal nature of Art is, in his view,
fundamentally at odds with the basic premises of Marxism, which
would entail the explanation of the form and content of literary
texts in terms of the economic, political and ideological relations in
which they are set.[1] It might therefore seem rather contradictory
to adopt an approach to criticism which has no qualms about the
viability of categories such as Art and Literature, and yet insists on
its own strict adherence to Marxist principles. The approach in
question is, of course, that of Georg Lukács, the most prolific and,
together with T. W. Adorno, the most sophisticated Marxist critic
and aesthetician of the twentieth century.

In order to bring out the intricacies and also the difficulties in
Lukács's position, I have chosen to focus on his classic essay of
1936, 'Narrate or Describe?'.[2] This has been described as 'one of
Lukács's finest essays'[3] and as 'possibly the most convincing
representation of the Lukácsian position',[4] and it raises a host of
questions central to any Marxist literary criticism and theory. It
was written when Lukács was in exile in the Soviet Union, and like
all Lukács's writings of the 1930s is marked by the debates and
controversies surrounding the development of socialist realism in
Soviet literary theory and policy at this time.[5] It presents itself as a

contribution to the ongoing discussion on naturalism and formalism in Marxist circles, but in fact is nothing less than a theory of the development of the European novel from its realist heyday in the earlier part of the nineteenth century to the experiments of modernism in Lukács's own day, which attempts to bring together both formal and sociological analysis. Lukács's central thesis in the essay is that in the wake of the victory of the bourgeoisie in the 1848 revolutions, a fundamental change occurs in the art of novel writing. Instead of continuing the great tradition of epic composition and embodying the principles of narrative, the novel becomes merely descriptive, and thus incapable of reflecting the true nature of society. This crucial distinction between adequate and inadequate reflection lies at the heart of Lukács's critique of descriptive writing, and is underpinned by Marx's differentiation between 'the material transformation of the economic conditions of production' and 'legal, political, religious, artistic or philosophic – in short, ideological forms in which men become conscious of this conflict and fight it out'.[6] Accordingly, developments in the novel are to be explained not on the basis of an autonomous evolution of artistic forms but with reference to a fundamental shift in the writer's life experience which is determined by socio-economic and political factors. At the same time, Lukács does not wish to view the human subject as a mere plaything of historical processes, and the somewhat abstract Marxian discourse of conflict between forces of production and relations of production is given a Hegelian turn, in the sense that Lukács emphasizes the importance of the actions of individual agents, however circumscribed these may be by their position in the struggle between opposing classes and by the encroachments of capitalism.[7]

The most striking feature of Lukács's account of *narrative* is his use of the metaphor of drama. The race in Tolstoy's *Anna Karenina* is characterized as a nodal point in a great drama, which presents events rather than images in a sequence of highly dramatic scenes which constitute turning points in the action of the novel as a whole. Indeed, the rhetorical flourish that opens the essay – 'Let's begin *in medias res*' – is itself presumably modelled on Scott's technique of plunging the reader into the heart of a decisive action which is about to unfold. Lukács, however, unlike other theorists of the novel, appears to construe the dramatic not as a technique of 'showing' rather than 'telling', but as a structural concept, as a way of characterizing the tightly knit and highly integrated relationship of the parts to the whole embodied in the organic unity of the self-contained work of art which alone is truly authentic.[8] However, this structural criterion can only be satisfied if certain other conditions are met. The causal interconnectedness and hierarchical organization central to the epic art of narrative can only be achieved if the events depicted are grounded in the dynamics of concrete human praxis and are set in the past. Lukács emphasizes the role of concrete human praxis because the driving forces of societal development, which the epic artist seeks to discover and depict, can only manifest themselves in the visible deeds and actions of human beings. Individuals in narrative must possess typical character features that manifest essential human traits, and the non-human world of nature and things can only attain true poetic status by mediating human destinies and relationships and by being connected with human struggle. The sequence of interactions to be depicted must be set in the past by the epic artist, because the past is his basic means of artistic organization. Complex interrelations in life can only be perceived retrospectively, Lukács argues, as can the essential rather than the accidental in society in general. Retrospection thus grounds the author's omniscience and his knowledge of the significance of each detail in the work for the work as a whole, so that although the reader is encouraged to share in the experiences of the characters from whose standpoint events are narrated, the overall contextualization of those experiences is never lost. As a result, the reader is enabled to feel at home in the work, secure in its illusory projection of life in all its breadth and wholeness.

The distinguishing features of the *descriptive* text radically distance it from the category of narrative. Instead of being tightly integrated into the work as a whole, its descriptions function as padding and are only loosely related to the total action. The text becomes episodic, the causality and sequentiality of narrative degenerates into chance and mere succession or juxtaposition, and events give way to occurrences. The reason for this tendency to atomization and disintegration is that things and descriptions are no longer closely interwoven with human praxis. Any intrinsic significance they might have had therefore disappears, and the artist is compelled to resort to the use of symbolism to impose poetic significance on them. Human beings themselves are reduced either to the level of dead objects or to a chaotic succession of moods or states. of mind which are but tenuously connected with their actions: instead of dynamically interrelating with the world, it is as if they are the spectators of their own lives, and the reader too is thus forced into the position of an observer. However, as an observer is contemporaneous with the occurrences which he is observing, he must soon become lost in a welter of information whose significance is as yet unknown, and so be incapable of correctly identifying events and giving an account of their relationship to the societal whole. The same applies in the novel, where the retrospection of narration is now superseded by the contemporaneity of description. The author/observer loses all sense of proportion and omniscience, sinks to the level of his characters' perspectives, and simply mediates a set of shifting points of view which are unrelated to any overall epic context. As a result, the descriptive text produces not a correct reflection of objective reality, which reveals its inner dynamism as grounded in the driving forces of human society, but a superficial and distorted reflection trapped at the apparently amorphous surface of life.

Lukács now defines narration and description as the two fundamental modes of representation in the modern novel, which correspond to the basic modes of behaviour of writers before and after 1848, involvement and observation. Narrative writers such as Balzac and Dickens were themselves involved in and actively experienced the process of development of bourgeois society in the first half of the nineteenth century, and were not specialist writers in terms of the capitalist division of labour. Descriptive writers such as Flaubert and Zola, on the other hand, started writing after 1848 when bourgeois society was already fully established. Their rejection of the status quo compelled them to become critical observers of their society, and they were professional writers, forced to compete in the capitalist market place. The writer's societal position conditions his artistic output because of the tight links Lukács wishes to establish between life experience, *Weltanschauung* and composition. Lukács's use of the term *Weltanschauung*, which normally means 'world-view' in an epistemologically and politically neutral sense, is rather idiosyncratic and expresses his conception of a Marxist world-view.[9] Lukács argues that a writer cannot produce narrative without a *Weltanschauung*, as it alone enables the writer to perceive the contradictions of life in a rich and ordered context. A *Weltanschauung* is the basis of any correct thinking, feeling and writing, and must embody the principle that society's development is governed by law-like regularities and is generated in and through human struggle. As a *Weltanschauung* is the concentrated and generalized sum of a writer's life experiences, not all writers will have a *Weltanschauung* in this strict sense. Flaubert, a major descriptive writer, was fully aware that he lacked a *Weltanschauung*, and Lukács argues that he was therefore led to confuse the boring monotony of everyday life in bourgeois society with life as such. Like the bourgeois intelligentsià in general after 1848, he was ignorant of the real driving forces of societal development and therefore incapable of producing narrative. However, this incapacity is not grounded in some personal failing, but is objectively determined by the structural position of the writer in mature capitalism. The dominance of description is also entailed by the fundamental nature of capitalist development: its increasing inhumanity, and the obliteration of the inner poetry of human praxis in the alienated 'world of Prose'.[10] Descriptive writers may well revolt against alienation, but their revolts will bear no fruit as long as they fail to grasp the real basis of the meaninglessness of human life under capitalism and do not actively experience the struggle of those who are seeking to give a meaningful shape to their lives. Until then, such writers are bound to capitulate to capitalist reality and to produce inauthentic art: the true art of narrative can only be achieved by writers committed to the class struggle of the proletariat, as this alone can provide the experiental basis for arriving at a *Weltanschauung*.

II

Lukács against Lawrence
In order to facilitate the application of theoretical principles elaborated in 'Narrate or Describe?' to *St Mawr*,[11] it is helpful to sum up Lukács's position in the form of a diagrammatic model which can then be used to generate categories and questions to which *St Mawr* can be related:

	Narration	*Description*
(i) the narrator	omniscient and retrospective	non-omniscient and contemporaneous

(ii) structure	hierarchical organization sequential causality	levelling and uniformity atomization and juxtaposition
	dramatic events	undramatic occurrences
(iii) the human subject	dynamic interrelation between humans, each other, the world	humans as dead objects or isolated observers
	unity of character through actions, essential human traits	arbitrary successions of states or moods
(iv) significance and symbolism	intrinsic significance grounded in natural symbolism	no intrinsic significance so imposed interconnections
(v) the writer	pre-1848 capitalism: non-specialist involved in society so *Weltanschauung* grounds correct reflection	post-1848 capitalism: specialist observing society, no *Weltanschauung* so distorted reflection
(vi) the reader	shares participant perspective, at home	distanced as observer by spectator perspective, lost

In attempting to assimilate *St Mawr* to these six categories, I shall for the time being assume them to be both valid and productive of insights, and delay any criticisms of Lukács until the textual analysis has been completed. Comments on the position of the reader will, however, be interspersed in discussion of the first five categories, rather than forming a sub-section in their own right.

(i) The narrator

The narrator in *St Mawr* appears from the beginning to be both omniscient and retrospective. The story is set in the past, and the narrator is a non-participant superior to the story being narrated, a typical configuration in omniscient or 'authorial' narrative. The narrator comments quite openly on the characters and events in the story, passing value judgements and expressing socio-cultural views, most strikingly in the history of Las Chivas, which the reader is clearly encouraged to share. There thus appear, on the face of it, to be no grounds for disputing the narrator's reliability, and in general terms the narrator has an overall view of events distinct from that of his/her characters. The only deviations from this principle seem to be relatively minor: Lou functions as a narrator internal to the story in her letters to Mrs Witt (pp. 116–23), and occasional use is made of free indirect discourse, in such a way as to blur the distinction between character and narrator perspective.

(ii) Structure

The status of the narrator in *St Mawr* would lead us to expect a highly integrated and densely concentrated account of dramatic events tightly linked in a causal sequence. However, although *St Mawr* clearly does incorporate material which is dramatic in the everyday sense of the word – most notably the St Mawr incident during the excursion to the Devil's Chair – the actual presentation of events or occurrences slides into the descriptive category. The text's linear structure betrays a tendency to parataxis and enumeration, and it is as if the happenings which do occur are rather like beads juxtaposed on a chain. In the opening pages, for example, the short paragraphs give an impression of bittiness, and the narrator makes striking use of coordinating conjunctions such as 'and' or 'but' to link sentences within paragraphs, and paragraphs themselves. When combined with enumeration, as in the depiction of Rico on page 12 ('But at the same time . . . suave, courier-like amiability') and in the account of Mrs Witt's ride on pages 16–17 ('In she sailed . . . everybody in sight'), the impression conveyed is one of atomization of detail into mere succession and juxtaposition, classic features of the descriptive text.

The above reflections also raise the possibility that, at the micro level at least, the text is structured spatially rather than temporally, and this suspicion is confirmed when one investigates the text's macro structure. The major sections of the text are indicated by significant changes of place, and although temporal references are made in the text, these tend to be imprecise. Despite the fact that the ordering of occurrences in text and story largely coincides,[12] the reader has difficulty in establishing a detailed overall perspective on their temporal relations. We know, for example, that pages 37–165 of the text cover a period of some five or six months, from summer to late autumn 1923, but it is far from easy to establish exactly when particular happenings take place. Similarly, although the first sentence of the text tells us that Lou is 25, we do not know precisely when she is 25 in story terms, when she and Rico married, or when Mrs Witt returned to London after her trip to America and the story's main action begins. This lack of perspective is intensified to some degree from the reader's point of view by the text's lack of chapter divisions and by the narrator's use of techniques which presumably fall into the category of levelling, namely scenic presentation and free indirect discourse. The depiction of Lou on the opening page could be read as proceeding directly from an authorial narrator, or as free indirect – 'Having one's own way landed one completely at sea', 'But she had "got" him. Oh yes!', 'So what sort of American was she, after all?' (p. 11). The same ambiguity arises in relation to Phoenix, Rico and Mrs Witt, and generally in the depiction of St Mawr, but we should also note that this issue only affects a relatively small proportion of the text as a whole.[13] Scenic presentation occurs more frequently, and involves larger sections of text, but not to the extent that one can argue that the narrator has a predilection for 'showing' rather than 'telling': if anything, the converse is the case.[14]

(iii)   The human subject

The status of the individual self or character, and the nature of individuals' relationships to themselves, each other, nature and society, are key issues in *St Mawr*. Each of the three main characters – Lou, Mrs Witt and Rico – undergoes a crisis in these relationships, which may be neither perceived nor resolved, and the text itself is fundamentally ambiguous as to the roots of this crisis, shifting uneasily from a socio-economic to a psycho-biological frame of reference. This is clearly exemplified in the case of Rico, whose inability to come to terms with his drives of aggression and desire appears to be explicable in psychoanalytic terms, but only after the text has proffered a sociological account of his predicament, as Rico's anxieties about his future and his place in the world are initiated by his insecure class position as the only son of an upwardly mobile colonial official, and are compounded by his relative lack of means. This ambiguity is crucial for any Marxist critique of the text, and also informs the presentation of Lou and Mrs Witt.

In Lukács's terms, Mrs Witt is a classic example of the critical observer distanced from society. She is filled with contempt and repugnance for the practices of European society: 'her terrible grey eyes with the touch of a leer looked on at the hollow mockery of things' and she scrutinizes her 'daughter's marriage 'as it were from outside the fence, like a potent well-dressed demon' (p. 14). However, the social isolation that grounds her venomous skirmishes with the world around her ultimately leads to her own psychic and critical dissolution. Her hatred of Europe crystallizes around the inadequacies of its men, which have perverted the quality of her own sexual relationships. These were based on sympathy or understanding rather than any erotic dynamism, but this sexual problematic is seen as having deeper socio-cultural roots. Modern culture and society, like modern men, have lost touch with Pan, and this loss is directly related to the development of industrialization: England is totally 'humanized', whether by coal smoke, or aeroplanes, or the artificial lights of its cities encroaching on 'the darkness of the old Pan' (p. 110). However, the text focuses on the psychological and interpersonal moments of this problematic, rather than on its socio-economic basis. The central issue for Mrs Witt is that in the emasculated society of modern Europe she cannot find a man able to counter her own innate destructiveness, her own will-to-power which, starved of worthy external opponents, is doomed to dissipate itself and drain away. In a world where there is nothing left to conquer, and conquest leads to contempt, she becomes aware of the increasing non-entity of her own being and her own experiences. Any firm and coherent sense of identity disintegrates, as she wonders where she is, whether she has ever been anywhere, whether the past events in her life have any substance. The full implications of her increasing social and interpersonal isolation dawn on her in conversation with Lewis, where she realizes that 'soon she would be left in an empty circle, with her empty self at the centre' (p. 107). She feels her power and dynamism gradually drain away, and the demonic observer of the early part of the text collapses into a state of silent, apathetic non-involvement in the world around her, no longer even capable of critique.

The text's initial presentation of Lou Witt suggests that the psychological disorientation which increasingly affects her also has a social basis. As the story proceeds, she is plagued by self-doubt, by questions about the reality of her social experience, and by intensifying alienation from the world around her, the 'cardboard let's-be-happy world' inhabited by all the people she knows (p. 35), the world of her own domestic surroundings which 'was turning ghostly' (p. 125). She becomes more and more weary, dazed, numb, time is a void she cannot fill, her life is futile and ridiculous. A possible explanation for her psychic state is suggested in the text's opening paragraph: Lou, we are told, 'had had her own way so long, that by the age of twenty-five she didn't know where she was. Having one's own way landed one completely at sea' (p. 11). However, this apparently individualistic account of her dilemma is given a sociological dimension as the opening page proceeds. The odd quirks and peculiarities enumerated in the third paragraph are seen to derive from her societal position as an outsider, as one 'who is at home anywhere and nowhere', who 'didn't quite belong' (p. 11), as she lacks the clearly defined social base that would enable her to know where she is and give her life the direction it so fundamentally lacks. At the same time the sociological is complemented and superseded as the text progresses by the psychological and the biological: her inner distress appears to be related to sexual problems, which are themselves seen as a manifestation of a crisis in modern culture.

The sexual dimension of her situation is introduced through the brief indication on the opening page that she had mastered Rico, and amplified a page later by references to the playfulness and pretence of their relationship and its foundation in fascination: their bonding is nervous rather than sexual, tense rather than spontaneous, and characterized by mutual destructive domination. Rico soon becomes associated in her mind with all the negative aspects of her experience outlined earlier, with the result that she comes to explain her inner decay in sexual terms. Tired of modern men and their sterile minds, sceptical of her mother's Cartesian rationalism, she advocates a reinvigoration of the male species through a return to intuition and animality, but without accepting that her argument entails primitivism as she slides between idealization of prehistory and abhorrence of its brute and degenerate barbarism. The problem with modern men is not that they are brute and degenerate, but that their animality has been domesticated, so that they become gutless slaves, and thus inappropriate partners in intimacy. Her sexual anxieties, expressed most graphically in her horror at penetration of her inner sanctuaries (p. 146), thus become the effect of a deep-seated cultural crisis, generated by the fact that we fail to 'get our lives straight from the source, as the animals do, and still be ourselves' (p. 57). Lou's conception of cultural crisis is given its fullest articulation in the apocalyptic vision she has during her ride to the farm after Rico's accident. She becomes aware of floods of evil overwhelming the world in a deluge of life-denying mediocrity, which masquerades as the ideal in order to poison and undermine natural creation, an evil which even underlies political phenomena such as socialism and fascism, and manifests itself in the mechanistic lives of those whose eunuch sensibilities wish to geld St Mawr. Once again, political and socio-economic factors are construed as effects rather than causes in a socio-cultural totality, and Lou's solution to the spread of evil is, appropriately enough, both quietistic and ostensibly a-political: the most the individual can do is

> depart from the mass, and try to cleanse himself. Try to hold fast to the living thing, which destroys as it goes, but remains sweet. And in his soul fight, fight, fight to preserve that which is life in him from the ghastly kisses and poison-bites of the myriad evil ones. Retreat to the desert, and fight. (p. 79)

Lou's vision and her more general views about how the crisis in western culture may be resolved are precipitated by St Mawr, who from her first contact with him catalyses both emotional release and revelatory insight. After their initial encounter, it is as if 'that mysterious fire of the horse's body had split some rock in her' (p. 22), and her vision of his head seems to signify another world – the world of Pan that preceded Hellenic western civilization, the prehistoric twilight world of danger and potency, demonic yet vital, but a world devastated by modernity. It is this world which she wishes to escape into, a world, unlike Texas, of intrinsic depth and meaning, the sustaining world of wild spirit which she believes she has found at Las Chivas – a world of concrete immediacy which had apparently been lost, where the individual can win through to 'the hard, lonely responsibility of real freedom' (p. 80) and attain true stillness and mastery in the arid refuge of the spirit.

(iv) Significance and symbolism

Lukács's meditation on significance and symbolism is a classic instance of his appropriation of Hegelian aesthetics in order to specify the problematic of modern art. In Hegel's view concrete works of art, which permit life to be felt as a totality and allow us to feel their situations in terms of individual human experience, can only be produced in societies whose elements are intrinsically meaningful to their members. Any loss of immediate comprehensibility in society has crucial aesthetic consequences: for Hegel the impossibility of epic writing, and for Lukács the impossibility of narrative, compensated for in the descriptive writer's recourse to symbolism. Hegel and Lukács both relate this loss of immediate comprehensibility to the emergence of industrial society, which is essentially abstract and prosaic. From Lukács's point of view, this loss is intensified under capitalism due to alienation, as the products of human labour are no longer felt to be the results of immediate, sensuous human activity. There can be no doubt that the world of western society as depicted in *St Mawr* is one of prosaic abstraction: but does this provoke an attempt to impose significance on objects and events by investing them with symbolic status? With the notable exception of its presentation of St Mawr, the text appears to be characterized less by recourse to symbolism than by a rather heavy-handed and laboured explicitness, which tends to manifest itself through adjunctive tropes such as expletion and pleonasm. We read, for example, of Mrs Witt's 'conceited, inquisitive, scornful, aristocratic-democratic Louisiana nose' (p. 16), of 'The slave, taking his slavish vengeance, then dropping back into subservience. All the slaves of this world, accumulating their preparations for slavish vengeance, and then, when they have taken it, ready to drop back into servility' (p. 80). Rather ironically, however, the attempt to imbue life with meaning and significance in this way could be seen as having the opposite effect, by increasing the degree of semantic redundancy in the text. And where experience is read symbolically in an explicit manner, for example when the pack-rats are described as 'symbols of the curious debasing malevolence that was in the spirit of the place' (p. 151), the effect once again is to foreground the lack of intrinsic significance in the rats' behaviour.

Similar strategies recur in the presentation of St Mawr. The repetition of epithets attributed to his physical features – his naked head, large black brilliant fiery eyes, ears like daggers, hot red-gold body – combined with the horse's eponymous status would of itself be sufficient to invite a symbolic reading, but St

Mawr's significance is explicitly posed and vehemently reasserted: dark, demonic, dangerous, and yet at the same time intensely desirable, even his neighing evokes 'another darker, more spacious, more dangerous, more splendid world than ours' (p. 34). This attempt to transpose experience into symbol is at its most striking in the double depiction of the single most dramatic event in the text, when St Mawr rears and Rico pulls the horse on top of himself:

> Then she saw a pale gold belly, and hoofs that worked and flashed in the air, and St Mawr writhing, straining his head terrifically upwards, his great eyes starting from the naked lines of his nose. With a great neck arching cruelly from the ground, he was pulling frantically at the reins, which Rico still held tight. (p. 74)

> It had come to her as in a vision, when she saw the pale gold belly of the stallion *upturned*, the hoofs *working wildly*, the *wicked* curved hams of the horse, and then *the evil straining* of that *arched, fish-like* neck, with the *dilated* eyes of the head. *Thrown* backwards, and *working* its hoofs in the air. *Reversed*, and purely *evil*. (p. 77, my italics)

Initially, the event is transmuted into a dynamic and vivid image of process. The use of the simple past in 'worked' and 'flashed' gives way to a sequence of continuous verb forms as the reader's attention is directed towards St Mawr's experience and activity, rather than his behaviour's moral or metaphysical significance. And then, in the second account, as the italics indicate, the emphasis is shifted from process and experience to idea and symbol. The verb forms are systematically reversed, as the description is dominated now by adjectival past participles, and the state of being reversed or upturned is foregrounded as an index of evil.

(v) The writer

D.H. Lawrence's societal position is, in many respects, a classic instance of that configuration of factors which Lukács takes to underpin the descriptive writer's output. Unlike Dickens or Balzac, he was not directly involved in, nor did he actively experience the process of development of his society. He was a non-participant in the major event of his age, the first world war, and for the greater part of his adult life he was a highly critical observer of a culture and society which he radically rejected. Although he himself related the crisis in contemporary art and culture to the threadbare nature of its metaphysic or philosophy,[17] the vitalistic alternative sanctioned in both his theoretical writings of the early twenties and in *St Mawr* does not meet Lukács's specification of a *Weltanschauung*. A *Weltanschauung* must accept that societal development is governed by law-like regularities and is generated in and through human struggle. Lawrence, however, rejected all attempts at explaining social life in scientific or mechanistic terms, and explicitly repudiates collective human struggle in his political comments, which are anti-democratic, elitist, and at times virtually Fascist. Although he was clearly aware of the increasing inhumanity and abstraction of modern industrial society, he was ignorant and even contemptuous of the real driving forces of societal development made manifest from a Marxist point of view in the class struggle of the proletariat, and was thus compelled, like descriptive writers in general, to 'capitulate without a struggle before the completed results, before the completed phenomenal forms of capitalist reality', and to 'see in these only the result, but not the struggle of opposed forces' ('Narrate or Describe?', p. 113).

Many of these points are borne out in *St Mawr*. We have already seen how the text gives grounds for construing individual disorientation and disaffection as a sociological problem, only to imply a more basic level of explanation in biological or psychological terms. Similarly, although the text is conscious of modern socioeconomic and political developments, it presents them in terms of a more general vitalistic critique of western culture, which mythologizes or ontologizes them, and thus tends to erase their specific historical determinations. Fascism and bolshevism are construed as manifestations of 'the secret evil' in Lou's vision (p. 78), and industrialization impinges on the text more often than not as a metaphor for the sterile monotony of modern life and the sexual inadequacies of modern men.[19] The text's few references to the first world war are more critical and certainly far less offensive than those in *Fantasia of the Unconscious*,[20] for example, focusing on the poverty and depredation it had caused, but even here the text fails to draw any clear socioeconomic conclusions from the war's effects, which instead are explained metaphorically in the language of pathology: 'Even on this countryside the dead hand of the war lay like a corpse decomposing' (p. 67). And when the war experience of combatants is referred to, it is integrated into the text's more general cultural problematic, most obviously in the case of Edward's minor facial disfigurement caused by the kick from St Mawr – 'To go through the war, and then get this!' (p. 79) – but also in the case of Phoenix and Lewis, whose war injuries reaffirm their alienation from urban industrial society in its devastation of Nature.

III

Lawrence against Lukács: Reflections in Conclusion
The results of the above application of 'Narrate or Describe?' would appear to suggest that, broadly speaking, *St Mawr* can be classified as a descriptive text. Although told by a retrospective omniscient narrator who has a clear evaluative overview, in structural terms it is characterized not by hierarchy and causality but by mere succession, juxtaposition and atomization, with the result that it is difficult for the reader to achieve an overall perspective on what happens. The text's main figures are outsiders, and in two cases observers, whose relationships to themselves and the world around them are in a state of crisis. Given the nature of their inner turmoil and disaffection, it hardly seems appropriate to look for any unity of self in their characters, though whether their behaviour and life experience manifests essential human traits must depend on one's concept of the 'essentially human': the text may well focus on what Lawrence takes to be the 'essentially human', but it does so at the expense of the ensemble of societal relations that his characters enter into. D.H. Lawrence himself comes across as an archetypal descriptive writer: an outsider, a radically critical observer aware of the increasing abstraction of industrial society, but because of his socio-political position quite incapable of grounding his work in an adequate *Weltanschauung* and therefore compelled to produce a text which gives a distorted reflection of capitalist society and which must resort to the imposition of significance, given Lawrence's lack of solidarity with those actively struggling to give a meaningful shape to their lives.

So far, then, Lukács's position would appear to be vindicated. His categories seem to have a high degree of descriptive validity, and have also made possible a reading of *St Mawr* that interrelates stylistic and sociological commentary in a way which meets Bennett's strictures as outlined in my introduction. Any disparities between *St Mawr* and Lukács's model would seem to imply that symbolism is only one strategic possibility for the descriptive writer attempting to counteract the prosaic abstraction of modern life, and that there is no necessary link between the presence of an omniscient narrator and key structural features of the narrative text. However, while the empirical application of Lukács's model suggests relatively minor criticisms of its viability, his position can also be subjected to a more general theoretical critique, and I should like to focus on three main areas: its account of the reader and narrator, its explanatory status, and its critical strategies.

Lukács's specification of the position of the narrator is inherently problematic. He systematically confuses author and narrator, and is not totally clear in his concept of point of view. While the omniscient author–narrator is commended for narrating events from the standpoint of the participants and thereby enabling the reader to share their perspective, the descriptive author–narrator is castigated for sinking to the level of his characters' point of view. Lukács also assumes, like Hegel, that the reader's response is entirely determined by the text, but if the writer's perceptions of reality are governed by his societal position, one wonders why the reader's, apparently, are not. The evidence of the other accounts of *St Mawr* in this collection would suggest that the reader's appropriation of the text is determined at least as much by the categories which the reader brings to bear on the text as by the text in itself, so that a crucial enterprise for any Marxist approach to texts must be the critical exploration and assessment of the categories in question, whether they be Freudian, Formalist, or even Marxist.[21]

Lukács's own explanatory model can be seen as working at two levels. At the level of the individual text, it purports to explain the occurrence of certain textual strategies rather than others (atomization and autonomization rather than integration and concentration), while in a more general sense it attempts to theorize a fundamental historical shift in the nature of textual production (from narration to description, or classic realism to naturalism and modernism). In both cases, structural and stylistic features of the text are ultimately to be accounted for in causal terms, with reference to the writer's socio-political position on the one hand,

and to overall societal developments on the other. Lukács's neo-Hegelian model of historical change, which theorizes capitalist development as a prosaic encroachment upon the realm of poetry, is fairly typical of the dualistic models of societal development common in nineteenth-century sociological theory, best exemplified in the *Gemeinschaft/Gesellschaft* model of Ferdinand Tönnies, but like all such models it oversimplifies the nature of the historical process and illegitimately valorizes a past social formation as a locus of harmony and organic unity. Furthermore, as far as the writer's position is concerned, Lukács is unclear as to how, precisely, to account for the writer's adoption of a perspective on reality which constrains his selection of specific textual strategies. Before 1848, the crucial factor appears to be the writer's active involvement in the the society of his day, whereas after 1848 (and, one might add, after 1917) the key issue appears to be not active involvement in society as such, but commitment to the struggle of the rising class.[22]

However, despite the fact that both these solutions beg more epistemological questions than they answer, the most contentious aspect of Lukács's position is his attempt to bring together Marxist theory and normative aesthetics. Lukács insists that the descriptive text is either bad art, or not even art at all, and once again his underlying assumptions derive from Hegel, but this time even more problematically, as he uncritically appropriates Hegelian criteria of artistic value and construes them not as being historically conditioned, but as timeless norms.[23] At the same time, the critical edge to Lukács's position is as much epistemological as it is evaluative: his attack on descriptive writers is far more trenchant when he exposes the inadequacies of their representations of capitalism, though here too his critique stands or falls with the validity of his basic sociological assumptions, of his Hegelianized version of Marxism. The problem for the literary critic is that none of the issues raised in the last two paragraphs can be resolved with reference to 'literary' texts or even 'literary' theory: the crucial test of any Marxist theory of literature or culture is not its ability to stimulate discussion in the literary salon, but its explanatory and critical power and its political bite, and the most fitting rejoinder to the cultural speculations of Lawrence and his acolytes comes from Lukács himself:

the sad fate that human beings exist without a dynamic inner life, without living humanity and human development, is far less outrageous and provocative than the fact that capitalism daily and hourly transforms thousands of living human beings with infinite human possibilities into 'living corpses'. ('Narrate or Describe?', p. 114)

Further Reading

(a) Works by Lukács

'Narrate or Describe?' is best read in conjunction with 'Art and Objective Reality', in *Writer and Critic and Other Essays*, trs. and ed. Arthur Kahn (London, Merlin, 1978), and *The Historical Novel*, trs. Hannah and Stanley Mitchell (Harmondsworth, Penguin, 1981). Lukács's classic treatments of realism and modernism are *Studies in European Realism: A Sociological Survey of the Writings of Balzac, Stendhal, Zola, Tolstoy, Gorki and Others*, trs. Edith Bone (London, Merlin, 1972), and *The Meaning of Contemporary Realism*, trs. John and Necke Mander (London, Merlin, 1979).

(b) Works on Lukács

The most useful recent accounts of Lukács's work on literature may be found in David Pike, *German Writers in Soviet Exile, 1933–1945* (Chapel Hill, North Carolina UP, 1982), and Eugene Lunn, *Marxism and Modernism: An Historical Study of Lukács, Brecht, Benjamin, and Adorno* (London, Verso, 1985), which also has an excellent bibliography. The best introduction to Lukács's literary theorizing remains Fredric Jameson's essay, 'The Case for Georg Lukács', in *Marxism and Form: Twentieth-Century Dialectical Theories of Literature* (Princeton, N.J., Princeton UP, 1971).

4 Feminism I: Sexual Politics
Henry James, *In the Cage*

Anne Jones

I

The publication of Kate Millett's *Sexual Politics* in 1969 created a new and polemical role for literary criticism. As one part of her wider analysis of the role of women in society Millett's use of literary material is inextricable from its theoretical context, and that context needs to be established before the implications of her approach can be drawn out.

Millett's views on the function of literary criticism are, for the most part, implicit in her practice, in which texts are examined as 'instances' or 'reflections' of the sexual politics she is theorizing. Thus, for example, a combination of plot summary and detailed sexual political analysis of extracts is used to support her reading of D.H. Lawrence's work as a progression from misogynistic homo-eroticism in *Aaron's Rod* to the narcissistic cult of male supremacy in *Lady Chatterley's Lover*.

If more immediately literary concerns (for example the literary value of a text) addressed by later feminist critics hardly figure here it is because the emphasis of the polemical first wave of feminist criticism was on literature as the product of social relations. Criticism thus becomes not simply another interpretive approach to the canonized texts but a part of women's liberation from oppression.

Fifteen years on Millett's remains one of the most detailed and lucid expositions of the nature and effects of this oppression. In her view women are oppressed, whatever their particular circumstances, by patriarchy, a social organization which 'guarantees superior status in the male, inferior in the female' and is political in the sense that it involves 'power-structured relationships, arrangements whereby one group of persons is controlled by another'.[1]

Women, she notes, are subordinate to men first of all in the home. Ideological pressures tend to encourage them to devote their energies to the family and to labour long after other workers have clocked off, for board and lodging only, servicing one generation of wage-earners and producing and socializing the next. These functions are central to the reproduction of society, yet the authority of generations is invested in the male 'head of the family' and although, as Millett observes, his legal priority has been modified in recent years women's 'chattel status continues in their loss of name, their obligation to adopt the husband's domicile, and the general legal assumption that marriage involves an exchange of the female's domestic service and (sexual) consortium in return for financial support' (Millett, pp. 34–5).

In order to highlight the enduring features of the social organization she describes, Millett gives less attention to differences in the nature of women's oppression than to similarities. The persistence of women's chattel status, for example, receives more emphasis than any historical modification of it. It is, however, important to note that by the end of the nineteenth century, when Henry James wrote *In the Cage*, this status was being undermined by women's wider participation in the new industrialized society. By this time production had been removed almost entirely from the home, drawing thousands of single working- and lower-middle-class women into factory, shop and government employment, as well as the more traditional teaching and domestic positions. Yet as Millett makes clear it was assumed then, as now, that reproductive would displace productive functions as soon as a suitable mate was found and that the usual domestic duties would be fitted around any outside employment in the interim. As a result the increase in the range of work theoretically open to women did not radically affect their subordinate status or domestic responsibilities.

As the twentieth century progressed the increasing numbers of women who wished to support themselves and seek a career of their own rather than working for the advancement of their partners found themselves competing on unequal terms for professional opportunities. They were (and continue to be) interviewed by men unaccustomed to working with women as equals and unlikely to rate a woman's competence or dedication as highly as that of a comparably qualified man because each was assessed according to different criteria. The unequal treatment and opportunities of women are grounded in an assumption of their inferior status which has, historically, gone largely unchallenged, based as it is on supposedly invariable physical and psychological factors held to derive from women's biology. In *Sex, Gender and Society* Ann Oakley demonstrates the dependence of this convenient and highly influential view on a conflation of sex and gender, the 'female' and the 'feminine', which has traditionally determined the treatment and representation of women throughout society. Physiological differences between the sexes must, Oakley states, be admitted 'but so also must the variability of gender'.[2] She concludes that

> in early upbringing, in education and in their adult preoccupations, males and females are pressed by society into different moulds. At the end of this process it is not surprising that they come to regard their distinctive occupations as predetermined by some general law ... despite the way in which other cultures have developed gender roles quite different from our own which seem just as natural and just as inevitable as ours do to us. (pp. 156–7)

It is not biology but the *social organization* of biological differences which produces and perpetuates gender differences. But if the relations of men and women are not dictated by biology, if they could be otherwise, then the fact that they are not is a political one. Millett reads literary texts as representations and developments of these relations and thus instances of sexual politics. In her analyses Millett attributes the prevailing differences in masculine and feminine gender roles to patriarchy, or the rule of men. 'The fact is evident at once', she states, 'if one recalls that the military, industry, technology, universities, science, political office, and finance – in short every avenue of power within the society, including the coercive force of the police, is entirely in male hands' (Millett, p. 25).

The significance of the universities' inclusion in this list is crucial for feminist literary criticism since, as critics such as Elaine Showalter point out, it is in the universities that literary values are codified, modified and replaced, and the literary canon established and policed in accordance with those values. Feminist interventions in critical theory and practice do not undermine the objectivity of academic criticism, since attributions of value are never simply objective. Like the social organization of sexual differences they involve choices and are thus political and designed, ultimately, to ensure women's participation in the creation of the canon and in the selection of the values it is to reflect. An indication of the range and aims of these analyses will help to contextualize sexual political literary criticism.

In a recent survey of feminist literary criticism Showalter isolates two dominant critical modes. The first, which she terms 'gynocritics', is concerned with 'the history, styles, themes, genres and structures of writing by women'[3] and relates its specificity to biological, psychic, linguistic or cultural features of women's experience. The second is broadly sexual political and examines the stereotypical representation of women in American male writing in what Cheri Register has called an attempt 'to deal with the reasons behind this proliferation of female stereotypes and the lack of realistic women characters; to discuss the political use of literary stereotypes; and to describe their effects on the individual female consciousness'.[4] This is clearly incompatible with the celebration of assumed psychic, biological or gender differences indulged in by some feminist approaches, for they serve only to perpetuate and reinforce stereotypes. Nor does sexual political criticism require an in-depth knowledge of linguistic or psycho-analytic theory. Its aims and methods are, in principle, quite simple. It seeks to probe the political aspect of sex and 'the role which concepts of power and domination play' (Millett, p. 3) in selected texts using a new, broader analytic framework that is 'capable of seizing upon the larger insights which literature affords into the life it describes, or interprets, or even distorts and which takes into account the larger cultural context in which literature is conceived and produced' (Millett, p. xii).

Before applying this framework to *In the Cage* it should be noted that the preceding outline of the feminist debate aims to establish a general theoretical context for a feminist reading of a particular text. Aspects have therefore been stressed, played down or omitted, while others will be dealt with as they arise in the course of the application. Like Millett's examples, *In the Cage* will be considered as an instance of sexual politics, and the implications of this procedure will be drawn out in the study's concluding section.

II

Since Millett's analyses require a constant movement between text and context, character and author, she restricts herself to primarily realist writers whose works appear to have a clear autobiographical focus. In *In the Cage* – where the protagonist is female but the author is not and where the narrator is barely perceptible – a patriarchal focus must be sought outside the text in prefaces, other narratives and other critical accounts as well as within it. Thus the first stage of the study will examine the telegraphist's constitution by critics, the second her constitution by James, the third the text's relation to the larger social and literary context, and the fourth the telegraphist's relation to other characters. These stages and their order are equally arbitrary. Sexual political criticism is not concerned with systematic or total readings and sets out no list of procedures the meticulous application of which would entail interpretive or methodological 'correctness'. In this and other respects the sexual political reading of *In the Cage* will be clearly distinguishable from the neat catalogues of structuralism, and from deconstruction's masterful reduction of the text to the same few problematic metaphors. It is with such critical mastery, its forms, motives and effects, that the study begins.

Kate Millett's major studies focus on twentieth-century writers and their texts, each involving vividly explicit descriptions of sexual activity. Henry James is an altogether different proposition. Like D.H. Lawrence, Henry Miller and the rest he is reacting to contemporary changes in sexual politics but the nature – and the form – of that reaction are at first sight obscure. In *In the Cage* action of any kind is minimal and nothing comes within a mile of explicitness, sexual or otherwise. The labyrinthine obliqueness of the opening sentences is a fair indication of what is to follow, and while they become intelligible retrospectively there are points in the narrative where hindsight doesn't help. In view of this the reader would probably expect a degree of circumspection in critical accounts of James's text. Here, however, is a representative selection of what she would find:

> [Everard] needs to be 'nailed', just as the telegraphist will benefit from being intermittently awed and put in her place by Mudge's masculinity. This will save her from her defensive inclination to hold herself superior to the male point of view....For too long, she has been taking

the benefits of masculine stimulation without the compromise of reciprocation.

> Stuart Hutchinson, 'James's *In the Cage*: A New Interpretation'.[5]

The whole affair finally betrays its sordidness, baffling the telegraphist's pathetic naïveté. Her comical stupidity . . . sets her apart from . . . other protectresses.

> Heath Moon, 'More Royalist than the King: the Governess, the Telegraphist, and Mrs Gracedew'.[6]

At the end we perceive that Mudge is a decent, courageous man and that the intrigue of Everard is unromantically sordid, and the clues which lead to his disillusionment come largely from Mrs Jordan. The girl now knows that she has meant nothing to Everard. Her adventure is over and she is ready to marry Mudge, no longer at some vague later time, but the very next week.

> Walter Wright, *The Madness of Art: A Study of Henry James*.[7]

'In the Cage' is a gay pitiless satire of the sort of person who slavers indignantly over gossip columns, simultaneously satisfying prurience, morality, and a bruised social consciousness . . . a social outcast – by reasons of birth, inexperience, and prudery – whose efforts to 'save' the world are really self-aggrandizing.

> Charles T. Samuels, *The Ambiguity of Henry James*.[8]

The cage-girl . . . is, in other words, confronted always by the realities of her condition – her poverty on the one hand and her job, and on the other the hints of the world's splendours about which she is so curious, and with which she must make her peace.

> Leon Edel, *The Complete Tales of Henry James*, vol. 10.[9]

[The telegraphist is] naïve, spiteful, and continually engaged in self-deception.

> E. Duncan Aswell, 'James's "In the Cage": The Telegraphist as Artist'.[10]

She was wrong about not seeing Everard again . . . she was wrong about Everard's supposed wealth, she was wrong about his desire to marry Lady Bradeen, she was wrong about Mrs Jordan's marriage to Lord Rye – in fact, as we shall soon see, she is wrong about everything.

> Ralf Norrman, 'The Intercepted Telegram Plot in Henry James's "In the Cage" '[11]

If James is to be blamed for anything it can only be for a misleading phrase in the Preface, where he speaks of the 'solution' depending on the girl's 'winged wit' . . . The 'solution' is not, as this might suggest, the solution of Captain Everard's perplexities; it is simply the telegraphist's – her final acceptance – of the bleakness of reality.

> L.C. Knights, *Explorations: Essays in Criticism, Mainly in the Literature of the Seventeenth Century.*[12]

So much for circumspection: the tone is patronizing, misogynistic, contemptuous or resigned but in every case authoritative and unequivocal; the problem of uncertainty simply doesn't arise. And what more proper object of those discrete and contradictory certainties than a woman – object par excellence and member of a class so habitually assessed and possessed that she can be constituted as pathetically naïve, comically stupid, prurient, self-aggrandizing or spiteful, in any combination, according to needs. Since the obliqueness of the material from which the critics construct their telegraphists belies the force of some of their reactions there must be other, extra-textual, factors involved: for example, the presence in the telegraphist of certain of the qualities patriarchy traditionally reserved for men (intelligence, a sense of self-worth, intellectual curiosity and ambition) to the detriment of the passivity, docility, humble virtue and ineffectuality that were encouraged in her contemporaries.

James, it must be said, does not have her deviate far from those norms but where they have been so thoroughly internalized as to appear natural any infraction of them seems perverse and can excite violent reaction, while compliance is taken as justification for the inferior status accorded to women in general. In Stuart Hutchinson's view, for example, Everard needs to be 'nailed' because he is passive and ineffectual, while the telegraphist must be disciplined, brought to order, for her want of the proper docility in her relations with male characters. Fellow feeling encourages critics like Hutchinson to let erring males off with a caution while sentencing the woman in the case to the most predictable of corporal punishments. Everard may have failed in his manly duty but his youth (he is, of course, older than the telegraphist) excuses him. Rendering James's 'between two journeys – duly bored with his evening and at a loss what to do with it'[13] as 'on the lookout for female diversion' Hutchinson describes Everard finding the telegraphist available and appa-

rently willing but, since he is 'not very mature', neglecting to whisk
her off to his rooms and have his proper masculine way with her.
Now in Hutchinson's terms this failure reflects less a triumph over
Everard's masculinity than an absence of masculinity to triumph
over, but since in the patriarchal view any semblance of power in a
woman – apart from that ceded to her for tactical reasons – is a
potential threat to male supremacy 'Mudge's masculinity' is finally
invoked to restore order and chastise her presumption.

Although Hutchinson's reaction to the telegraphist seems at first
rather idiosyncratic it echoes what Shulamith Firestone has called
the 'Virility Inc.' school of writers for whom woman is an
exclusively sexual object yet must be constantly punished for her
sexuality. The rhetoric of Aswell and Norrman and the misogynist
laughter of Moon and Samuels reflect the same exasperation at the
telegraphist's presumption. But there is another, less overtly
inimical, critical tendency at work in the excerpts selected.
Sighing, as the telegraphist relinquishes her ambitions and bows to
the inevitable, Knights, Edel and Wright resign themselves to her
fate. Speaking in priestly tones of 'the world's splendours . . . with
which she must make her peace' (p. 10) Edel commends
renunciation of this world, presumably with a view to some reward
in the next. It may be that the celestial hierarchy is radically unlike
its patriarchal equivalent, but it doesn't do to rely on it.

To reject male critical constructions of the telegraphist is not to
assume that the real telegraphist would step forward if asked to do
so by a member of her own sex. Female critics – many of whom use
male critical theory as if it were Critical Theory – are not to be
confused with feminist critics, nor male truths with Truth. At its
surface *In the Cage* seems to interrogate the possibilities of
knowing and imagining, but this surface must be penetrated if
feminist readers are to use the text as an illustration of their truths,
rather than simply accepting it, or the male critical version of it.
Whether these versions are New Critical, structuralist, deconstructionist or whatever matters little. Concerned less with questions of
literary value and textual complexity than with the relation of one
half of the population to the other, Millett would reject them all in
order to concentrate on what each of them takes for granted,
ignores or suppresses: the power relations that license the male to
impose meanings on the female and thus to perpetuate those
relations.

James's role in this process is uncertain. As a male writer he can hardly avoid imposing meaning on female characters but, as demonstrated in his preface to *In the Cage*, it would be difficult to do so more obliquely. His central characters are frequently females endowed with qualities that he professed to admire and whose predicament is described with sensitivity, even sympathy. Judith Fetterley's feminist reading of *The Bostonians*, for example, celebrates James's analysis of the 'situation of women' and his 'ability to place himself on the side of women and in line with their point of view';[14] Patricia Stubbs, struck by the fact that even the most sympathetically portrayed of James's heroines are always in predicaments of one kind or another, speaks of 'pure ideology and an anti-feminism so subtle and fused so completely with the form and texture of the novels that it can be overlooked altogether'.[15] A sexual political reading of *In the Cage* must attend to these subtleties so as to comment on patriarchy's place in the relations of women and men in general in the belief that, as Millett puts it, like all power systems 'when its workings are exposed and questioned, it becomes not only subject to discussion, but even to change' (Millett, p. 58).

In a text where aristocratic protagonists have a wealth of names it is certainly something to have no name at all. Critics have noted that anonymity, by inhibiting the crystallization of character effects around the name, makes the text's central consciousness more powerfully diffuse.[16] Perhaps, but it also enables James to manipulate reader response to the telegraphist with a subtle economy. Where social status derives (through the name) from the father or husband the affiliations of the girl who has neither are exceptionally 'tangential, vicarious, and temporary' (Millett, p. 38), as epithets applied to her indicate. About to encounter Everard at Park Chambers she is 'our young lady'; contrasted with the elegant classes or in the company of Mrs Jordan she is 'the betrothed of Mr Mudge'; according to context she ranges from 'our heroine' to 'our poor young friend'. And each epithet subjects her to the patronage of Mr Mudge, the narrator or the reader implied in its possessive adjective.

The telegraphist, one of the few working heroines of the time, is also patronized by the customers of Cocker's. References to 'her ladies' and 'her gentlemen' (p. 23) echo the commercial formula which assumes possession by the servant of the served but there is a stronger sense in which they might be said to be hers. In his preface to the New York edition of *In the Cage* James observed: 'To criticise is to appreciate, to appropriate, to take intellectual possession, to establish in fine a relation with the criticised thing and make it one's own'.[17] By dint, therefore, of an obsessive attention to the ladies and gentlemen who visit Cocker's 'our young critic' (p. 31) makes them her own. However, the telegraphist's 'winged wit', as James puts it in the Preface (p. 157), her large imagination and 'small retentive brain' (p. 22) provide James with a rich source of guesswork and intuition. Moreover, the limited focus he allows her (compared with what he refers to in the Preface as his own 'large intellectual appetite' (p. 155)) deprives her of an interpretive context and renders all but her romantic object a blur. The resulting combination of imagination, memory and myopia make the telegraphist concerned and able to help Everard's romance along in trivial matters of names and numbers but ignorant of the exact nature of his circumstances. With Everard cleverness thus maintains her in a relation of servitude; with Mudge it tends to be suppressed altogether. Within patriarchy the general prejudice of male superiority teaches women who are more intelligent than their partners to conceal that fact (the telegraphist for example likes Mudge 'to think her silly' (p. 35)), but since women who are known to dissimulate simply incur a different form of animosity – directed at 'the scheming woman' – it is not always easy to see what benefits are to be derived from cleverness. In James's narratives it serves chiefly to make his female characters more acutely aware of the restrictions imposed on them.

Like the imagination and refined sensibilities bestowed upon her, the telegraphist's cleverness compounds the social restrictions which derive from her sex and her circumstances. Driven from a domestic cage to a commercial one by pressing financial need the telegraphist, a 'picture of servitude and promiscuity' (p. 29), is subjected to the most galling effects of both enclosure and exposure. Under Buckton's surveillance at Cockers, in the park or on the beach her encounters are all equally public, until the final revelatory meeting at Mrs Jordan's lodgings that is peopled with new names and new definitions of old ones.

In the meantime, shut out and shut in, the telegraphist daydreams. Since the calculation and conjecture that the narrative is designed to dramatize occupy the whole of her imaginative energy and resources there is little else she can do. Nothing so vulgarly functional as a plan is allowed to enter her head. The undirected and unproductive nature of this endless mental activity is clearest in the telegraphist's relation to Everard. Though freely indulging her resentment and revulsion at the activities of the leisured classes (a somewhat ambivalent antipathy – widespread at the time – which James shared) the telegraphist pursues her vocation in the service of one of its members to whom she is as 'sand on the floor' (p. 40). The clash between this 'petty slave mentality'[18] and her otherwise critical and independent spirit highlights James's use of old stereotypes to construct the new woman. But this, in turn, reflects a larger tendency: having been socialized into conformity with stereotypes prescribed by an earlier patriarchal phase women found themselves ill-prepared for sudden changes in their roles and circumstances in the wake of the Industrial Revolution. Reacting to these changes, James allows the telegraphist a measure of independence but the enduring effects of patriarchal conditioning on author and character alike ensure that the servicing of men remains one of the few forms of 'useful' activity which she is permitted or socially or psychologically prepared for.

Isolated from her peers and educated largely by popular fiction (whose stereotypes are particularly resistant to change) the telegraphist is punished for expecting reality to coincide with her novelistic models – rash no doubt since James, the source of her 'reality', is concerned to distinguish his own radically non-popular narratives from her 'ha'penny-worths' (p. 14). Fiction told her what Lady Bradeen was like. At the same time it offered an escape from dreary routine into a fantasy grounded for the most part in the same patriarchal assumptions. However, despite their regulatory social functions James clearly sees popular novels as potentially enervating, corrupting morals and arousing unrealistic expectations in their impressionable (female) readers, and his telegraphist suffers accordingly. The telegraphist's problem is that she and James simply do not read the same books. Endowed with middle-class sensibilities by a middle-class writer of middle-class fiction but assessing the world in terms designed for the literate working-classes the telegraphist's disappointment is pretty well guaranteed.

There are, of course, points on which character and author appear to coincide. For example, they share an ambivalence towards the leisured classes and this has been put down to a limited acquaintance with the classes in question, for James too was marginalized – by nationality, by profession, by temperament, even, it has been suggested, by sex. According to Alfred Habegger – who is himself ambivalent towards non-members of the Virility Inc. school – James 'had a very big stake in the argument that you could know the world without being of it. Like Victorian women novelists he lacked access to vast areas of masculine experience'.[19] Certainly James is not of Mailer's or Miller's bristling macho world; as Philip Rahv points out, he subordinates experience to consciousness and energy to sensibility.[20] But for all his imagination and discrimination he is not of George Eliot's or Charlotte Brontë's world either. No doubt he admired certain of the qualities conventionally assigned to women, especially those he shared, but if he wasn't a 'masculine' writer he was certainly a male one.

James's interest in 'the situation of women' and its oppressive character, his admiration for the heroines whose qualities and strategies so often mirror his own, are beyond question. The nature of that interest and the use made of the awareness are not. As a male and as a writer he was free to romanticize the characteristics prescribed for the oppressed sex and throw them into relief with a few restrictions of his own – Milly Theale's invalidity, Maisie's youth and ignorance, the telegraphist's cage. The telegraphist's baroque thoroughness; narratorial irony at her attempts to free herself or derive what comfort she can from her circumstances; the apparent inevitability of her final rout and capitulation and the archness with which they are described: none of these suggests a sympathetic, or even neutral, observer of the situation of women. They suggest a writer whose stylistic predilections require a subject; typically a specimen with a fine, sensitive, imaginative and highly reflective head and no body.

But for the sexual political critic James's sympathy or otherwise with contemporary feminist movements finally matters less than the effects of patriarchal ideology in his texts. In Millett's examples in *Sexual Politics* these effects are most revealing in the construction of sexuality, but in James's text the role of sexuality is altogether more obscure. According to Patricia Stubbs in *Women and Fiction*, 'James's heroines . . . tie themselves into knots of inhibition and self-consciousness at anything resembling a sexual encounter' (p. 162). The telegraphist is endowed with a detailed knowledge of literary boudoirs and a virtuous ignorance of any other kind. This ignorance is, in part, depicted as wilful: she shies away from any detail that would offend her virtue or her sensibilities by making those boudoirs 'too real'. In this text, unlike many of James's, this tension seems to be resolved quite unambiguously. The innocent adolescent becomes a more knowledgeable, chastened and thus marriageable young woman through an unexpected insight into the mysteries she had previously shunned. What she had sought to preserve in the imaginative intensity of romantic fiction degenerates at the first shaft of daylight into ignoble detail.

Yet this need not be the daylight conventionally equated with 'reality'. It may simply be a different light, or the same light from a different angle, deflected via Mrs Jordan and Mr Drake through the door he holds open on to the barely visible boudoir of Everard and Lady Bradeen. The 'details' themselves could hardly be more obscure, and something needs to be said about James's refusal to shed more light on them. It could be argued that he is representing the uncertainties of an innocent consciousness at work, and that is probably the only way of defending his own indulgence in the coy omissions and obliqueness he censured more than once in British – as compared with French – fiction. In his essay on *In the Cage* Ralf Norrman refers to an occasion when a friend asked James what Everard had actually done wrong and was told that the author 'did not know, would rather not know' (p. 427). James, too, was clearly not interested in any 'nearer vision of discovery or shame' (p. 82). The suggestion of sordidness remains as veiled as fine minds and contemporary morality could have wished.

Ranged against the romantic fantasy of the 'possible' is the 'irremediable' presence of Mr Mudge, which produces unfocused stirrings in his betrothed. When he bodily removes two violent customers 'the neatness of his execution' leaves her 'without resistance' (p. 34) for the physical power it bespeaks will in turn engage her own body. Yet imagination too (represented as freer than her body but ultimately as restricted as the experience it feeds on) must be subdued if Mudge's wife is not to harbour socially undesirable aspirations. Thus, having shunned the 'vulgar' and

'horrid' reality of physical contact, its sudden eruption into her
fantasies causes her to panic and turn away from the imaginative
possibilities of romance altogether when it is subsequently
revealed to be a veil she has thrown over sexual activity.

Between the early yearnings and the final disenchantment lies a
transitional state of what has been called anxious half-knowing or
'apprehension'.[21] In the park, when daydream and reality appear
to merge, the telegraphist is thrown into confusion. But perhaps
they are never clearly distinguishable. The contrast between her
situation and that of the couples in the 'vulgarly animated gloom'
(p. 62) indicates how much her transactions with Everard owe to
books. Thereafter she knows how to go on. When Everard places
his hand on hers she makes no objection and restraint alone
prevents her from doing the same when conversational manoeuvres give *her* the upper hand. Having announced her absolute
devotion to his service she 'bravely and magnificently left it; and
little by little she felt him take it up, take it down, as if they had
been on a satin sofa in a boudoir' (p. 58). The seduction scene is
every bit as clichéd, metaphorical and controllable as its basis in
telegrams and fiction could lead one to expect. Well acquainted
with the manuals, the telegraphist conquers, metaphorically
pushing, even striking, Everard before commanding him to
remain, unmoved by his pleas to accompany her.

When the romantic tableau fades the telegraphist senses the
obscurer motivation that was concealed behind Everard's 'awfully
good manners' (p. 20), that complacent chivalry which treats even
'gaping slavies' as ladies or, as Millett puts it, as female members
of 'that fraction of the upper classes and bourgeoisie which treated
women to expressions of elaborate concern while permitting them
no legal or personal freedom' (Millett, p. 73). This reparation for
social inequities enables the telegraphist to imagine herself a
'lady', outside the cage, rather than a 'shopgirl at large' (p. 52),
and it is to the fineness of her sensibilities and emotion that
Everard responds. Within the cage she is, for Everard's less
chivalrous peers, sub-human, a letterbox (p. 61), and after the
park seduction scene his own attitude to her also changes. Where
any action on the part of a single woman is a sign of forwardness
even metaphorical unchastity licenses her constitution as a whore
by means of covert sovereigns. These she rejects with the fineness,
not of the virtuous lady she imagines herself to be, but of the

deluded *ingénue* she is for James. Since, according to Stuart Hutchinson, a refusal to be seduced can be at least as culpable as permitting it, patriarchal prescriptions don't leave the telegraphist much room for manoeuvre. But *In the Cage* is no tale of repressive Victorian norms being undermined by the heroine's nascent sexuality: female innocence entails dependence but female sexuality does not entail power, and Mudge, like Basil Ransome in *The Bostonians*, is summoned to escort his 'heroine' to the conventionally (procreatively) sexed niche reserved for her once the perils of ingenuousness and indeterminacy have been overcome.

Lady Bradeen, the one woman in James's text who is permitted to be both romantically and sexually active – another luxury generally reserved for the leisured classes – is first and foremost a source of sexual interest for the man she wishes to marry and who has, we are told, no intention of marrying her in exchange for those favours until obliged to do so by the threat of discovery and the intervention of his young admirer. The details of this affair derive from Mrs Jordan who is, in theory, the telegraphist's obvious – perhaps only – ally. The fact that they generally relate competitively in practice thus needs to be accounted for. Sexual political critiques, though they tend to focus on the relations of male to female characters, can highlight the workings of patriarchy with equal clarity in the relations male writers ascribe to female characters. 'Women', Juliet Mitchell has observed, 'directed from childhood towards marriage, living in a "man's world", relate primarily to men and mainly competitively with each other.'[22] Whether comparing herself with 'the kind of low barmaid person who rinsed tumblers and bandied slang' (p. 39), 'brazen women' (p. 22), or Mrs Jordan – social inferiors, superiors or equals in her own terms – the telegraphist is hypercritical. This tendency underlies her ambivalent dislike of 'brazen women' as, conditioned into repressing sexuality yet intrigued to know what it might entail, she monitors their activities. Moved by attraction and pity for their defenceless male game she pours love, service, 'the only magnificence she could muster' (p. 61) into the already overflowing hands of her hero. He, able to move freely among the virtuous and the brazen and enjoy the favours of both, can play one off against the other. In view of the foregoing the fact of having been 'bereaved, betrayed, overwhelmed' (p. 11) at the hands of men (and, one might add, of being conceived by one with this in mind) will not prevent the telegraphist from assessing the males she encounters with an indulgence that varies only according to their suitability as potential husbands.

Where the status of women is concerned Mrs Jordan is, the telegraphist feels, 'her only equal' (p. 26). At a time when female heads of households were 'undesirable . . . a trait of poverty or misfortune' (Millett, p. 33), the women are marginalized by both sex and class. Social status is determined solely by males, and loss of males entails loss of status, since a woman without a man cannot expect to maintain her place in a society in which domestic and reproductive functions alone are assigned to her. Away from the tutelage of the male the telegraphist's mother turns to alcohol: her elder sister, another weak vessel, 'succumbed to all but absolute want' (p. 11) with all that the phrase's ominous obliqueness suggests. Like her friend, Mrs Jordan will not fail to marry, however disappointing the opportunities available to her, since any man is, of course, better than none. Her 'new career for women' (p. 11) promises well at a time when more women were seeking work outside the home but in fact hardly differs from the old ones; interior and domestic in nature, determined by the requirements of males (as, for example, surrogate wife/mother for all those bachelors) and designed primarily to postpone or advance the pursuit of the oldest legal one, marriage. But without the protection of a man economic independence is not available to Mrs Jordan, and she escapes from poverty into the arms of a man who falls well short of her aspirations. In the interim the women seek to elevate themselves not only by exaggerating their own opportunities and responsibilities but also by dignifying the other (as when Mrs Jordan's late husband is elevated to a bishopric) or by humiliating her (as, for example, in the telegraphist's lack of mercy where Drake is concerned). At the same time, and like the telegraphist's, Mrs Jordan's social status depends not only upon the male she ultimately weds but on the company she keeps in the interim. In Lord Rye's service she acquires what her friend perceives as a 'super-eminent air' (p. 27) so that the girl is overwhelmed at once by Mrs Jordan's social mobility and by her own exclusion. Having felt she would 'almost hate' (p. 33) her friend on the day of her betrothal to Lord Rye the telegraphist is hardly warmer when Mrs Jordan reveals her betrothal instead to Mr Drake. For all their shared disadvantages this constant jockeying for position is made to displace any sense of common cause, in accordance with the principle of 'divide and rule' on which the continuance of patriarchal government depends.

It is on the 'safe sentiment' (p. 43) of Mudge that the telegraphist's cleverness and aspirations are finally dashed. The legal and conventional controls of marriage will ensure that any talents she may have are directed exclusively towards his social and economic advancement. Part of the personal frustration this arrangement tended to produce in her more talented contemporaries could be dissipated by means of the higher function ascribed to women – that of providing culture and refinement in the life of her preoccupied husband, 'serving as the male's conscience and living the life of goodness he found tedious but felt someone ought to do anyway' (Millett, p. 37).

The sexual political critique must ask whether the subordination of the telegraphist's talents and individuality is the only alternative to romantic fantasy, whether imagination and sexuality need be mutually exclusive, whether, in short, her end is as inevitable as we have been led to believe. The policeman who, in the narrative's closing sentences, 'paused and watched' (p. 101) the telegraphist as she stood on the bridge is monitoring the activities not just of the potential suicide or prostitute he presumably imagines her to be (and we too speculate on whether the woman has fallen, is about to jump, or whether James has pushed her) but of all her peers. Women's upholding of patriarchal law is by no means inevitable – however skilfully texts such as this make it appear so – and agents are required to ensure compliance with the truculence of a Hutchinson, the wise resignation of an Edel, the subtlety of a James. It is precisely in these subtler and more resistant texts, where patriarchal ideology is least obtrusive, that its effects are most powerful. Sexual political criticism is concerned to question these representations. It reassesses the qualities assigned the telegraphist, among them an imaginative power (frequently conceded to women, presumably because the majority of men don't need it) whose focus is so limited that it can only contain one object at a time: courting couples or Everard but not both (p. 56), with all the distortion and misconception this entails. It seeks, too, to foreground the limits of the telegraphist's independence – whether to serve this rather than that male object, whether to choose this or another chocolate cream (p. 68) – in a society and a text that constitute women as dependent. It probes the ignorance on which such strategies depend and which is at once encouraged as basic to male control and censured so that control may be more complete.

Once challenged, these representations and the assumptions they embody can be traced to the power relations that motivate them in order to 'make available to consciousness that which has been left largely unconscious and thus to change our understanding of these fictions, our relation to them, and their effect on us' (Fetterley, p. 24). Whether we see the telegraphist finally as a victim of social conditioning or of plot convention we should bear in mind that she has not simply been described but 'absurdly constructed' (p. 12) by James. Unlike many of her literary contemporaries she is granted a mind (which serves to intensify her awareness of oppression) and in exchange forfeits a body. James can thus indulge his 'settled pessimism about the fate of women' (Fetterley, p. 117) by bringing another incomplete one to a personally tragic, patriarchally desirable end and invoking human destiny, in accordance with the assumption of Knights, Edel and Wright that even in fiction reality is a given which must be faced with stoical acceptance, on the part of women at least.

III

The sociological basis of Millett's sexual political theory has considerable internal coherence, and the explanatory power of its critical form is also undeniable. It can account for features that are lost in the study of structures or of the machine of history, and whose vitality escapes textual critics and threatens supposedly apolitical ones. Difficulties in both its sociological and literary forms have, however, emerged from the preceding application and need to be accounted for. Chief amongst these is Millett's emphasis on what has been called a 'universal and trans-historical category of male dominance'[23] which appears to leave little room for the resistance she advocates. In Millett's defence it must be said that in subordinating the distinctive features of women's oppression at a given historical moment to the similarities she is not ignoring or denying modifications in the nature of patriarchy but highlighting its resistance to change – rather as James, consciously or otherwise, highlights the persistence of the old patriarchal prescriptions in the new working girl. Then there are other feminist approaches which reject the view implicit in *Sexual Politics* that women and men would be all but identical if it were not for what she conceives as patriarchy. Instead, it is maintained that there are differences which are significant and should be suppressed or repressed no longer, not least because to do so would be to perpetuate existing male values. Many of these dissenting voices employ psychologically or biologically deterministic arguments that Millett would deplore. Such issues do not arise directly from the application of sexual political theory and may be followed in the suggestions for further reading.

The most widespread objection to sexual politics as literary criticism is that it tends to conflate character and author, text and world. The result is a reflection theory in which literature is portrayed as having 'a formal homology with the working of patriarchy, except in literature the male writer can, presumably, have it all his own way'.[24] However, the emphatic literariness of *In the Cage* poses difficulties when treating characters as living subjects of social relations and, as this essay demonstrates, a more circumspect approach may be needed than Millett employs on realist or autobiographical texts. In the end, though, objections to sexual political criticism, like charges of reductionism and insensitivity to literary values, must be weighed against its objectives. Millett's application of sexual political theory to texts was not designed to produce subtler or more complete readings of, for example, D. H. Lawrence. Instead, it sought to highlight certain tendencies and assumptions within his work in the context of the first polemical wave of feminist consciousness-raising. Since then the appropriation and adaptation of these insights by feminist literary critics has shifted emphasis from women's oppression to textual subtleties and highlighted the tension between the means and ends of feminist criticism. Elaine Millard's essay in this collection is a case in point. Although their validity fifteen years on and in a specifically literary context remains a much-debated issue, Millett's own priorities are unequivocal and remain the starting-point for most contemporary British and American feminist theory.

Further Reading
Among the early radical feminist texts the following are indispensable reading: Simone de Beauvoir, *The Second Sex* (first published in French in 1949), trs. H. M. Parshley (Harmondsworth, Penguin, 1972); Betty Friedan, *The Feminine Mystique*, first published in 1963 (London, Gollancz, 1972); Germaine Greer, *The Female Eunuch* (London, MacGibbon and Kee, 1971); Juliet Mitchell, *Women's Estate* (Harmondsworth, Penguin, 1973); and Ann Oakley, *Sex, Gender and Society* (London, Temple Smith, 1972). *Feminist Theorists: Three Centuries of Intellectual Traditions*, ed. Dale Spender (London, Women's Press, 1983), provides useful background material. Her own essay in the collection summarizes recent developments which are dealt with in greater detail in Michelene Wandor, *The Body Politic: Writings from the Women's Liberation Movement in Britain, 1969–72* (London, Stage 1, 1972) and Hester Eisenstein, *Contemporary Feminist Thought* (Boston, G. K. Hall, 1983). Eisenstein's study is of particular interest as it discusses the use made of Kate Millett's sexual politics by writers such as Adrienne Rich and Mary Daly.

For analyses of patriarchy's relation to capitalism see, for example, *Capitalist Patriarchy and the Case for Socialist Feminism*, ed. Zillah R. Eisenstein (New York, Monthly Review, 1979) and Christine Delphy, *Close to Home: A Materialist Analysis of Women's Oppression*, trs. and ed. Diana Leonard (London, Hutchinson, 1984), both of which are discussed in Michèle Barrett's admirably clear survey, *Women's Oppression Today: Problems in Marxist Feminist Analysis* (London, Verso, 1980).

The best introduction to feminist psychoanalytic theory is still Juliet Mitchell, *Psychoanalysis and Feminism* (Harmondsworth, Penguin, 1975). A more recent overview of feminism's relation to French psychoanalytic theory (especially Jacques Lacan's) is Jane Gallop, *Feminism and Psychoanalysis: The Daughter's Seduction* (London, Macmillan, 1982). The influence of both psychoanalytic and linguistic theory on French feminism emerges clearly in the anthology *New French Feminisms*, eds. Elaine Marks and Isabelle de Courtivron (Brighton, Harvester, 1981), the introductory sections of which form quite a detailed survey of French feminist thought.

For additional reading on the scope of feminist literary criticism see *The Authority of Experience: Essays in Feminist Criticism*, eds. Arlyn Diamond and Lee R. Edwards (Amherst, Massachusetts UP, 1977) and *Feminist Literary Criticism: Explorations in Theory*, ed. Josephine Donovan (Lexington, Kentucky UP, 1975). Toril Moi, *Sexual/Textual Politics: Feminist Literary Theory* (London, Methuen, 1985) is a good introductory survey of both Anglo-American and French theory and includes a discussion of Millett's *Sexual Politics*. Her essay in *Modern Literary Theory: A Comparative Introduction*, eds. Ann Jefferson and David Robey (London, Batsford, rev. ed., 1986), pp. 204–21, clearly defines such terms as 'feminist', 'female' and 'feminine'.

Of the feminist critiques which focus on James's work probably the most useful are Judith Fetterley, *The Resisting Reader: A Feminist Approach to American Fiction* (Bloomington, Indiana UP, 1978) and Patricia Stubbs, *Women and Fiction: Feminism and the Novel, 1880–1920* (London, Methuen, 1981), but see also Judith Fryer, *The Faces of Eve: Women in the Nineteenth Century American Novel* (New York, OUP, 1976) and Elizabeth C. Allen, *A Woman's Place in the Novels of Henry James* (New York, St Martin's Press, 1984).

5 Psychoanalytic Theory
D.H. Lawrence, *St Mawr*

Roger Poole

I

There is something so compelling in the story that Freud tells that
everyone interested in the human mind wants to read it. Even if,
on reflection, much of the story that Freud tells seems too
primitive or too sophisticated, the story lingers on in the
imagination, and no reader can remain unchanged in the way he
perceives the world after reading it.

So it is perhaps not surprising that Freud enters, invited or not,
into literary critical discourse at every level. Freud is omnipresent.
He has saturated the discourse òf literary theory to the point
where that theory itself seems to be little more than a further set of
revisions in Freud's own writings.

We have to start with two questions. What is the nature of the
'Freudian' insight itself? And secondly, why is that insight
particularly well adapted to the needs of literary criticism and
literary theory? Elizabeth Wright offers a clear formulation about
the first question:

> Freud's original insight centred upon the determining force of the
> unconscious aspect of utterance which revealed that mechanisms
> working in dreams, puns and slips of the tongue can be shown to be
> analogous to certain mental and linguistic processes. [1]

So the dream itself is a language, though it appears in the first
instance to be a translation, and sometimes even a bad translation,
of a text which has been composed in a more comprehensible form
elsewhere. Jacques Lacan, Freud's leading modern commentator,
achieved fame by stating that 'the unconscious is structured like a
language', but Freud himself would have found this only a slightly
surprising account of his idea. It is Lacan too who has without

doubt the most elegant description of what is going on in Freud's *Interpretation of Dreams*:

> Take up the work of Freud again at the *Interpretation of Dreams* to remind yourself that the dream has the structure of a sentence or, rather, to stick to the letter of the work, of a rebus; that is to say, it has the structure of a form of writing....The important part begins with the translation of the text, the important part that Freud tells us is given in the elaboration of the dream – that is to say in its rhetoric. Ellipsis and pleonasm, hyperbaton or syllepsis, regression, repetition, apposition – these are the syntactical displacements; metaphor, catachresis, autonomasia, allegory, metonymy and synecdoche – these are the semantic condensations in which Freud teaches us to read the intentions – ostentatious or demonstrative, dissimulating or persuasive, retaliatory or seductive – out of which the subject modulates his oneiric discourse.[2]

Cumbrous as that may appear, it is in fact quite accurate. The dream, according to Freud, is a rhetoric with transformational rules of its own. Through displacement and condensation of the elements, the dream can, as Lacan says, show or demonstrate, lie or persuade, take revenge or seduce – that is to say, the dream is an active intending force with a will of its own. It happens, though, to speak in our own mother tongue, and to observe the rules of our grammar.

It is in his early, founding works on method that Freud gives the literary theorist his tools. In *The Interpretation of Dreams*, which ushered in the new century in 1900; in *The Psychopathology of Everyday Life* (1904); and in *Jokes and their Relation to the Unconscious* (1905), Freud shows in detail how the unconscious manages to get its messages past the repressing censor, and which manoeuvres it has to carry out in order to escape that censorship. The 'latent content' of the dream in the unconscious gets 'scrambled', through condensation, displacement, the various means of representation and the secondary revision of the dream-work, so that what issues out into the 'text' of the dream is far from the optimum form that the unconscious would like to present. The basic difficulty the unconscious has, apart from the obvious one of avoiding censorship, is the grammatical one, for a dream does not dispose of a grammar or a syntax, neither can it directly imply cause and effect, nor can it show its materials in a temporal sequence. Perhaps the most brilliant single device Freud invents in *The Interpretation of Dreams* is what one might call the dream semaphore. With only two flags the unconscious can, through combinatorial expertise and substitution alone, manage to express itself in a 'dream grammar' which the analyst can eventually comprehend and analyse.

Logical connection between one thing and another, for instance, is reproduced in the dream-semaphore by mere co-presence in time. Events, people or ideas from widely different periods of the dreamer's life, will appear together in the dream, because they have something to do with each other, something which has been material to the activity of the unconscious.[3] Causal relations may be represented in the dream by the presence of two sections of material of unequal lengths, of which one section may well be an attempt to explain or account for the other section (p. 315). This function of the dream grammar will be essential in a final consideration of the two 'parts' of *St Mawr*. Freud is inclined to believe that 'the more extensive part of the dream always corresponds to the principal clause', though he is cautious enough to add that this is not always necessarily so, and that sometimes 'it seems as though the same material were being represented in the two dreams from different points of view' (pp. 315–16) – which again will affect our judgement of the structure of *St Mawr*.

The alternative 'either/or' cannot be expressed in a dream in any way whatsoever, says Freud. Both alternatives are expressed in the dream as if they were of equal importance, and it is up to the waking mind to discover the relation between the two (p. 316). The dream-censor thus avoids the necessity of expressing a preference, and all the responsibility is left to the conscious waking mind. Similarly, contraries and contradictions are 'simply disregarded by the dream'. 'Dreams feel themselves at liberty to represent any element by its wishful contrary: so that there is no way of deciding at first glance whether any element that admits of a contrary is present in the dream-thoughts as a positive or as a negative' (p. 318). All this shows just how subtle and evasive the dream-work and its secondary revision can be. The mere co-presence of two elements in the dream is the best that the unconscious has been able to do under the repressing conditions.

Freud lists several other figures which rely on condensation for their effectiveness, amongst which is the figure of reversal. This particular device will turn out to be central to an understanding of

St Mawr. Reversal serves 'to give expression to the fulfilment of a wish in reference to some particular element of the dream-thoughts. "If only it had been the other way round!" ' (p. 327). Freud goes on to say that if a dream refuses to give up its secret meaning, it is worth while permutating the elements in the dream sequence, to see if a reversal of the order of the elements will make more sense to the message. The same thing applies to time. '*Chronological* reversal must not be overlooked. Quite a common technique of dream-distortion consists in representing the outcome of an event or the conclusion of a train of thought at the beginning of a dream and of placing at its end the premises on which the conclusion was based, or the causes which led to the event' (pp. 327–8).

If the unconscious in its workings can be compared, then, to the play and slippage of rhetorical devices in a literary text, then there is also a second analogy which partly answers our questions about why Freud's theory lends itself so well to the needs of the literary theoretician.

Freud laid down his pen, of course, before the explosion of 'structuralism' in Paris in the 1950s and 1960s, but he formed a useful conceptual data-bank for those literary and psychoanalytic structuralists who drew on the linguistic models of Ferdinand de Saussure and of Roman Jakobson, in order to evolve the new type of literary critique. Along with Dante, de Sade, Marx, Rimbaud, Artaud, Bataille and others, writers who emphasized the mere facticity of the literary text as opposed to some essentialist or idealist content it was supposed to have, Freud was easily located as a writer whose interest lay predominantly in how a tale got itself told, and the reasons for why it chose *this* form to get told in, rather than *that* form. The massive bifurcation between text and meaning was supported philosophically, by the early structuralists around *Tel Quel* for instance, by an appeal to Nietzsche, who was interpreted as saying that all philosophy is but a metaphor pretending to refer to something other than itself. Abusing slightly the famous line of Gertrude Stein, one could aver that, for the structuralists, if philosophy was nothing but a metaphor and truth nothing but an illusion, then a text is a text is a text or, in the famous formula of Jacques Derrida, 'Il n'y a pas d'hors texte'. If a text was nothing more than the sum of its tropes, its strategies and even the very form of lettering upon the page, in the manner of

Mallarmé's *Un Coup de Dés*, then who could be more useful than the Freud of *The Psychopathology of Everyday Life*, who could show, in a luminously exciting diagram, how to get across a page from Signorelli via Botticelli and Bosnia to Boltraffio?[4]

When Jacques Lacan brought out his massive *Ecrits* in 1966, he gave official doctrinal support to this mood. Never was a book more elegantly timed. Like Derrida in his three books of 1967, Lacan denied the reality of the individual subjectivity of the patient and by extension of the creative autonomy of the writer. He offered a re-reading of Freud in terms of a linguistic phenomenology of deferred or impossible desire. Since desire was anyway confounded by the Phallus, the marker of absence, lack, deprivation and oppression, the failure of desire was capable of a merely textual demonstration, and this Lacan proceeded to carry out.

Inverting and personalizing the formula of Ferdinand de Saussure, whose linguistic sign is represented as the unity of the signifier and the signified, where the signified is the concept and the signifier is the acoustic image, Lacan insists upon taking his purely linguistic distinction out of the realm of linguistics, and asserts that not only is there a different order of reality involved in the relationship between signifier and signified, but that, much worse, the signifier cannot refer to a signified at all. The signifier does not refer, in the unconscious discourse or anywhere else, to a signified, as we all naively assumed, but merely to another signifier, which in its turn refers to another signifier in an endless chain.

Thus Lacan doubles, or intensifies, the Freudian proposition itself, which is that in dealing with the rhetoric of the dream or of the art work we are dealing with an agency, an unconscious discourse which proposes and negates its own truth. Later critics, like Paul de Man and Harold Bloom, have pushed this Freudian assumption to the point where the undecidability of the dream work or the art work ends up in *aporia*, the necessity of a decision where, on internal grounds, no decision is possible.

Unfortunately, Lacanian influence on literary theory has not been all benign. Apart from his deliberate refusal to deliver up a plain literal sense in anything he writes, Lacan has also imposed an empirically false and intellectually grotesque mythology of his own on his epigoni, who very often cannot distinguish between what is living and what is dead in the work of Lacan. Literary critics influenced by Lacan have very often been damaged by accepting Lacan's queer and idiosyncratic myth of origins without daring to disbelieve it, and have then spent much time imposing or mapping this myth of origins on to works of literature which do not need such an interpretation and are indeed positively obscured by it. Yet at the same time these critics are convinced, in a naïve and unconscious way, that Lacan's insights are, or ought to be, fruitful for the literary theorist.

So indeed they are. The difficulty though is the same with Lacan as it is with Freud. The myth of origins, personal and eccentric in both cases, can be, and ought to be, distinguished from what Freud and Lacan teach us about literary theorizing. To derive this benefit, though, is not easy. In a few words, one could hazard the generalization that, both with Freud and with Lacan, the literary theorist could derive a great deal from the implications of the praxis, while he or she ought to remain ruefully unconvinced by the monstrous theories that lie behind it.

The great emphasis on undecidability engineered by Freud and then after him by Lacan has been of immense value for literary theory, and it is this emphasis that we should at first make clear for ourselves, and then jealously guard and develop. It is the Freud who shows a reader the analogies between the workings of the unconscious and the workings of the literary text who is invaluable, Freud the technician, Freud the student of dreams, jokes, slips of the tongue, Freud the student of poetry and rhetoric, Freud the collector of Egyptian statuary, who provides the instruments of translation and decipherment. It is the 'linguistic' and 'rhetorical' Freud who never fails.

II

But a Freudian reading of D.H. Lawrence's short novel *St Mawr* has to be undertaken with caution. What, at first sight, could be more 'Freudian' than this magnificent virile horse, prancing and plunging in front of two disappointed and sexually dissatisfied women? 'Vulgar Freudianism', of the kind that Freud himself was the first to animadvert against, would attribute an obvious phallic meaning. And one has to use the more circumspect Freud against the more early and naive one, in order not to fall positively into a trap. What could be more obviously 'symbolic', in the sense in which Freud describes phallic symbols in his first book, than a passage like this, when the heroine, Lou, first encounters St Mawr?

> In the inner dark she saw a handsome bay horse with his clean ears pricked like daggers from his naked head as he swung handsomely round to stare at the open doorway : . . . She laid her hand on his side, and gently stroked him. Then she stroked his shoulder, and then the hard, tense, arch of his neck. And she was startled to feel the vivid heat of his life come through to her, through the lacquer of red-gold gloss. So slippery with vivid, hot life![5]

It is the head of the horse, with his 'clean ears pricked like daggers from his naked head' and his 'great, glowing, fearsome eyes, arched with a question, and containing a white blade of light like a threat' (p. 22) that sets up a series of almost undeniable assonances in the reader's mind with matters sexual. 'Naked' is an odd word to apply to a head, and 'pricked' has it own punning force. 'Daggers' and 'blade' reinforce the pun subliminally.

When Freud, then, in the sixth chapter of *The Interpretation of Dreams*, asserts that certain symbols in dreams correspond to sexual meanings, he seems to be offering us the answer to many of the questions raised in Lawrence's tale:

> Steps, ladders or staircases, or, as the case may be, walking up or down them, are representations of the sexual act . . . Tables, tables laid for a meal, and boards also stand for women . . . a woman's hat can very often be interpreted with certainty as a genital organ, and, moreover, as a *man's* . . . Nor is there any doubt that all weapons and tools are used as symbols of the male organ: e.g. ploughs, hammers, rifles, revolvers, daggers, sabres, etc. In the same way many landscapes in dreams, especially any containing bridges or wooded hills may clearly be recognised as descriptions of the genitals . . . (pp. 355–6)

An invitation, it would seem, to a kind of one-for-one 'matching', which Freud however was quick to foresee and to forbid:

> What is the meaning of such dreams? It is impossible to give a general reply. As we shall hear, they mean something different in every instance; it is only the raw material of sensations contained in them which is always derived from the same source. (p. 393)

But surely the horse as such is an immemorial symbol for energy, force and passion? It would seem difficult, even perverse, to deny meanings to a symbol that it traditionally has. Departures from the traditional symbolic usage of the horse are striking precisely because of their inversion, as when Swift makes his Houyhnhnms into noble rationalists,[6] or when Kierkegaard disputes the rationality of the democratic assembly by comparing those who take part in it to horses in a hippodrome.[7]

Lawrence himself had already used the horse as a symbol of phallic pride, when he makes Gerald, in *Women in Love*, rein in his terrified horse by the railway crossing in order to impress on two young women with fervid imaginations the full extent of his virility. The stallion St Mawr goes on looking like a highly interpretable symbol, even if Freud forbids us to attribute any *a priori* signification to him.

This is where Freudian literary criticism needs to make some critical justification and take up a certain defined critical distance. Of course, a stallion is 'also' a 'Freudian' symbol, but the distinction the critic has to make is that this stallion is not found in a dream-discourse, but in a work of art. This stallion is placed there with a conscious intention. Freud's own attitude to literature was both affectionate and condescending. The writer was for him a neurotic who was trying to solve his repressed problems in terms of an art form. This was the form the artist's 'sublimation' took, and therefore Freud could only read literature as if it were a case history. Freud does not ever fully allow a literary work autonomy, since he regards the writer himself as in thrall. Early Freudian critics, Princess Marie Bonaparte certainly, and in a thorough way too Ernest Jones, refused to allow that art is not a dream, even if, as Calderon insists, life is.

But art, unlike a dream, is both historical and inter-textual. *St Mawr* takes its place in a tradition which reaches from Blake and Wordsworth through Dickens and Carlyle to Morris and Ruskin. The opposition of nature and culture has been through so many transumptions that the deliberateness of Lawrence's symbol cannot be questioned. It relates to the underlying symbolism of *The Woman That Rode Away* and the horses, 'the two horses that draw the chariot of the soul, the savage, rough-eared, unmanageable black one, and the delicate beautiful white one' which form the hidden ground of the debate between Clifford and Connie in *The First Lady Chatterley*.[8] Neither can we ignore a certain rough literalness in Lawrence. Freud, too, in his celebrated case history of Little Hans, takes the impressiveness of the genital equipment of a horse as being obviously symbolic in the formation of little Hans's 'phobia'. If then we are to read *St Mawr* with Freud, we have to read it against Freud.

At the beginning of the story, Mrs Witt and her daughter Lou are represented as dissatisfied, disappointed, resentful against men. The stallion St Mawr is given antithetical qualities, he is full of life, glowing, apparently positive in his undisputed vitality. So, at the beginning of the story, St Mawr appears to be some kind of direct 'answer' to the quest of the two women. The two grooms, Lewis and Phoenix, seem to be interchangeable with the horse in the structure, representing as they do a kind of free-floating, mysterious otherness, which both women are inclined to read off, from time to time, as sexual attractiveness. Both the horse and the grooms, however, turn out to be less than satisfactory from the feminine point of view. Rico, Lou's husband, is the least satisfactory of all, from that point of view, and he plays only an inciting sort of role, maddening Lou by his effeteness, in much the same way as Sir Clifford maddens Connie in *Lady Chatterley's Lover*. Rico, like Clifford, is external to the action, what Henry James would have called a fifth wheel. The structure of strong oppositions is this one:

Mrs Witt (Lou) : St Mawr (Lewis) (Phoenix)

This structure allows various substitutions to take place on either side of the sexual divide. Rico, when attacked so bitterly by Mrs Witt, is often no more than a substitute for her daughter. Likewise, as in the nocturnal ride with Lewis after Mrs Witt's decision to return to America, all the dissatisfactions and self-reproaches that Mrs Witt feels are substitutes in the structure for Lou's own.

Let us trace one single strand in this rich texture, the symbol of the head. We have already noted how the first impression Lou has of St Mawr is of 'a handsome bay horse with his clean ears pricked like daggers from his naked head' (p. 19) and noted the oddness of the word 'naked' in this connection. But reading with a Freudian eye for repetitions of this motif, we are struck again and again by the re-emergence of this matter. St Mawr's head is linked in the chain with his 'terrible, gleaming, questioning eyes arching out of darkness' (p. 22) and this alternation head : eyes will always provide the opportunity to unravel a chain of substitutions. Indeed, the whole penumbra of meanings around Peter Shaffer's play *Equus* will be relevant.

Mrs Witt asks Lewis the groom, early on in the story, 'Supposing now, that Lady Carrington wanted you to shave off that beard, what should you say?' (p. 30). The question is to be made actual later. Both grooms are reported to possess very good heads of hair. Lewis, indeed, 'like Phoenix . . . rarely had any cap or hat on his head. His thick black hair was parted at the side and brushed over heavily sideways, dropping on his forehead at the right. It was very long, a real mop...' (p. 46). It is no doubt this arrogantly masculine head of hair which leads Mrs Witt to insist on barbering Lewis the groom, in a way which is proleptic of the manner in which the horse, St Mawr, after he has reared and injured Rico, is threatened with castration (though in that case, by inversion, it is Mrs Witt who intervenes to save the horse's sex).

The scene of the barbering of the groom Lewis at the hands of the castrating Mrs Witt is one of the central symbolic acts of the novel:

at last he sat with a black aureole upon the floor, and his ears standing out with curious new alertness from the sides of his clean-clipped head. (p. 53)

The verbal assonances with earlier passages about St Mawr's head and ears is deliberate, of course, and Mrs Witt offers to compound her crime by depriving Lewis of his beard as well. Offended to the soul, the groom summons strength to refuse this final indignity. Mrs Witt pretends to be quite unconscious of her own motives: 'And even those poor boys in hospital: I have shaved them, or cut their hair, like a mother, never thinking anything of it' (p. 54).

It is at this point that a Freudian reading in terms of penis envy and the castration complex offers itself insistently, but once again a contemporary Freudian reading would read against Freud. Lawrence's textual ploy is to lead the reader directly from this scene to the exchange between Mrs Witt and her daughter on the faculty which is peculiarly lacking in the modern man. Hair leads to head, head leads to thinking, thinking leads to mind, and the opposition between 'mere animal' and 'real mind' leads to Lou's passionate affirmation of the value of lived intelligence (p. 56) which must surely be Lawrence's central theme. Yet to gain the needed insight into structure, we need to read the chain of textual substitutions as clues leading *away* from a Freudian symbolic centre, and *not* towards it.

This attention to the interrelation of signifying units in the text, rather than to the theory of the Master, is what a modern Freudian praxis consists in. The reader has to keep on making textual connections, and avoiding the sacrifice of the intellect to some specific Freudian doctrine. For instance, the 'head' theme is continued when Rico comes back from his domineering ride on St Mawr just a few pages after the barbering scene, and Lou's first impression of the horse in his sweaty and humiliated state is:

> He seemed a little bit extinguished, as if virtue had gone out of him.
> But when he lifted his lovely naked head, like a bunch of flames, to see who it was had entered, she saw he was still himself. For ever sensitive and alert, his head lifted like the summit of a fountain. (p. 60)

The text tells its own story. 'Naked head' and 'alert' should recall 'pricked like daggers' from the earlier passage. But now there is a new element added to the code, 'his head lifted like the summit of a fountain'. A fountain can only have a summit when the water is flung up into the air in an arc, and Lou's opening perception of the horse is that 'he seemed a little bit extinguished, as if virtue had gone out of him'. This apparently artless reference to Mark 5, v. 30 must indicate a link between the precious life-force that Jesus can feel has been taken from him by the woman who has had an issue of blood for twelve years, and some comparable sort of lost essence. But at what level is the connection to be made? At the level of Lou's unconscious? Or might this doubled effect of signification be operated by the textual unconscious itself?

As a symbol, the stallion St Mawr is overdetermined. Freud used this term to describe the fact that a single element of behaviour can sometimes express a complex motivation. A single dream image, for instance, could signify a preoccupation with several different desires and preoccupations. St Mawr in the tale certainly has this 'many in one' symbolic function, and this creates considerable problems for any one consistent interpretation.

First and foremost St Mawr seems to represent maleness and life-giving positivity, and yet he is 'not keen on the mares' and only plays the role of being the stallion when near them (p. 82). In fact he holds off, lacking desire, disdainful. It seems to be suggested in the text that the mere act of generation is somehow below him, that it would be debasing for him. Consequently he begins to take on a quality of wonderful, wasteful excess. The value of his symbol thus shifts constantly from positive to negative and back again. This oscillation is reflected in the ambiguous relationship which Mrs Witt and Lou have to the horse. Neither of them is wholly positive, yet neither of them is wholly negative, towards this incarnation of male power. Both women seek to locate the positive in St Mawr, yet neither can find it satisfactorily there. Likewise, both women seek to avoid the negative and the disconcerting in St Mawr, yet cannot help noticing its presence, which seems to reinforce their own deepest self-doubts and to force into being their worst repetition-compulsions. Finally the stallion's refusal to mate is brought into the proximity of the term 'bad':

> 'That St Mawr, he's a bad horse,' said Phoenix....
> 'Why don't he never get any foals?'
> 'Doesn't want to, I should think. Same as me.'
> 'What good is a horse like that? Better shoot him, before he kill somebody.' (pp. 39–40)

The ambiguous nature of the horse is re-emphasized in the ill-fated excursion to The Devil's Chair, when Rico is thrown by St Mawr and his leg crushed. Lou's reaction to the scene is apparently quite inappropriate: 'she had a vision, a vision of evil. Or not strictly a vision. She became aware of evil, evil, evil, rolling in great waves over the earth' (p. 76). The horse with its 'wicked curved hams' and the 'evil straining' of its neck, is perceived by Lou as 'reversed and purely evil'. Yet surely St Mawr, seeing a snake in its path', was not acting evilly in rearing and attempting to dislodge its rider? The cause of the fall may be a snake, but this is no Fortunate Fall.

It is the evil of modern society as such that Lou suddenly constellates, the *kind* of evil which modern society typically generates. This evil is *mean*. And of this kind of evil the horse is suddenly seen as symbolic. Lou sees it as a mean horse, and its revolt against Rico is indirect and in a certain way cowardly. Like Kierkegaard a hundred years before him, Lawrence lambasts the secret 'levelling' evil of a society which does not dare to attack a fellow-man openly, but 'injures him secretly, makes a fool of him, undermines his nature' (p. 77).

Lawrence's references to the 'two bad breaks the secret evil has made: in Germany and in Russia' locates the story securely in 1924, but Lawrence obviously sees both 1914–18 and 1917 as outbreaks of 'outward loyalty, inward treachery, in a game of betrayal, betrayal, betrayal' (p. 78). The threefold repetition of the word 'rhymes with' the threefold repetition of 'evil' in Lou's vision, no doubt, showing incidentally how careful a craftsman Lawrence is, down to the very details. But this doubled acoustic effect, at the level of the text, pushes the symbolic meaning of St Mawr one step further towards uninterpretability.

The whole novella indeed has a strong tendency to increase the difficulties of interpretation wherever it can. This is nowhere more in evidence than in the interestingly lopsided imbalance of its structure. The story divides up into two very unequal parts. The first section is in England (pp. 11–132) and seems to propose a 'problem', while the second section is in America (pp. 132–165) and seems to propose some kind of 'answer'. The ratio of the story is thus 4 : 1.

Might not the whole story be an example of reversal in the sense in which Freud described it in his chapter on the dream-work? There are so many examples of reversal in the narrative and its symbolism, that one begins to perceive them everywhere, for example during that strange three-day trek through the English countryside which Mrs Witt undertakes, in the company of Lewis, after she has decided to return to America. There is an extended stream of consciousness which takes us into the heart of Mrs Witt's own dilemma, which starts at p. 100. This is very unexpected, as Mrs Witt is the one character to whose occluded identity we had long ago settled. Now, however, we move right into the centre of Mrs Witt's disappointments with men. As she rides along, she begins to notice Lewis, the groom. Mrs Witt is in a mood where she 'wants to be defeated in her own eyes. And nobody had ever defeated her. Men were never really her match' (p. 102). And it is in this mood, of wishing to be defeated by a man, that she begins to become aware of the silent groom, riding morosely by her side. It is the deliberate distance which he insists on keeping from her which eventually provokes in her a desire for intimacy with him. At first he does not respond to her. The day is hot, and Mrs Witt decides to put up at an inn, to eat and rest before they continue. So that it is not until evening is beginning to fall that the odd pair set out again. The section which follows, like the 'night music' in the second movement of Bartok's third piano concerto, contains one example of reversal after another.

First, there is the quite dislocating experience of Lewis's breaking the silence, something which, knowing what we do about Lewis, we could never expect. And secondly, there is the incredible nature of what he chooses to speak about: ' "You ask me about God," he said to her, walking his horse alongside in the shadow of the wood's-edge' (pp. 109–10). It is almost too uncanny, and the reader suspects for a moment that Lawrence has pushed out beyond what story-telling can bear. But the figure of reversal, now set into motion, brings up all sorts of strange things from the unconscious of this tale:

> 'I think I hear something, though I wouldn't call it God.'
> 'What then?' said Rachel Witt.
> 'And you smell the smell of the oak-leaves now,' he said, 'now the air is cold. They smell to me more alive than people.' (p. 110)

Having utterly upset readerly expectation by speaking at all, and confounded it even further by talking of an abstraction like God, Lewis then reverses the entire accepted form of discussion about God by attempting to define Him in terms of the five senses, the fairies, the magical properties of ash-tree seeds, the people in the moon and the proper contents of the mind:

> 'A man's mind has to be full of something, so I keep to what we used to think as lads. It's childish nonsense, I know it. But it suits me. Better than other people's stuff.' (p. 113)

To reverse civilized expectations of how one should think and talk, and on top of this to refuse civilized norms because these are inherently unsatisfactory and actually inferior to folk-wisdom, is to carry out, in a set of further magical reversals, a chain of thinking which chimes in exactly with what Mrs Witt most longs to hear. It is not surprising then if these reversals directly provoke the most unexpected reversal in the whole story, when the powerful and intellectual Mrs Witt suddenly decides to propose marriage to her own groom:

> 'Now don't be surprised, Lewis, at what I'm going to say. I am going to ask you, now, supposing I wanted to marry you, what should you say?' (p. 113)

This enquiry, shocking as it is, probably reminds Lewis of a previous question put to him by Mrs Witt, all that time ago in the Park: ' "Lewis!" she said. "I want to ask you a question. Supposing, now, that Lady Carrington wanted you to shave off that beard, what should you say?" ' (p. 30). This new proposal from Mrs Witt is no doubt felt to be as violent an attack upon his masculine pride as that first insulting question had been, and he rejects Mrs Witt's offer because: ' "I couldn't give my body to any woman who didn't respect it" ' (p. 114). To imply that those who demand respect are those who don't in fact show it to others is a yet further reversal of the social expectations of the scene. Even more surprising, perhaps, are the three eloquent pages (pp. 114–16) where Lewis advances an entire philosophy of the respect due to the body and the necessity of inner inviolability. The only unreversed aspect of this scene is that Mrs Witt should end up by being offended at his 'empty, male conceit' of himself.

This nocturnal dialectic between Mrs Witt and Lewis contains *in nuce*, I suspect, the major formal property of the whole novella. The story employs reversal throughout, but it is itself a reversal, when by chiasmus, section A (in England) changes place with section B (in America) and the apparent cause of action (dissatisfaction) and the apparent conclusion of the action (askesis) also change position in the economy of the whole. But reversal and chiasmus keep all the elements in the kinetic work of art in constant relations of substitution, and this leads to the necessity of inventing a figure which does justice to the real effects of the tale, and I will call it, for the sake of argument, oscillation.

Oscillation may not figure as such in the rhetoric books as a device, but it is a definite textual effect of a modernist kind, which may well be coeval with some of the techniques of Impressionism. It is also a reality in the unconscious, which the modernist text attempts to imitate by whatever rhetorical means it can. Since the meanings between which St Mawr oscillates are life and death, Freud's own theory of Eros and Thanatos seems to impose itself eventually as a possibility with which the reader has to deal. In *Beyond The Pleasure Principle*, Freud distinguishes between the 'ego-instincts' and the 'sexual instincts'. The former, he says, 'exercise pressure towards death and the latter towards a prolongation of life'.[9] Speculating from the famous example of 'Fort-Da', Freud comes to the conclusion that repetition compulsions are useful in that they create retrospective anxiety in the psyche, such that the subject, by living again and again through his or her problems in the unconscious, be they recalled events or recurrent states, manages to build up, little by little, a sufficient defence against them.

The struggle between the two sorts of instincts, then, is advanced, in late Freudian theory, to the status of a major conflict within each psyche, one might even say, punning a little, a struggle 'to the death'. For it is towards death, curiously enough, that the 'ego-instincts' tend in a curiously self-destructive way. The origin of the instinct is 'the need to restore an earlier state of things' (p. 331).

This is a very useful hint, for it is noticeable that it is with 'an earlier state of things' that both Mrs Witt and her daughter are constantly preoccupied. Freud's paradoxical formulation, 'The aim of all life is death', would thus take on a precise significance as an interpretive tool in the reading at *St Mawr*. The compulsion to repeat, in which the subject chooses to face again his or her most traumatic experience, in an attempt to master it, reduce it, and find psychic resources to contain it, may be the origin of the many returns that both Mrs Witt and Lou have to the stallion. Both women track down St Mawr to repeat the unpleasant experience of having to face the reality of emptiness, nothingness and failure. In facing, in challenging even, the powerful male reality of the stallion, over and over again, Lou attempts to come to terms with memories of her sexual failure, attempts to build up a sufficient defence against it. For Mrs Witt, the stallion is the endless re-encounter with the inadequacy of the men she has known, of the maleness which failed to be sufficiently that.

The horse seems to oscillate in its significance, it swings between benign talisman and cursed fetish. In so far as both women are attempting again and again to 'fix' the meaning of St Mawr in their own psychic economies, in so far as, in a state of diremption, both women are attempting to re-integrate their own personality under the powerful influence of St Mawr, the theory of Jacques Lacan seems to impose itself at this stage.

III

Lacan's version of how things happen is his own personal re-telling of the story of the Fall. In his phenomenology, the consciousness of the newborn baby (the 'homelette') is basically happy. The neonate has a satisfied relationship with its mother, and desire (for milk, for the teat) is immediately followed by satisfaction of desire. This is the realm of the 'Imaginary' which is also the realm of metaphor, where things correspond (by transposition) to each other.

The time scheme is always obscure in Lacan, but at some point there occurs a crisis in which the baby is separated from the mother. The withdrawal of the breast causes need and desperation in the baby, and longing for the breast becomes transformed into the experience of desire. The breast, though, has already been made an impossible object of desire, and hence has become the 'mark' of the impossibility of satisfaction in the chain of signifiers which makes up the child's new insertion into the public world. The search for this lost and impossible object of desire will, however, follow and torment the adult all his life. Buñuel's film, *That Obscure Object of Desire*, is an elaboration of this dilemma.

At some later point (again the chronology is obscure) a second crisis occurs, which reinforces the first, and which corresponds to Freud's Oedipus Complex. The child gets itself involved in a battle of take-over bids for the love and exclusive possession of its mother and father. This, too, is a doomed effort: parents cannot be colonized and possessed or enjoyed as objects of desire in that sense. The child is suddenly made aware of the fact of sexual difference, and the Phallus (a word which has no 'content' of any kind, but which stands as a symbol for all that is lost and all that is at risk, for all the satisfaction that is no longer possible and all the frustrations that are to come) imposes the harsh realm of the Symbolic.

Now the child has to learn the meaning of exclusion, absence, lack and default. The signified slips from the signifier, the centre cannot hold. The Symbolic is the world of socialized public consciousness, and this implies that it is the *language* of *others* that will henceforward shape the way you see yourself. It is also the world of metonymy, where the part stands for the whole, and yet does not correspond in kind or nature *to* that whole. In this new hostile world of the language of others, one signifier leads to another, in an endless displacement of possible meanings, and the 'subject' will attempt to track down the 'real' significance of any signifier in vain. The plight of Oedipa Maas, in Pynchon's novel

The Crying of Lot 49, is a perfect literary illustration of Lacan's point. The search for a possible 'signified' for the mass of signifiers takes place in a split subject, who desires to find a meaning among the signs that they cannot in fact ever provide. Indeed, this split subject is not even a subject at all, but built up out of the linguistic suggestions of others, and hence cannot even conceive what the object of his or her own desire is, and hence, as in the Pynchon novel, is doomed to the endless deferral of satisfaction.

This myth of origins, however, while endowed with a certain poetic charm, is a Circe to the theoretician. The theory is empirically unverifiable, of course, but it also looks to be actually false on many issues. It often seems as if Lacan wishes, for instance, to assert that a child does not even have an unconscious until he or she is possessed of the words to have it in – a contention so paradoxical as to set up a contradiction in terms, for if the unconscious is not pre-verbal and infra-verbal, it is difficult to imagine what content it could possibly have. Likewise, Lacan gives the period between six and eighteen months for the 'mirror stage' and yet seems to imply at the same time that this is the period when the child settles to some definite opinions about itself, when it comes to define his or her reality in terms of the mirror's reflection. But surely such explorations would be precocious, even for a French child, at six to eighteen months?

Struggling with some of these problems, Anthony Wilden protests, a bit desperately it seems, that 'the *stade du miroir* never "occurs" at all . . . it is a purely structural or relational concept'.[10] Connected with this, there is the problem of when the transition from the Imaginary to the Symbolic actually occurs. Again, Lacan is never precise, and again Wilden tries to act as honest broker: 'We must ask how he actually relates the Imaginary to the Symbolic, and the question would be unfair only if he had not claimed to have answered it' (p. 175). Nevertheless, Wilden eventually concludes 'Thus the Symbolic coexists with the Imaginary' (p. 177). That is to say, there is no distinction possible because the two stages are co-temporal and co-extensive. In what way, then, might we say that they differ? Such problems are bound to remain unanswered.

The second danger in taking Lacan's theory on board is that it is theoretically useless in the form in which Lacan proposes it, since it cannot be 'applied' unless in the same servile way the old

Freudians 'applied' the theories of Freud. To apply it unexamined would be to repeat, at a later stage in history and therefore more culpably, the mistakes of those who superimposed the Oedipus Complex on everything from Hamlet to Edgar Allan Poe. To do this is to carry out what Harold Bloom would call a 'weak misreading' of the original texts. There are, alas, many such 'Lacanian' readings of literary works, and every one of them darkens counsel.

The third danger derives from the fact that, for all Lacan's pronouncements about the supremacy of the linguistic signifier in the chain, his most distinctive characteristic is his refusal to look at any text, as such, at all, and one can only wonder how his patients fared in their dealings with him. On one unique occasion he does carry out a reading of Poe's *The Purloined Letter*, but he makes it clear that he is using the story only as an analogy to show how the unconscious works, not the other way round. He does not even offer to be enlightening for literary critics, and his failure to make such an offer on this one occasion ought to have been seen as significant by those who want to use his theory to theorize in a more general way. Lacan does not in fact derive his theories from the linguistic structure and rhetoric of the text (whichever text is in question) but rather, ignoring these, imposes a metaphysical theory on the text from above.

These three aspects of Lacan's thought severely limit its usefulness for literary purposes. If however we are prepared to 'bracket' the myth of origins, the 'system', then the individual poetic insights are invaluable.

Lacan's theory (however bizarrely derived from the myth of origins) to the effect that the object of desire is always deferred, belated or irretrievable, has a poetic suggestiveness which seems peculiarly well adapted to the sensibility of the contemporary Western world. Buñuel's film *That Obscure Object of Desire* has, in our current modernity, a truthfulness to experience which seems to be undeniable. For some reason (and it does not seem to matter which myth of origins one refers to), it does seem as if what the psyche most longs for is what has been made impossible for it. *St Mawr* is a text which is massively overdetermined in this respect: there is nothing in it which is not, in one way or another, a portrayal of a state of longing which cannot be assuaged. We can never get to know what Mrs Witt and Lou 'lack' – the tale has made that impossible for us.

The second insight is that the subject is created in terms of the language of others. Its reality is reflected back to it from what others *say*. Reality is very largely linguistic, and we define what we want in terms of words (signifiers) and thus become a signifier in our own chain, and get lost in it. What we feel we are allowed to desire is already an achievement of the language of others. Our subjective reality is very largely 'real' because it is mirrored back to us from what others say. We define what we want in other people's words, and thus become to some extent a signifier in a chain of other people's making. Oedipa Maas in *The Crying of Lot 49* is a perfect demonstration of this, and she proves incidentally as well that the 'mirror stage' can last until one is 45 and beyond!

Applied to *St Mawr*, this Lacanian insight allows us to see to what an extent both Mrs Witt and Lou are defined by, and define themselves in terms of, a certain social 'set'. They take their place in a world of country life, riding in the Park, horses, and international travel. So deeply does Mrs Witt, for example, accept the rightness of this sort of economic superiority that any escape from it has been made impossible. The signifiers of others, in which she colludes, have claimed her for good. Lacan's claim that we have *no* 'subjectivity' is obviously false, but that a subjectivity is set up and maintained to a much greater extent than we believed by the defining words and rhetoric of others is given proof in Lawrence's tale.

The third valid Lacanian insight is that we are advised to look at a literary text (dream, poem, unconscious discourse) as a mere extended set of signifiers, and that there is no one transcendentally derivable 'signified'. This is freeing. No longer need the reader search for that one right, original, founding and ultimate 'meaning' which a text has so long been assumed to possess. We are now entirely free not to worry about why Hamlet hesitates, what sort of girl Emma 'really' is, and what *The Waste Land* 'really' means. For this relief much thanks.

But this Lacanian insight is in fact not derived from linguistics any more than his other insights are. There is an uneasy sense, indeed, that this theory of the impossibility of the 'signified' may fit in just a bit too easily with fashionable modern scepticism about all 'truth' and 'reality', etc. Lacan may be giving us sophisticated reasons for arguing what most people believe by instinct. Nearly the totality of contemporary fiction and film presents us with a world view so similar to Lacan's that critical suspicion ought to be aroused. It remains the fact that if we did not believe in 'signifieds' we could not get through a single day.

But, as in the previous two cases, Lacan's insights are valuable however faulty their extraction. Reading *St Mawr*, for instance, what possible final 'signified' could that stallion have? When Lou goes to stare at St Mawr, after it has thrown Rico and thus disgraced itself irrevocably (p. 82), she is obviously using the horse as a 'mirror' in which she is trying to piece together the contours of her own problem. But St Mawr, who tries to 'bluff' Lou by neighing to the mares which he does not desire, is an unsatisfactory mirror for her, and far too multiform. All that Lou can read in the mirror of St Mawr is that the mirror is shattered and blind.

The interrogation of St Mawr in England, though, does allow of a certain hardening of sentiment when Lou arrives in America. She is more explicit now about the necessity of rejecting men as sexual partners, and her buying the ranch is obviously a triumphant statement about the rightness of her decision. The isolation of the ranch and its almost monastic order of life, slung between the desert and the Rockies, is a recognizable symbol of her new decisiveness. Even as she is being driven by Phoenix to inspect the ranch with a view to possible purchase, she reinforces her will in its rejection of the sexual dimension:

> 'No, no,' she said to herself, 'I was wrong to ride in the front seat with him. I must sit alone, just alone. Because sex, mere sex, is repellent to me. I will never prostitute myself again. Unless something touches my very spirit, the very quick of me, I will stay alone, just alone. Alone, and give myself only to the unseen presences, serve only the other, unseen presences.'
>
> She understood now the meaning of the Vestal Virgins (pp. 145–46).

Lou's dilemma about the oscillating value of the sexual life leads us to the enigma of the closing section, the section about the ranch she determines to buy. The description of the ranch, its first two owners, and its setting half way between mountains and desert is a veritable mass of signifiers.

The very first thing that we learn about it, for instance, is that it is dry (p. 147). Yet the first owner concludes that he has civilized the ranch when he has imposed taps, running water, wash-hand basins and a bathtub (p. 149). Lacan's 'structural' reading of this would offer us an undecidability between desert and water, nature and culture. Neither reading is final. There is 'a strange invisible influence coming out of the bowels of those uncreated Rocky Mountains . . . A curious disintegration working all the time, a sort of malevolent breath, like a stupefying irritant gas, coming out of the unfathomed mountains' (p. 151). Yet, beyond the mountains, there is 'pure beauty, *absolute* beauty', which reassures the New England woman who is trying to settle the ranch. Nature as malevolent, then, and nature as benign. The pine-tree which is the 'guardian of the place . . . a bristling almost demonish guardian' is struck down by lightning, and thus causes the destruction of the New England woman's Christian faith (p. 156). Lacan would have us read the opposition between the demonic and the theocratic worlds. Some flowers are aggressive and dangerous, they come up 'bristly, and many of them were fang-mouthed, like the dead-nettle'. The mariposa lily, in order to survive, has to become 'invisible' (p. 157). Is Nature then primarily destructive–aggressive, or beautiful and helpless? On a grander scale, the 'seething cauldron of lower life' is 'working for ever against man's attempt at a higher life' (p. 159). This, in the context of the beauty and peacefulness of the setting, is a paradoxical signifier. But Lawrence intensifies his paradox: 'every civilization, when it loses its inward vision and its cleaner energy' becomes, he says, 'an Augean stables of metallic filth' (p. 160). In the course of these few pages of description, Lawrence has scattered so many conflicting signifiers that Lacan's theory about the undecidability of any signifier in a chain is evidently right.

Might it just be that death itself is the positive value in *St Mawr*? We would be ill advised to abandon the Lacanian principle that a signifier can never be tied down to a single signified, but that the other signifiers in the text are all involved in each individual signifier. Yet there is a great deal about the stallion which has death-associated values, and the ranch itself is explicitly given those values.

There is the possibility that Lawrence may be involved here in writing a prophetic text, one which seized the Freudian paradox. 'The aim of all life is death' in a way whose contemporaneity is only just beginning to appear. Lawrence was sensitive to that sort of death wish which seeks the quiet of the grave, a sort of post-orgasmic peace, where the nervous system can finally give up the struggle and rest. The poems are our best testimony for this strain in Lawrence, poems like 'Bavarian Gentians' or 'The Ship of Death'. It could be that Lawrence is presenting his form of the Freudian paradox in his description of Lou's fatal fascination for torpor, a sliding back towards infancy and the womb, which would represent final peace. It would be significant, if this return to the womb and its security and happiness is in play, that Lou's major interlocutor is her own mother.

Let us suppose for a moment that Freud's Eros and Thanatos are in subtly twined *agon*. It could be that the fascination of the stallion for Lou is his association with death. Lou's recollection of childhood bliss, wired into her body through her whole life as a sense of aching absence, compounded by repeated disappointment, can only be recalled or imagined as death. If then Lawrence is working at the same paradox as Freud, one could say that for Lou (and by substitution throughout, Mrs Witt) since all satisfaction has lost its savour, then all that is desirable is connected with death. 'The aim of all life is death.' In Mrs Witt, who insists that she wants death, *at least*, to be real for her (p. 93), to 'hurt her enough', it has become a positive longing.[11]

If one were to read the signifiers in the chain *this* way, then the meaning, or at least *a* meaning, of the ranch and its emplacement in the death-dealing mountains would emerge. It is however a testimony to the strength of Lacan's insight about the undecidability of the signifiers that this remains only a possibility. The way to a hermeneutic of the story along these lines would make perfect sense, but it could only be an arbitrary privileging of certain signifiers over others.

In the end, it is Lou herself who refuses to define:

'Very well, daughter. You will probably spend your life keeping to yourself.'
'Do you think I mind! There's something else for me, mother. There's something else even that loves me and wants me. I can't tell you what it is. It's a spirit. And it's here, on this ranch. It's here, in this landscape. It's something more real to me than men are, and it soothes me, and it holds me up. I don't know what it is, definitely' (p. 165).

In the face of a refusal to define of this order, it would seem that the most tactful ploy is to accept Lacan's case and to cease to look for precise signifieds. The story virtually instructs us to leave Lou as she is, as a still unravished bride of quietness, and to turn literary theory from a hasty rushing-in to a politic holding back.

Further Reading

There are good introductory studies by Elizabeth Wright in *Modern Literary Theory: A Comparative Introduction*, ed. Ann Jefferson and David Robey (London, Batsford, rev. ed., 1986) and *Psychoanalytic Criticism: Theory in Practice* (London, Methuen, 1984); by Terry Eagleton in *Literary Theory: An Introduction* (Oxford, Blackwell, 1983); and by Meredith Anne Skura in *The Literary Use of the Psychoanalytic Process* (New Haven, Yale UP, 1981). For Lacan, see Anika Lemaire, *Jacques Lacan*, trs. D. Macey (London, Routledge and Kegan Paul, 1977); Anthony Wilden, *The Language of the Self: The Function of Language in Psychoanalysis* (Baltimore, Johns Hopkins UP, 1968) and sections of his *System and Structure: Essays in Communication and Exchange* (London, Tavistock, 1972); Gary Handwerk, 'Irony as intersubjectivity', in *Comparative Criticism*, vol. 7 (Cambridge, CUP, 1985); Juliet Mitchell, *Women: The Longest Revolution: Essays in Feminism, Literature and Psychoanalysis* (London, Virago, 1984), and with Jacqueline Rose, *Feminine Sexuality: Jacques Lacan and the Ecole Freudienne* (London, Macmillan, 1982); and Julia Kristeva, *Desire in Language: A Semiotic Approach to Literature and Art*, trs. T. Gora, A. Jardine and L. S. Roudiez, ed. L. S. Roudiez (Oxford, Blackwell, 1980).

Freud himself is not a very rewarding literary critic. His account of Hoffmann's *Der Sandmann* (Collected Works, vol. 17) shows Freud too much as an early Freudian. See Malcolm Jones, '*Der Sandmann* and "The Uncanny": a sketch for an alternative approach' (*Paragraph*, Spring 1986). The powerful rhetorical innovations come with the series on Edgar Allan Poe's 'The Purloined Letter'. See Jacques Lacan, 'Seminar on "The Purloined Letter" ', trs. Jeffrey Mehlman (*Yale French Studies*, 48, 1972); Jacques Derrida, 'The purveyor of truth', trs. Willis Domingo, James Hulbert, Moshe Ron, and Marie-Rose Logan (*Yale French Studies*, 52, 1975–6); Barbara Johnson, 'The frame of reference: Poe, Lacan, Derrida' (*Yale French Studies*, 55–56, 1978); and Norman Holland, 'Re-covering "The Purloined Letter": reading as a personal transaction', in *The Reader in the Text* (details below).

The single most important revision of Freud has come in a series of books from Harold Bloom, starting with *The Anxiety of Influence: A Theory of Poetry* (New York, OUP, 1973). His *A Map of Misreading* (Oxford, OUP, 1980) establishes the critic in a new function altogether, while *Wallace Stevens: The Poems of our Climate* (Ithaca, Cornell UP, 1977) introduces major new existential criteria into Freudian reading. *Agon* (New York, OUP, 1982) and *The Breaking of the Vessels* (Chicago,

Chicago UP, 1982) put Freud to the service of a religious hermeneutic.
Particularly useful collections involving the application of Freudian methodology to texts, some from a feminist angle, are: Joseph W. Smith, ed., *The Literary Freud: Mechanisms of Defence and the Poetic Will* (New Haven, Yale UP, 1980); and, in the same series and with the same editor, *Kierkegaard's Truth: The Disclosure of the Self* (New Haven, Yale UP, 1981); *Literature and Psychoanalysis: The Question of Reading: Otherwise*, with special editor Shoshana Felman (*Yale French Studies*, 55–6, 1977); and *Feminist Readings: French Texts/American Contexts* (*Yale French Studies*, 62). See also the interesting selection from the English Institute entitled *The Representation of Women in Fiction* (Baltimore, Johns Hopkins UP, 1983); and Susan Suleiman and Inge Crossland, eds., *The Reader in the Text: Essays on Audience and Interpretation* (Princeton, N.J., Princeton UP, 1980).

The sheer difficulty of reading is emphasized in the fascinating work of Paul de Man (*Allegories of Reading*, New Haven, Yale University Press, 1979). In particular, de Man has shown how key texts end up by forcing the reader into an *aporia*, the necessity of deciding upon one of two possible solutions and the imposed impossibility of finally choosing either. *Aporia* is rhetorically similar to what I have called 'oscillation'. See also William Empson (*Seven Types of Ambiguity*, London, Chatto and Windus, 1956) whose fourth, sixth and seventh types of ambiguity correspond strikingly to what I have called 'oscillation'.

Very interesting indeed, and far too little known in Britain, is the work of the Buffalo School of psychoanalytic criticism, led and inspired by Norman Holland. See his *Poems in Persons* (New York, Norton, 1973) and *Five Readers Reading* (New Haven, Yale UP, 1975). Holland has reclaimed theory from the theoreticians to examine the process of reading itself, examined with Freudian assumptions, and to re-situate the text between writer and reader. See, in this connection, the rich and varied *Reader–Response Criticism*, ed. Jane P. Tomkins (Baltimore, Johns Hopkins UP, 1980).

Perhaps the most interesting work being done right now in Freudian method is by the post-Marxists, such as Fredric Jameson. See his *The Political Unconscious: Narrative as a Socially Symbolic Act* (Ithaca, Cornell UP, 1981). Starting from absurdly metaphysical political premises, Jameson nevertheless has introduced a new dimension into Freudian criticism by insisting on the textual unconscious itself, cajoling 'Conrad', for instance, to yield up its own 'unconscious'.

The learned world awaits with bated breath the long-considered work from Harold Bloom, the 'Freud' book, which will present Freud as the greatest novelist of the twentieth century. After that, 'Freudian criticism' will take on a quite new meaning, where novel, novelist, and critical approach will at last be one.

6 Dialogics
Joseph Conrad, *Heart of Darkness*

David Murray

I

'Dialogics' is a term primarily associated with Mikhail Bakhtin (1895–1975), whose work has only relatively recently been made available in English translation. Even now a quantity of his work is untranslated, and we must rely on Slavist scholars to fill out our picture of Bakhtin's work. Apart from translation problems, though, there are peculiar difficulties in establishing any comprehensive view of Bakhtin. Because of the dangers of Soviet intellectual life, Bakhtin found it easier to get published under the names of friends who were more in favour with the authorities, so that we have at least two works under the name of V.N. Voloshinov and another one under the name of P.N. Medvedev, which, together with some articles, are now generally accepted to be substantially Bakhtin's work.[1] These confusions over authorship, as well as the close cooperation and interchange of ideas amongst Bakhtin and his friends, have led some critics to refer to the 'Bakhtin school' (though in this essay I refer simply to Bakhtin as author of all disputed texts). To this difficulty in locating Bakhtin's own voice – appropriate, perhaps, for a man who emphasized the dialogue of voices in texts – must be added another. Because of the piecemeal way his work has emerged in the West, he has tended to come to us under the aegis of particular critical positions, of which he has been presented as an early exponent. Bakhtin would be the first to recognize that texts can only take on meaning for us in dialogue with our current concerns, but he would also alert us to the struggle of voices in dialogue for *dominance,* and we need therefore to be aware of the uses to which Bakhtin is put in presenting him as, in different quarters, post-structuralist, Marxist or liberal humanist.

The best way to handle this situation is, perhaps, to introduce very briefly Bakhtin's key terms and ideas, and to look at their intellectual and literary ramifications, in the hope of clarifying them before their application to *Heart of Darkness*. At first sight some of Bakhtin's terms, like 'dialogics', 'heteroglossia' and 'carnivalization' may look daunting. In fact, though, even a simple grasp of these three terms and how they relate takes us to the heart of Bakhtin's ideas. For Bakhtin we experience and represent the world to ourselves and others not in a single shared language, but in a multiplicity of overlapping and often conflicting versions of that language (official, vernacular, technical, literary, the jargons of different age-groups, etc.). This multiplicity of interacting languages (*heteroglossia*) is always *implicitly* present when any one of them is used, and any utterance takes its meaning from its relation to the various other languages with which it is inevitably in dialogue. Dialogics, then, is the study of the way meaning is constructed out of the contending languages within any culture – contending because there is a constant cultural tendency to try to *unify* languages within an official or unitary language, which is undermined by the endlessly changing conditions of the society, which generates new languages and new relations between them. Bakhtin sees the overturning of official unitary languages as coming from the unheard, unofficial voices generated in the less-recognized areas of society, and this life-enhancing debunking of the official he calls *carnivalization*, after the model of medieval carnival with its release of folk energies. In terms of literature, then, Bakhtin is interested in those forms which seem to him to offer most room for explicit dialogical activity, as opposed to those which tend toward a unitary language.

These are the bare bones of Bakhtin's ideas, but to grasp their implications and their importance they have to be seen in relation to Formalism and Marxism, the major intellectual movements within which his work is situated. While much of his work is an explicit use of Marxist argument to criticize the limitations of Formalism, with its assumptions of the autonomy of art and 'literariness', it is also possible to find a less explicit but no less powerful critique of a Marxist literary criticism which would ignore the formal characteristics of a work of art in its haste to find its ideological context. For Bakhtin both of these approaches distort the way that language works in literature, and the way that literature functions in society, and his dialogue with these two positions has maintained its relevance in relation to later confrontations between Marxist, structuralist and post-structuralist critical approaches.

Bakhtin's fundamental disagreement with Formalism and, later, structuralism can best be approached through the issue of the problematic relation between a general system of rules and individual performance within those rules. In terms of how language works this means that whereas Formalists and structuralists would stress the *system*, the synchronic whole which enables meaning to emerge within individual utterances, Bakhtin, while not rejecting the existence of the system, insists that it offers no way of explaining how *particular* meanings are generated within particular utterances. In other words, it ignores the diachronic nature of language in actual use, in its concern to understand it as an abstract system: 'The actual reality of language – speech – is not the abstract system of linguistic norms . . . but the social event of verbal interaction implemented in an utterance.'[2] As well as a diachronic event, language is also a *dialogical* event, in that the meaning of an utterance is given not by the intention of a sovereign individual (he rejects the idea of the speaker as Adam, naming the world, in an originary way), but by its specific context. It is addressed to another, and, more fundamentally, since we do not invent our language is already *quoting* another. Meaning, then, is socially produced: 'Not a single instance of verbal utterance can be reckoned exclusively to its utterer's account. Every utterance is the product of the interaction between speakers and the product of the broader context of the whole complex social situation in which the utterance emerges.'[3] Within the huge range of meaning which the *system* of language makes possible, particular meanings are triggered off, and others suppressed, by the actual historical situation of each individual utterance. This is *not* the same as the more traditional and common-sense objection to the structuralist approach, which resists the dissolution of meaning across a field of signifiers by insisting that meaning resides in the intending subject. This humanist approach, which would want formally to find meaning residing *in* a word or statement guaranteed by the intention of its author-utterer, would find little comfort in Bakhtin, since the idea of dialogue, when developed, radically decentres the speaking subject as guarantee

[handwritten margin note: Study of a subject (esp. being) through its historical development]

[handwritten margin note: truth of meaning]

of the essential meaning of a statement.[4]

To insist on the primacy of the social does not in itself, though, solve the problem of how meaning is created in specific situations, and this is particularly so where the relation of language to the social and historical world is by definition problematic, as in the case of literature. Bakhtin rejects any crude conflation of language in literature and in ordinary discourse via a reduction to the 'content' of a work of art, but he also rejects Formalist concepts of 'literariness', defined exclusively in terms of technical characteristics, deviations and estrangements from earlier systems of literary language. This, in his view, allows no room for changes to take place at a social rather than purely literary level, which would change the whole context in which the language was received. Bakhtin opposes to this several interlocking ideas centred on the concept of genre.

Genre offers him a way of dealing with literature on a broader social and historical scale than the detailed concern for stylistic variations between works or between individual authors. It is not just a way of defining timeless literary norms and expectations, since genres are profoundly responsive to, and formed by, the whole social configuration. As Clark and Holquist put it, genre for Bakhtin is 'a crystallisation of the concepts particular to a given time and to a given social stratum in a specific society'.[5] This is not an abstract *Zeitgeist*, then, but a concrete expression of the changing sense of a developing material reality. In looking at the way that narrative genres differ, Bakhtin is at pains to show how they embody different historical concepts of time and of space. In Greek romances, for instance, the sense of time – what he calls 'adventure-time' – involved no clear progression, whereas in later narrative forms, organized in terms of the duration of an individual life, events are not reversible in time, and the sense of place is not arbitrary, being directly related to this sense of time. To take another example, Rabelais, a key figure for Bakhtin, inherits a world-view in which material reality is seen as inferior to the transcendent world of the spirit. This view is undermined, though, as is its social counterpart, the corrupt hierarchy of the Church, by a new sense of material reality, which Rabelais is able to represent. Hence Rabelais' destruction of all the normal connections between things and ideas, best illustrated in his intensely material presentation of the human body, which focuses everything around it into new configurations: 'the entire remaining world also takes on new meaning and concrete reality, a new materiality: it enters into a contact with human beings that is no longer symbolic but material'.[6]

Bakhtin is concerned to isolate the distinctive and historically specific ways in which the temporal dimension of narrative interacts with space and matter, and he calls this concrete embodiment 'the place where the knots of narrative are tied',[7] the *chronotope*. Chronotopes would range from unlocalized 'adventure-time' to the castle in Gothic writing, seen as a spatial locus intensively inhabited by different historical periods, and on to the salon and the provincial town in the French novel. The whole idea of the chronotope, and its concern for the specific ways in which materiality and temporality fuse in different periods and genres, is a suggestive one, but will not be developed in this essay except, as here, to illustrate Bakhtin's view of genre as historically rooted in the material realities of its society.

Bakhtin's account of genre, though, is not merely a descriptive account of changing chronotopes or narrative genres. He shows a marked preference for some forms over others, and to account for this preference we need to remember his insistence that language, far from being a synchronic and abstract system, is a material and constantly changing practice in which two contending forces are constantly operating. These he calls 'centripetal', working towards a unified and static language, and 'centrifugal', endlessly developing new forms which parody, criticize and generally undermine the pretensions of the ambitions towards a unitary language. Bakhtin distinguishes between different literary genres and forms in terms of these conflicting impulses, arguing that poetry (which he apparently takes, for his purposes, to be quintessentially lyric) aspires towards a unitary language that will suppress the opposing forces inherent in language in the interest of the particular artistic formal whole. It is because literary critics have tried to use this idea of stylistic unity as a prerequisite of artistic form that they have completely failed to cope with the novel, either denying it full artistic status or setting up absurd rules for it. Once one accepts the importance of the centrifugal as well as centripetal forces in language, it is possible to see the artificially closed discourse of poetry or epic not as the *essence* of literary form, but as one choice among many. Thus the carefully erected barriers between artistic and ordinary discourse are eroded: 'Style organically contains within itself indices that reach outside itself, a correspondence of its own elements and the elements of an alien context. The internal politics of style (how the elements are put together) is determined by its external politics (its relationship to alien discourse). Discourse lives, as it were, on the boundary between its own context and another alien context.'[8]

Novelistic discourse has developed the capacity to open itself to the multi-languaged, or heteroglot world in which it exists because of its growing acceptance within its form of the way that any language we use is neither neutral (belonging to no one) or completely one's own: 'The word in language is half someone else's'.[9] Rather than try to erase this characteristic the novelist builds on it. He 'does not strip away the intentions of others from the heteroglot language of his works, he does not violate those socio-ideological cultural horizons . . . that open up behind heteroglot languages – rather he welcomes them into his work'.[10] In his studies of the development of novelistic discourse, which stretches well beyond, temporally and generically, what we usually mean by the novel, he distinguishes different lines of development in terms of the degree to which they incorporate heteroglossia into the very fabric of the text. Early parodic forms, for instance, are seen as undermining official unitary language, using the resources of the living diversity of languages within the society, and Bakhtin sees the culmination of this scepticism turned upon itself in the novel as 'the expression of a Galilean perception of language, one that denies the absolutism of a single and unitary language – that is that refuses to acknowledge its own language as the sole verbal and semantic center of the ideological world'.[11]

The effect of this in the novel, though, is not just the open-ended inclusion of untreated slices of people's speech, a simulacrum of actual experience, but a *representation* of it. This is an important distinction which rests on the co-presence in the text of both the author's and the character's voice. The character's language is always dialogized, set in relation to at least one other, creating a polyphony of voices in dialogue, with the effect that we are made aware of any utterance both as particular speech produced by an individual and as a type of utterance. We place it in relation to other speech in such a way that the whole ideological provenance is revealed, and we are made aware of both the particular and the general.[12] The author, then, ultimately makes the different languages serve his purpose, but it is a purpose that is expressed within, and by means of 'the concrete social context of discourse' of his time, and 'expresses the differentiated socio-ideological position of the author amid the heteroglossia of his epoch'.[13]

The various novelistic methods involved in this dialogization, centring on the many forms of reported speech, are extensively illustrated by Bakhtin, particularly in his work on Dostoevsky whose work represents, for him, the culmination of the polyphonic novel. The speech of Dostoevsky's characters is profoundly dialogized by the author's ability to dialogize his *own* relation to their words, so that the thought of his characters 'is not impelled toward a well-rounded, finalized, systematically monologic whole. It lives a tense life on the borders of someone else's thought, someone else's consciousness.'[14] This precarious ideal balance, where all positions are in dialogue and equally available, should not lead us to see dialogism as tending towards a stable equilibrium, a balance of contending forces. Bakhtin makes clear that one of the characteristics of language is that it changes, and it is this change which throws the dialogical possibilities of language into relief. The decentring of particular official languages is made possible with 'a disintegration of stable verbal-ideological systems, and with an intensification and intentionalization of speech diversity . . . an activity that goes on both within the limits of the literary dialect itself, and outside it'.[15] This speech diversity reflects social diversity and the struggle for dominance which is the relation of social classes, and it is when we give this fact its due weight that we realize the inadequacy of our usual sense of the word dialogue, with its implications of give and take. For Bakhtin the dialogical nature of language clearly *included* this struggle, as can be seen in his view of folk culture and its overturning of official values in carnival and generally in his opposition of official and unofficial languages. Indeed, it has been objected that some Western versions of Bakhtin have tended to give a sense of dialogics closer to a polite liberal pluralism than to the materialist view of language and society which informs all of Bakhtin's work.[16]

It should be clear by now that we can take the idea of dialogism on a number of levels. On the most general level it is a description of language and its operation as a social and shared act. An individual utterance, like the language of a particular group, is inevitably capable of being dialogized, made provisional, shown to be only one part of the social whole, by an increased awareness of the part played by the unheard voices which make up the whole and, therefore, implicitly shape the utterance. Changes at all levels of society, then, will bring about this endless process of dialogization, against the best efforts of monologism. At a much more specific level, dialogism is a quality most fully developed in a particular literary form, novelistic discourse, which is equipped formally to relativize and dialogize monologic utterance and, therefore, offer a fuller and truer version of the way things are. Bakhtin's faith in this form may need to be questioned in the light of later developments, as may his faith in the inevitable dialogization and carnivalization of monolithic or official language, and as a way of trying out Bakhtin's approach I want to apply his ideas about dialogism and reported speech closely to Joseph Conrad's *Heart of Darkness*, with the intention of showing how dialogism works, but also what historical factors operate to shape and limit the possibilities of dialogue.

II

The most obvious way to begin an application of Bakhtin's ideas is to look at the reporting of speech within *Heart of Darkness*. Marlow, the central figure and narrator of the great bulk of the book is, in fact, not the 'I' who is telling the whole story, since his story is itself reported and framed by the scene on the Thames where, we are told by the 'I' figure, Marlow tells his story. But this 'I' is almost inseparable from the 'we' of the little group on the boat – in fact, 'we', 'our', 'us' dominate the opening pages. 'I' only appears briefly, three times in the book, once in the middle, once at the end, and very fleetingly and obliquely, in the opening section: 'Between us there was, as I have already said somewhere, the bond of the sea'.[17] The sentence seems to trail after it the idea not of earlier speech, but of earlier texts ('some*where*', not at some *time*), and of an already existing context which we are belatedly joining. It would seem, then, to identify 'I' as a writer, and what we are reading as writing rather than speech, but there is hardly here a claim for authority or presence which might be expected to go with the idea of author, since other than this hint, the 'I' is even

Marlow's reported dialogue by the frame narrator

less differentiated than the rest of Marlow's auditors. They are identified individually by their professions (director of companies, lawyer, accountant) and jointly, not by what they say – which is almost nothing – but by the way that, at certain points, their presence explicitly dialogizes Marlow's narrative. The most obvious instance is when he enters into a dialogue with their expected objections: ' "You wonder I didn't go ashore for a howl and a dance? Well, no – I didn't. Fine sentiments, you say? Fine sentiments, be hanged! I had no time" ' (p. 69). It is perhaps worth noting the double set of quotation-marks here. In later passages cited there are three and even four – the most obvious reminder of the constant dialogization at work in the book, of which Marlow's relation to his auditors is a clear instance.

Throughout, though, we can say that his narrative is shaped by their presence, their implicit speech, so that Conrad has *placed* Marlow's speech very carefully as the product of a social and historical situation, and we need to stress at this point the curious nature of the little community in which it is produced. We are told of the 'bond of the sea' uniting them, and this could lead us to see Conrad re-creating an archaic world of shared values. Much has been written about the aristocratic/organic values behind this code of the sea in Conrad and its expression in Marlow and elsewhere, but what we have here is a community identified more specifically in terms of the 'monstrous town' of London and precisely those commercial and legal interests which had made it 'the biggest, and the greatest, town on earth' (p. 27). This will be of importance later, but what can be stressed for the moment is the fact that Marlow's speech is placed, subjected both explicitly and implicitly to dialogization, and that the context which dialogizes it is itself available for *us*, as readers to place in yet another, larger context. An awareness of this can at least prevent the direct conflation of Marlow and his values with Conrad, which leads F. R. Leavis to tick Conrad off for Marlow's abstractness of language, but it can also head us off from the opposite position of having to set up a clear authorial position *behind* the (unreliable) narrator – an exercise which may have more to do with protecting the figure of the author as absolute authority and presence rather than anything else.

If we see Conrad's production of *Heart of Darkness* dialogized in the same way as Marlow's story by its potential readers, contemporary and later, we can look not so much for a single authorial intention as a changing set of parameters or dialogues within which the meanings emerge. To respond to Leavis's strictures by arguing Conrad's *separation* from Marlow tells us nothing if to do this we have implicitly to posit an omniscient and ironic author. In Edward Said's view, Conrad's use of utterance (reported *speech*) as the basic narrative mode is a way of dissolving the author into a multiplicity of voices and allowing a clear approach to a reality which is, nevertheless, fundamentally unrepresentable in language. Said recognizes that in Conrad 'every narrative utterance . . . contests another one'[18] but interprets this, in Freudian terms, to be Conrad confirming his authorship by denying validity to any one of the visions he creates. Said thus recognizes the relativity and dialogization of voices, and the *problematic* nature of the implied author as more than the sum of their parts, but the danger is that the author can then be left as a non-determinate presence rather than a man with particular discourses available, or otherwise, to him. Making the author determinate in this case would mean, for instance, exploring what Marlow's abstractions mean or what they conceal, what purpose they serve, within the larger historical and ideological dialogue in which Conrad's work takes place, because it is here that the author is situated, rather than in an Olympian realm of artistic invention and autonomy. To take us nearer to this broader context, though, we can return to the reporting of speech.

A characteristic feature of the book is the way that major characters and their languages merge into each other rather than sharply define themselves. The relation of this to Bakhtin's view of the self as *decentred* in language should be clear by now. This important psychological aspect of Bakhtin has been developed by Julia Kristeva,[19] but can only be handled indirectly in this essay through the issue of reported speech and dialogue. Clearly, though, we have some significant mergings and transferences of character within the book. When, for instance, the 'I' reappears at the end of the book he does so not in distinction to Marlow, but as a way of extending Marlow's pervading gloom. We are still within Marlow's view which is now extended to the Thames. 'Marlow ceased .... "We have lost the first of the ebb," said the Director, suddenly. I raised my head...the tranquil waterway leading to the uttermost ends of the earth...seemed to lead into the heart of an immense darkness' (p. 121).

[Handwritten marginal notes, left margin:] it's me! nor that I'm him, I mean that I'm here, well I was.. when I was writing this obviously but I'm not now obviously. I was just saying that because it was changed to fraud it must be me. Do you see? Gosh, it's very strange isn't it! still I'm off on my way now, well by the time you read this I'll be dead. well not really but the me I am now will be dead coz by the time you read this I will have finished the chapter and not really be that particular me any more. Do you see? Bye then!

[Handwritten notes, bottom:] I just tried to write with my fag then - silly me! → all this time and I could have been writing proper notes! silly me! bye!

More prominently, we have the relation of Marlow to Kurtz. Marlow's whole narration is full of other people's languages, and the way that they are incorporated enables them to be held up to the light and, in varying degrees, dialogized. When, for instance, Marlow sees the ship pointlessly ' "firing into a continent" ' he tells us that the absurdity ' "was not dissipated by somebody on board assuring me earnestly there was a camp of natives – he called them enemies! – hidden out of sight somewhere" ' (p. 41). Soon afterwards on land when he encounters Africans in chains, he is prompted to make a connection by the noise of explosions he hears: ' "It was the same kind of ominous voice; but these men could by no touch of imagination be called enemies. They were called criminals" ' (p. 43).

This trying-out of language to see if it fits is continued at the end of the same paragraph in the description of his non-verbal communication with their guard, who ' "with a large, white, rascally grin, and a glance at his charge, seemed to take me into partnership in his exalted trust. After all, I also was a part of the great cause of these high and just proceedings" ' (p. 43). This language has its origin neither in Marlow nor in the guard, but in the official language of empire, and is labelled as such in all its hypocrisy by being dialogized, made relative to other more appropriate languages. There are many instances of this throughout the book, but the main area where the idea of voice and language is most problematic *and* where it is explicitly thematicized is in relation to Kurtz. Kurtz is regularly characterized by his eloquence, but of course we never experience its force directly, since his actual reported speech is heavily dialogized by what surrounds it. Early on, for instance, Marlow overhears the corrupt administrators discussing Kurtz. ' " 'And the pestiferous absurdity of his talk,' continued the other; 'he bothered me enough when he was here. "Each station should be like a beacon on the road towards better things, a centre for trade, of course, but also for humanizing, improving, instructing." Conceive you – that ass!' " ' (p. 65). Here the idealistic language is ridiculed, but from a totally unacceptable position which Marlow has already made us mistrust. More often, we are given Kurtz's speech from the more ambivalent position of Marlow, for whom the voice is powerful and somehow sympathetic as the expression of ' "a sense of real presence" ' (p. 83).

For Marlow, Kurtz's tragedy lies precisely in the isolation of that voice, the fact that it is only ever a monologue. What takes the place of the other side of the dialogue is, in fact, the wilderness, which 'had whispered to him . . . things of which he had no conception till he took counsel with this great solitude – and the whisper had proved irresistibly fascinating. It echoed loudly within him because he was hollow at the core' (p. 97). This seems to contradict Marlow's earlier claim for presence in Kurtz, and the implications will be dealt with later, but for now it is worth stressing the way that the echo here, and the ambiguity of outer and inner involved in the whole idea of the 'heart' of darkness provides a useful contrast to the idea of dialogue, where one expresses oneself, finds oneself in the words of others, where self-expression and self itself are relativized and historicized. The echoing hollowness here is a good image of the ultimate emptiness of monoglossia, language which excludes all others, and Kurtz's self-expression through voice is expressed as a destruction of everything else, when Marlow remembers him speaking, ' "opening his mouth voraciously, as if to devour all the earth with all its mankind" ' (p. 116).

In the isolation Kurtz's view involves the world becomes more and more monolithic and abstract, and instead of the real world of society and history, it becomes a world which vacillates between the empty ideas of progress and white destiny expressed in his report, and the equally absolute and empty evil expressed in his ' "valuable postscriptum" ' as Marlow calls it, ' "Exterminate all the brutes!" ' (p. 87). This is not dialogue, but self-cancelling opposition. His last words, ' "The horror, the horror" ' could equally well be seen as an expression of a perverted and monomaniac sense of evil, but Marlow here dialogizes his words with a vengeance, in insisting that they represented, as an expression of ' "that supreme moment of complete knowledge" ' (p. 111), ' "an affirmation, a moral victory, paid for by innumerable defeats, by abominable terrors, by abominable satisfactions" ' (p. 113). Many readers have felt uneasy about the plethora of abstractions surrounding Kurtz's, and increasingly Marlow's, vision of moral and metaphysical darkness, and have taken Conrad to task for vagueness, but if we continue to examine the text in terms of reported speech we can offer another way of tackling this issue.

refer to Towson's text why does it excite M so much? English + Cipher

Why does Marlow become the repository of the confidences of ' "this initiated wraith from the back of Nowhere" ' (p. 86)? Why can Marlow be so influenced by the vision of Kurtz? The most obvious answer may seem banal: ' "This was because it could speak English to me" ' (p. 86). The absolute importance of this, though, is revealed in Marlow's account of the death of the helmsman, since the helmsman and Kurtz are specifically connected by Marlow in a long and important digression from the main narrative line. After the death of the helmsman, when Marlow's shoes are still filled with his blood, his mind races off at a panicky tangent to Kurtz, and the later, narrating Marlow follows this tangent by interrupting the narrative with some of his most important statements about Kurtz which anticipate the end of the book. ' " 'He is dead,' murmured the fellow, immensely impressed. 'No doubt about it,' said I, tugging like mad at the shoe-laces. 'And by the way, I suppose Mr Kurtz is dead as well by this time'. For the moment that was the dominant thought" ' (p. 82).

Then comes the preview of the rest of the story, with an emphasis on Marlow's responsibility to understand Kurtz and tell his story, and the remark about speaking English quoted above, which comes back to the main narrative, and the crisis-ridden situation on the boat with ' "No; I can't forget him, though I am not prepared to affirm the fellow was exactly worth the life we lost in getting to him. I missed my late helmsman awfully....a subtle bond had been created, of which I only became aware when it was suddenly broken. And the intimate profundity of that look he gave me when he received his hurt remains to this day in my memory – like a claim of distant kinship affirmed in a supreme moment. Poor fool! If he had only left that shutter alone. He had no restraint, no restraint – just like Kurtz" ' (pp. 87–8). It is 'that look' which is at the back of this compulsive excursus and the nervous elliptical connection between Kurtz and the helmsman, as we see in the account of his death: ' "We two whites stood over him, and his lustrous and inquiring glance enveloped us both. I declare it looked as though he would presently put to us some question in an understandable language; but he died without uttering a sound" ' (p. 82). The total lack of communication, the impossibility of dialogue here is not just because of the helmsman's agony, but is a particularly vivid instance of the general impossibility of dialogue because of lack of a common language. Here we come up against the limits of dialogization. Following Bakhtin, I have talked of the different 'languages' within English, but of course this depends on a degree of communication and mutual intelligibility between them. Elsewhere in the book we have a clear demonstration of how Marlow's understanding is limited by language, or its absence, when he assumes that the Russian marginal notes in the book he finds are in cipher. In this case, the ' "extravagant mystery" ' is eventually solved since the unnamed Russian speaks English, and the event is of little consequence, but the inability to communicate with the helmsman is final and has crucial political implications.

In the various identifications of Kurtz and the helmsman here, there seems to be a pressure both to distinguish (Kurtz had a voice) and to identify (ultimately one was worth no more than the other) but the actual implications of this are nervously suppressed. When we look elsewhere in the book for dialogue between whites and Africans we find a similar strategy of evasion taking place, as for instance in the account of the boat steaming past native villages and encountering ' "a black and incomprehensible frenzy. The prehistoric man was cursing us, praying to us, welcoming us – who could tell? We were cut off from comprehension of our surroundings....We could not understand because we were too far and could not remember, because we were travelling in the night of first ages" ' (pp. 68–9). What they are passing are actually human communities with a perfectly comprehensible language, but characteristically the issue is transposed on to a metaphysical level. Again and again the specific and historical, that is, African communities and individuals, are conflated with an a-historic Nature, which is then curiously re-anthropomorphized: ' "Could we handle that dumb thing, or would it handle us? I felt how big, how confoundedly big, was that thing that couldn't talk, and perhaps was deaf as well" ' (p. 56). Marlow is right to fear the lack of dialogue but it is with people that one has it, not impersonal forces, not inanimate objects, and it is finally because the natives are seen as objects rather than subjects that dialogue is blocked off. It is here, then, that there is the need to dialogize Marlow's voice, but the most relevant voices that should do it are unavailable to him *and* to Conrad, since the situation out of which Marlow's narrative arises, and out of which Conrad's work arises, too, is a specific type of colonialism. Knowledge of the 'natives' could only be from outside, objective, rather than dialogical, and some recent severe self-examinations undertaken by anthropologists have tended to stress the inextricability of the forms of possible knowledge of other groups from the political situation in which they are studied.[20]

Marlow recognizes monoglossia and the tyranny that goes with it, in Kurtz's voracity and monomania. He is himself subjected to it and manipulated by it at the end of the book when Kurtz's fiancé *forces* him to lie, and obliterates any possibility of the truth forcing itself into their conversation, and dialogizing her version of Kurtz. He recognizes only too clearly the evil and oppression carried out in the name of the official language of white domination, but he literally has no adequate way to dialogize it, since he has no adequate language to oppose to it. The other end of the dialogue, the voices that would lead to an overturning, a carnivalizing of the official language, cannot adequately be represented by the language of the sea – we have already seen that his auditors are deeply implicated in the city which is at the heart of the Empire – and the other and most obvious place to look, the subjected people themselves, is closed for social and historical reasons that neither Marlow nor Conrad can individually overcome. In this context, it is interesting to look at Marlow's response to Kurtz's last words. As has often been pointed out, Marlow loads Kurtz's cryptic outcry with a particular meaning which has the effect of validating and redeeming Kurtz. He is suggested by Marlow to have expressed a moment of self-knowledge. A clear enough case, then, of reported speech being dialogized within someone else's speech, but we need to look more closely at what *else* Marlow is in implicit dialogue with here. Only a paragraph later we are given – almost uniquely in the book – the actual speech of an African. ' "Suddenly the manager's boy put his insolent black head in the doorway, and said in a tone of scathing contempt – 'Mister Kurtz – he dead' " ' (p. 112). Here is the exact opposite of Marlow's empathy. Kurtz is seen from the outside, almost as object. This is the last word *on* him, not by him, the true dialogization of his words, and it is with this implied – and unacceptable – truth that Marlow struggles, in insisting on Kurtz's worth. ' "I like to think my summing-up would not have been a word of careless contempt. Better his cry – much better" ' (p. 113). Here Marlow is, whether he likes it or not, in dialogue with the manager's boy, and his 'word of careless contempt' and it is surprising that so many critics ignore this fact, seeing the word of contempt as emanating generally from Marlow and his disillusionment.[21] The boy's view must be opposed, by salvaging some moral value from Kurtz's words, because the alternative is recognizing that there may be an African view which is unknowable to Marlow or the other whites, but which could have the last word on them, could be the expression of a subject rather than a dumb object.

III

In sticking very closely to the issue of dialogue and its forms and possibilities within *Heart of Darkness*, I have tried to show that it can lead us to the fundamental contradictions engendered by its historical situation and can, therefore, account for the move into vagueness and abstraction that has worried so many critics. This approach, while distinguishing between Marlow and 'I' and Conrad would not elevate Conrad to a position above and outside the historical contradictions of his time, but would insist on Conrad's own place within the available languages of his time and, more importantly here, within the limitations of the languages. Bakhtin's admiration for the polyphonic novel of Dostoevsky, his view of the progressive dialogization of discourse in the novel and the positive role of carnivalization has itself to be historicized, and we must ask what a polyphonic novel of colonization could possibly look like at the end of the nineteenth century. That is, we need to stress that if the novelistic discourse is genuinely to attempt to incorporate and be open to the heteroglossia of the time, this cannot be achieved either by an act of transcendence on the part of the author or by the magical possibilities and open-endedness of the novel form. The normal relation of languages in unequal and oppressive societies is that of struggle for dominance rather than peacefully co-existing dialogue. As Bakhtin has pointed out, at certain periods of rapid change suppressed languages suddenly get the chance to be heard, and even to overturn the official language. Even at other times these languages are still there at the level of unofficial and folk culture. In stressing the positive dialogical aspects of the novel, the way that it can relativize languages and the ideologies they represent, Bakhtin has provided us with a very useful tool, but if we take this as a celebration of an inherent capacity within novelistic discourse, and follow him in seeing Dostoevsky's polyphony as the culmination of this, we go only part of the way, since what then becomes interesting and even crucial is, given this capacity for dialogization, what are the limiting conditions which have shaped the development of the modern novel, and caused the displacements and blocking of true dialogism.

James Joyce has often been seen as the culmination of Bakhtin's views of heteroglossia, but it would be misleading to see Modernism in general continuing the line of development traced by Bakhtin up to Dostoevsky. Certainly there is the social upheaval and flux which should enable carnivalization, and even the sudden availability of new, formerly suppressed languages, but these languages are not necessarily used to overthrow the official language, and it might be more productive, therefore, to see Modernism and what comes after it as a series of strategies to contain carnivalization.[22] One of the most multivoiced works of Modernism and one of the most celebrated, Eliot's *The Waste Land*, attempts to bind together the disparate voices and explicitly to counter the centrifugal social and cultural forces of the time. Disorder is an appalling prospect for Eliot, and Babel is more a threat than a liberating possibility. His original intention of using Kurtz's last words as the epigraph for *The Waste Land* is, then, entirely appropriate, another way of dialogizing his words, and the use of images and phrases from the opening section of the book remains clearly in evidence in the descriptions of the Thames in the poem. Where, though, in Conrad, the relation of the modern *conquest* Thames to earlier times and to other rivers is presented in terms of empire and conquest, in Eliot it is transposed into myth, and the relations between the elements of the poem are dehistoricized throughout. Eliot almost begins at the point of mystification to which Marlow and Conrad are forced, and his use of 'Mistah Kurtz, he dead' as an epigraph to *The Hollow Men* confirms this reading of Conrad since the words and their original tone are dialogized so that they represent the end of Kurtz's 'sense of real presence', leaving us only with hollowness, and the alternative language here is a banal and corrupted rather than a liberating one.

Bakhtin's distinction between prose and poetry might perhaps lead us to expect this sort of reduction to monoglossia and the tight control of other voices in poems, but when we look at the characteristic techniques of Modernist fiction we find many parallel strategies. William Faulkner's *The Sound and the Fury*, for instance, may seem to offer voices in dialogue, but the central concern of Faulkner's work is the tension between these many voices and the desire to hold them all, and his fictional world, together by a style which overrides these voices and a myth which contains their history. In terms of reported speech and the particular approach used in this chapter, it could be argued that the development of point of view, notably in Henry James, offers an ambiguous response to the decline of any central or official world-view. It could be seen as a provisionalizing of all voices, a development Bakhtin would applaud, but it could equally well be seen as a way of affirming precisely that sense of individual psychology and separation which Bakhtin questions. Fredric Jameson's description of Jamesian point of view as perpetuating 'an increasingly subjectivized and psychologized world, a world whose social vision is one of a thorough-going relativity of monads in co-existence'[23] is an interesting reminder of the danger of reading Bakhtin in terms of the bourgeois psychology which he explicitly rejected, since it could lead us to seeing Bakhtin's ideal of dialogue as precisely what Jameson here criticizes in James.

This is only possible, of course, if Bakhtin's own stress on the social and historical determinations of dialogism is ignored, and in stressing these aspects, this chapter has dialogized Bakhtin in the context of recent Marxist criticism rather than the perhaps more psychological stress which would see more elements of liberal pluralism. The continuing relevance and increasing urgency of the issues raised by Conrad's relation to colonialism, and the problem of dialogics, are specifically demonstrated in Francis Ford Coppola's and Michael Herr's transposition of *Heart of Darkness* to Vietnam in the film *Apocalypse Now*. Once again the only dialogization of American official language is by other Americans. The Vietnamese remain silent, unknown, and history dissolves into mystery and metaphysics. The conditions under which the Vietnamese, or the Africans, or whoever, *can* speak, and can differentiate themselves not only from whites but from each other, and become subjects rather than symbolic objects cannot be created by literature or criticism alone. But criticism can chart in detail where and how it operates or breaks down in literature, and the social and historical situations under which this happens. This is where my use of Bakhtin would fruitfully approach the ideological analyses of Macherey, Jameson and others, and where this chapter enters into another dialogue.

Further Reading

The single best way into Bakhtin – or, at least, into those aspects of his work utilized here – is the essay 'Discourse in the Novel' in M. M. Bakhtin, *The Dialogic Imagination*, trs. Caryl Emerson and Michael Holquist (Austin, Texas U P, 1981). This whole volume is probably a better general introduction than Bakhtin's two full-length literary studies, *Problems of Dostoevsky's Poetics*, trs. Caryl Emerson (Manchester, Manchester U P, 1984), and *Rabelais and His World*, trs. Helen Iwolsky (Cambridge, MIT Press, 1968). Indispensable for understanding Bakhtin's relation to Marxism is V. N. Voloshinov, *Marxism and the Philosophy of Language*, trs. L. Matejka and I. R. Titunik (New York, Seminar Press, 1973), and *Freudianism: A Marxist Critique*, trs. I. R. Titunik (New York, Academic Press, 1973). For a more general statement of his approach see P. N. Medvedev, *The Formal Method in Literary Scholarship*, trs. A. J. Wehrle (Baltimore, Johns Hopkins U P, 1973).

The most comprehensive secondary account of Bakhtin in English is Katerina Clark and Michael Holquist, *Mikhail Bakhtin* (Cambridge, Mass., Harvard U P, 1984), which combines a great deal of biographical information and Russian intellectual background with a clear and forceful account of his ideas. The other full-length work, Tzvetan Todorov, *Mikhail Bakhtin: The Dialogical Principle*, trs. Wlad Godzich (Minneapolis, Minnesota U P, 1984), is less informative on the Russian context and tends to stress those aspects of Bakhtin most relevant to recent critical theory, but gives a concise account of dialogics, often using Bakhtin's own words, skilfully edited. Two useful collections are *University of Ottawa Quarterly*, 53, January–March 1983, a special edition covering disparate aspects of Bakhtin and including a bibliography of criticism on Bakhtin, and *Critical Inquiry*, 10, December 1983, which includes a forum on Bakhtin edited by Gary Saul Morson. There are several responses to the latter in *Critical Inquiry*, 11, June 1985.

Bakhtin's relation to Formalism and to Marxism is still a contentious issue. For a clear account of the issues see Tony Bennett, *Formalism and Marxism* (London, Methuen, 1979), and Graham Pechey's review of Bennett in *Oxford Literary Review*, 4, 2, 1980, which extends his discussion of Bakhtin. Bakhtin's critique of Formalism is treated specifically in, and developed interestingly by, Julia Kristeva in 'The ruin of a poetics' in Stephen Bann, ed., *Russian Formalism* (Edinburgh, Scottish Academic Press, 1973). Kristeva represents the most interesting development of Bakhtin's ideas, as evidenced in several essays in *Desire and Language: A Semiotic Approach to Literature and Art*, trs. T. Gora, A. Jardine, and L. S. Roudiez (Oxford, Basil Blackwell, 1980), most particularly 'Word, dialogue and novel'. Paul de Man's brief article 'Dialogue and dialogism', *Poetics Today*, 4, 1, 1983, unlike most of the work cited so far, takes Bakhtin's importance for granted, and asks some searching questions in terms of his own tropological concerns.

7 Feminism II: Reading as a Woman
D H Lawrence, *St Mawr*

Elaine Millard

I

The woman reading

My intention in this essay is to appropriate for a feminist reading a
textual strategy originating from the French theorist, Roland
Barthes, whose texts, whether classified as semiotic, structuralist,
or post-structuralist, have radically altered the role of the critic. In
re-reading D.H. Lawrence's *St Mawr* I intend to concentrate not
on what F.R. Leavis has called its 'poetic evocation of scenes,
environments, and atmosphere' but on the codes and conventions
which underlie these 'reality effects', most specifically on those
which seek to impose a preferred reading of the nature of women.[1]
The particular model for this reading is *S/Z* (1970), a text in which
Barthes analyses a French classic realist narrative, 'Sarrasine', a
short story by Balzac.[2] In both its methodology and presentation
S/Z offers a challenge to orthodox critical practice. Instead of
searching for thematic unity, Barthes' method is to divide the work
sequentially into small units of meaning, termed lexias, analysing
them in terms of the cultural codes, myths and conventions which
sustain meaning. Because these codes refer outward to a far wider
web of significance than that of the text they cannot be rounded off
or completed. They are not the text's structure but participate in
its structuration. Barthes identifies five codes operating within
what he calls the tutor text. These are the hermeneutic, the semic,
the actional, the referential (or cultural) and the symbolic codes.
They form systems of literary and cultural knowledge which the
reader draws upon to make meaning. I shall explain each code in
more detail as I subject two fragments of the Lawrence text to a
seme-analysis, where seme implies the smallest unit of meaning.

These named codes are, however, in no way exhaustive. It is the arbitrariness of the reader's selection from an infinite possibility of codes which allows the 'free play' that is most characteristic of Barthes' analysis, whose purpose is not to say what texts mean but to unpick the way that meaning is produced.

A text which can be consumed passively is, in Barthes' typology, *lisible* (the English translation renders this 'readerly' but it is best understood as 'readable'). Its antithesis, the *scriptible* or 'writerly' text, involves the reader in the active production of meaning from the collision/collusion of two interconnecting networks, the reader and the text. Barthes discusses this interaction in *S/Z* under the heading 'Reading, Forgetting':

> *I read the text.* This statement, consonant with the 'genius' of the language (subject, verb, complement), is not always true. The more plural the text, the less it is written before I read it; I do not make it undergo a predicative operation, consequent upon its being, an operation known as *reading*, and *I* is not an innocent subject, anterior to the text, one which will subsequently deal with the text as it would an object to dismantle or a site to occupy. This 'I' which approaches the text is already itself a plurality of other texts, of codes which are infinite or, more precisely, lost (whose origin is lost). (p. 10)

The reader 'creams off meanings' in an open-ended process of structuration which assists in the dispersal, rather than the unification of codes. Barthes' model, which gives equal status to the competing ideologies of text and reader, frees both from charges and counter-charges of distortion or misreading, for both can be revealed, as the text is unravelled 'step by step', to be caught up in a multiplicity of codes, each in itself dependent on a cacophony of voices off-stage.

A woman observing herself in role, reading as a woman, particularly if the reading is 'academic', cannot be unaware of certain ambiguities. Elaine Showalter has defined the problem as one of dual affiliation: 'We are both the daughters of the male tradition, of our teachers, our professors, our dissertation advisers and our publishers – a tradition that asks us to be rational, marginal and grateful; and sisters in a new women's movement which engenders another kind of awareness and commitment . . .'[3] Put plainly, the difficulty is how to reconcile competencies that have been learned within a patriarchal institution and which guarantee academic relevance, with the experience of being other than this.

S/Z can be read as a declaration of the rights of readers over the tyranny of authorial intent, a feature I can adopt for a feminist purpose. Barthes' strategies will allow me to substitute for the practice of interpretation a 'science' which is able to call its own discourse into question. His method allows for reference to literary and general history, but the emphasis on plurality, which includes 'psychological, psychoanalytical, thematic, historical, structural' possibilities (p.14) blocks the temptation to claim a definitive reading. Before beginning the analysis, however, I want to reconsider the ideological dangers for the feminist implicit in the adoption of a counter model of reading whose roots lie in structuralism, a scientific methodology, which many women distrust as being more macho, less sympathetic than the liberal humanist tradition from which much feminist literary criticism has evolved. It is important to ask whether I am replacing former patriarchal habits of interpretation with newer, more fashionable, but no less male-oriented modes. Barthes remained for most of his productive life at the margins of academic certainty and each of his texts appeared as a fresh assault on the complacencies of conventional criticism. Yet for many feminist critics both author and methodology embody in their structuralist and linguistic origins patriarchal power, which is perceived as engaged in a perpetual colonization and re-definition of knowledge in favour of male interests. Elaine Showalter's essay, important for feminist theorists because it attempts a typology of feminist criticism, accuses the 'new sciences of the text' of serving the interests of a dominant male ideology inasmuch as they 'have offered literary critics the opportunity to demonstrate that the work they do is as manly and aggressive as nuclear physics — not intuitive, express-ive and feminine, but strenuous, rigorous, impersonal and virile' (p.38). Brief encounters with *S/Z* are likely to increase this anxiety.

(1) *SARRASINE* * The title raises a question: *What is Sarrasine?* A noun? A name? A thing? A man? A woman? This question will not be answered until much later, by the biography of the sculptor named Sarrasine. Let us designate as *hermeneutic code* (HER) all the units whose function it is to articulate in various ways a question, its response, and the variety of chance events which can either formulate the question or delay its answer; or even, constitute an enigma and lead to its solution. Thus, the title *Sarrasine* initiates the first step in a

sequence which will not be completed until No. 153 (HER. Enigma
1–the story will contain others–: question). ** The word *Sarrasine* has
an additional connotation, that of femininity, which will be obvious to
any French-speaking person, since that language automatically takes
the final "e" as a specifically feminine linguistic property, particularly
in the case of a proper name whose masculine form (*Sarrazin*) exists in
French onomastics. Femininity (connoted) is a signifier which will
occur in several places in the text; it is a shifting element which can
combine with other similar elements to create characters, ambiances,
shapes, and symbols. Although every unit we mention here will be a
signifier, this one is of a very special type: it is the signifier par
excellence because of its connotation, in the usual meaning of the
term. We shall call this element a signifier (without going into further
detail), or a *seme* (semantically, the seme is the unit of the signifier),
and we shall indicate these units by the abbreviation SEM, designating
each time by an approximate word the connotative signifier referred to
in the lexia (SEM. Femininity).

For the numerous academics whose community of readers is
limited to members of departments of English Studies, the text is a
confirmation of their worst fears concerning the barbarity of
scientific methods. Typographical novelties such as the asterisks
starring the text to indicate each new coding, extensive use of
italics and abbreviations, coupled with an unfamiliar structuralist
lexicon, deter those accustomed to the smooth prose style of L. C.
Knights or F. R. Leavis. It would, however, be difficult to find a
self-consciously feminist strategy that engages with the text as
'intuitively or expressively' as Barthes' re-reading of classic realist
texts, or an analysis which questions as radically the classification
of gender difference.

Feminist criticism is itself inscribed across a wide range of
positions that resist synthesis into a unified voice. Historically, an
overtly feminist approach to the discussion of literature can be
traced back fifteen years to Millett's re-readings of male texts in
Sexual Politics.[4] The strengths and limitations of her analysis have
been recorded elsewhere in this volume. The major concerns of
feminist theorists since then have been, on the one hand, to
register dissent from prevailing norms of interpretation, revealing
literature as yet another instrument of patriarchy, and on the
other, to assert a counter tradition of women's writing, a practice
for which Elaine Showalter has coined the name 'gynocriticism'.

Neither mode of criticism deals satisfactorily with reading as text production. Although the archaeological task of unearthing the neglected history of women's culture is important, the concept of a woman reader has far greater strategic importance for an assault on patriarchy in its textual manifestation. Male theorists, such as Jonathan Culler, have been quick to see its power of leverage. It is in fact Culler's essay, 'Reading as a Woman', which underlies the choice of title for my own re-reading of Lawrence's novella.[5] In it Culler has adopted the strategy of a hypothetical woman reader as a staging-post in a movement from a structuralist to a post-structuralist position. He distinguishes three moments in feminist criticism by tracing developments from an initial appeal to the experience of women as guarantee of a difference in reading, through the hypothesis of a woman reader by an analysis of male misreadings, to a radical questioning of all the procedures, assumptions and goals of current criticism. Culler further cites the writing of French feminists for whom '"woman" has come to stand for any radical force that subverts the concepts, assumptions, and structures of traditional male discourse' (p.61). It is however 'reading as', rather than 'the woman reading', that concerns him: his interest is meta-critical, focusing on the leverage that reading in role allows for 'displacing or undoing the system of male criticism'. He admits that feminists are 'rightly disturbed' that deconstruction makes use of the sign 'woman' as a 'horizon of a critique identifying "sexual identity", "representation", and the "subject" as ideological impositions' (p.175). For a feminist this is sophism; she must return to the textual construct to resist its cultural power.

Feminist theory demands that a distinct stance be taken in relation to its object and therefore is intentionally interventionalist within culture. Barthes' strategies, in comparison, are concerned to lay out possibilities and to affirm plurality rather than to arrive at a meta-meaning. However, because within this plurality the 'semantic substance' of several kinds of criticism is proposed by the codes, it allows the opportunism of feminism entry to appropriate the methodology for its own (political) purpose. Barthes has said that 'it will then be up to each kind of criticism (if it should desire) to come into play, to make its voice heard, which is the hearing of one of the voices of the text' (*S/Z*, pp. 14–15). I shall be giving hearing to those codes which serve a feminist criticism, adapting Barthes' model for my own purposes in order to 'mistress' rather than 'man-handle' Lawrence's text. In the process of textual production the intention is to make room for myself in which to reflect on the competing systems of male text, woman reader and male theorist.

II

'Lawrence could only write where one's imagination could have grace and free play, where the door was not closed to the future.' Frieda Lawrence, *Not I, But the Wind*, 1935.
'Bech could only say, "Kate you've never read my books they're all about women."
"Yes," she said, "but coldly observed. As if extraterrestrial life."' John Updike, *Bech: A Book*, 1970.
'I am offered a text. This text bores me. It might be said to prattle.' Roland Barthes, *Roland Barthes on Roland Barthes*, 1975.

I Approaching the text

The text is not of my choosing and yet it exerts its fascination as a remembered classic of an English degree course, which bestowed on Lawrence's writing both an academic and a patriarchal seal of approval. This novella has been singled out for particular commendation by F.R. Leavis who, in *D.H. Lawrence: Novelist*, claims canonical status for it by comparative reference to T.S. Eliot's *The Waste Land*, itself a paradigm for modernism: '*St Mawr* seems to me to present a creative and technical originality more remarkable than that of *The Waste Land*, being, as the poem is not, completely achieved, a full and self-sufficient creation' (p. 271). Leavis reads the work as a proof of the author's 'supreme intelligence' in his 'deep insight into human nature'. Such confident (and largely unsupported) assertion is a challenge to careful re-examination of the tutor text.

A further spur to a re-reading is the fact that Lawrence has been a focus for feminist debate, largely because his writings, both fictive and polemical, obsessively interest themselves in the essential nature of sexual difference. Indeed it is largely as prophet of a new sexuality that he figures in popular consciousness. His texts ascribe primacy to the intimate relationship of men and women, and frequently convey harsh criticisms of the institutional-ization of sexuality through a feminine consciousness. On the one hand, women readers have been attracted by the importance accorded the personal in his writing; on the other, repelled by doctrines of a dominant masculine sexuality mouthed at them through the women characters. Some, like Anais Nin, who desired for herself 'a feminine sensibility that would not threaten man', admire the mimicry. Interviewed on her choice of Lawrence as subject for her own writing, she is reported as saying, 'I found someone whose work I wanted to develop further because he was trying to write very much what a woman felt. He wrote very much as a woman.'[6] Others, however, most notably Simone de Beauvoir and Kate Millett, have sought to unmask the manipulation. Yet by directly challenging only the interpretation of what is assumed to be represented, these feminist readings remain glued to the tutor text in a complicitous fashion. Left unquestioned by their readings are the conventions which sustain the activity of both writer and reader.

My own re-reading utilizes Barthes' method of structuration in order to establish the codes and myths which constitute gender within the text and to resist the kind of dangers that Judith Fetterley has uncovered in male narrative contracts.[7] In accordance with Barthes' own practice I shall describe each code as it arises in the process of reading. The tutor text is reprinted in italics and from time to time larger *divagations* (Barthes' term for the digressions that punctuate his own analysis) are indicated by sub-headings and roman numerals.

(1) *St Mawr*[8]

The function of a title is to announce a piece of literature and point to its content. The proper noun should, advises Barthes in his analysis of Poe's 'Valdemar', 'always be properly questioned'; it is 'the prince of signifiers; its connotations are rich, social and symbolic'.[9] This name poses the text's first enigma: who or what is St Mawr? A place? A religious leader or martyr? A church? An island? An aristocrat? The answer is withheld from the reader for several pages, by a convention that governs the appearance of the protagonist of a tragedy (is this tragedy?), serving to whet the appetite with a mystery to unravel. Barthes names this code of enigmas and mysteries which is common to all narrative, the HERmeneutic code. It motivates the consumption of the readerly by raising questions and withholding the truthful answer (*S/Z* p.17). *HER, question: Who or what is St Mawr? St is a religious signifier *par excellence*; it has connotations of spirituality and mysticism that link with Lawrence's popular image as the 'Priest of

Love'; it brings connotations too of fleshly transcendence, a seme that will be repeated in connection with the stallion elsewhere in the text. Such signifiers which deliver multiple meanings (connotations) make up Barthes' SEMIC code. Semes appear to be 'fleeting' citations with no real significance, 'a galaxy of trifling data', but in fact coalesce into thematic importance through repetition (*S/Z* p.22).

**SEM: spirituality. Mawr: 'wr' as noun ending signifies otherness, non-Anglo-Saxon, in antithesis to the other surnames; Witt, which suggests the Old English verb *witan*, to know – witt, then, signifies the knower (always a negative value in the Lawrentian canon, where to know another is to suck the life from that being) – and Carrington, which as surname suggests the English aristocrat. The saint's name nearest in spelling to 'Mawr' is St Mawnan, Cornish in origin; attributed to him is the following warning against 'pert' girls: 'A time shall come when girls shall be pert and tart of tongue; when there will be grumbling and discontent among the lower classes and lack of reverence to elders; when churches will be slackly attended and women shall exercise wiles'.[10]

Such cultural fragments (although this particular example is unusually esoteric) go to make up the cultural or ***REferential code, which Barthes also calls the voice of science. They are drawn from the proverbial wisdom, or cultural stereotypes of the age. These codes are so familiar, Barthes claims, that they have an 'emetic virtue'; they 'bring on nausea by the boredom, conformism, and disgust with repetition that establishes them' (*S/Z*, p.139). For the purposes of this analysis I intend to give particular hearing to fragments of ideology, inverted into a natural reference, an accepted value, and call it MIS, a code of MISogyny. In arbitrarily choosing a new code (or rather, sub-code of REFerence) I am still following Barthes, whose own selection of relevant codes is an arbitrary choice from an indefinite number of possibilities. (Though five major codes are traced in *S/Z* these are subsequently modified in 'Textual Analysis of Poe's "Valdemar"'.) The voice of misogyny contains all the patriarchal wisdom accrued through time on the nature of women, spewed out as stereotype. *St Mawr*, as title, at once announces and demonstrates for the woman re-reading, a covert phallocentric and misogynist intent.

(2) *Lou Witt had had her own way so long, that by the age of twenty-five she didn't know where she was.*

The opening sentence plunges us at once into the semes that will settle on the proper name, Lou Witt, to create character. Such semes will be repeated several times in combination with each other to determine the complexity of the character's personality for, explains Barthes, 'The proper name acts as a magnetic field for the semes' (*S/Z*, p.67).

*SEM: wilfulness/cocksureness, an anathema in the patriarchal distribution of attributes between the sexes; Juliet Mitchell has demonstrated how male typologies from Aristotle to the present constitute woman as non-male, impotent, passive and incapacitated.[11]

Here the text implies antithesis of the male-dominating female principle to a subordinated male; a transgression that will lead into the text's thematics, harping again on the struggle for ascendancy between antithetical pairings: male/female: husband/mother-in-law; mother/child. Just as Barthes discovers in 'Sarrasine' an empty space in the family chronicle, that of the mother, in this text it is the father whose absence is significant, indicating a vacuum of patriarchal power. **SYM: mother and daughter/son: the absent father. In *S/Z* Barthes notes Sarrasine's turbulence as 'a larger, vaguer and more formal signified' than a character trait (p.91). In this text it is wilfulness that expands in chains of signification, marking the thematic importance of the flawed antithesis of gender. ***SYM: antithesis of male/female. Twenty-five (for a Jane Austen heroine it would have been younger); ****SEM: marital status: the age of the woman is also connotator of sexual availability; marriageability and possibilities for adultery are announced in terms of age. *****REF: 'the amorous typology of women'. This is articulated into the chronology of women's lives and is a Book created by men (The Book of Love?). Barthes identifies this typology in connection with Mme. Lantry (*S/Z*, p.35). Lawrence's text offers the reader a similar typology of women, namely Lou, married woman, would-be adulteress; Mrs Witt, mother/mother-in-law; the servant girl Fanny, as child/woman and sexual subordinate; Phoenix's Mexican squaws, as primitive woman/mate; Flora Manby, the virginal; a New England settler, woman as pioneer. All are defined in relationship to the male, their lives determined by their biological role and degree of desirability, a relationship further determined by age. REF: typology of women. MIS: gender constituted as biology.[12]

(3) *Having one's own way landed one completely at sea*
*SEM: wilfulness. Who speaks? Who knows Lou? The questions Barthes puts to classic realism in 'The Death of the Author' can be put to this text. Who is speaking this? Is it Lawrence as individual, with experience of women, or Lawrence as author, professing literary ideas of women, or is this universal wisdom? The voice of the narration in the opening sentence is collective and anonymous. It speaks authoritatively, with its book, as it were. 'One' however denotes, in Gérard Genette's terms, the internal focalizer, rather than an external focalizer, in this way presenting the focalized from within. This trangression of narrative voice works to make the female complicit in her own censoring, so that the opinions of the narrator (discourse) are foisted on to the character and to the reader. The text constrains the women characters to share the derogatory societal stereotyping of their actions, assuming agreement from the reader. It exemplifies the process that Mary Daly has described as 'man-made and man-controlled pseudo-feminism'.[13] **MIS: the code of actions dissolves in the code of cultural reference; Lou's actions confer her 'fallen' female nature.

(4) *To be sure for a while she had failed in her grand love affair with Rico. And then she had had something really to despair about. But even that had worked out as she wanted. Rico had come back to her, and was dutifully married to her. And now, when she was twenty-five and he was three months older, they were a charming married couple.*
What is being formulated here is a sequence, the progress of a relationship, the development of a marriage. This is part of the proairetic code, or code of ACTIONS, whereby 'whoever reads the text amasses certain data under some generic titles for actions' (*S/Z*, p.19). The code is founded on sequence. Barthes uses as an example the expected sequences of a '*stroll, murder, rendezvous*' (p.19) to illustrate how actions in narrative are systematically coded by a dependence on the logic of the already-seen, the already-read and the already-done. By this system a cultural code

of actions is established. *ACT: break-up of marriage. This code mingles here with a further code, the code of irony. Reader and narrator are made complicit in a perspective on marriage which is cynical and debunking. Irony is one of the strategies of the *lisible* that Barthes identifies as used to combat boredom arising from the naïveties of the referential code. In principle irony is an explicit quotation of what someone has said; but who is it in this instance who first spoke? It remains in doubt whether this is society's opinion of the marriage, or Lou's; the effect is again to place Lou in judgement on herself and make the irony uncertain.

II A modest plurality
In digression XX (*S/Z*, p.41) Barthes argues that 'the more indeterminate the origin of the statement, the more plural the text'. Here the undecidability of the voice quoted ironically creates a very modest plurality opened up by following *S/Z*'s 'step by step' method. This slow 'decomposition', coupled with a systematic use of digression, meets a feminist need to challenge the superiority of rational, controlled discourse as a patriarchal value. *S/Z*, as model, allows entrance into a network, a web of inter-textualities determined by the will of the reader. Lawrence claimed freedom for the act of writing, Barthes' method on the other hand liberates the reader from the text's preferred encoding and effects a radical shift in the balance of power.

(5) *He flirted with other women still, to be sure. He wouldn't be the handsome Rico if he didn't.*
*SEM: Femininity. Barthes comments of Filippo Lanty that 'saying a boy is handsome is already sufficient to feminize him' (*S/Z*, p.37). So the epithet 'handsome' coupled to Ricardo, the diminutive Italianate form of the Christian name, Richard, and the addition of flirtatiousness, mark the husband as feminized. At a later point he is described by Lou as like Adonis, an archetype of the androgyne (*St Mawr*, p.120). This is part of a structure that draws together disparate elements of the narrative into a network of antithesis. **SYM: reversal of (natural) role, feminized male. This is the first occurrence in my analysis of the symbolic code. All such lexia belong to a huge network of antithetical pairings which work to structure gender in a binary opposition of nature versus culture, instinct opposed to civilization.

(6) *But she had 'got' him. Oh yes!*
*ACT: Progress of a relationship; the woman traps the man. **SYM: reversal of natural (biological) role. *** SEM (MIS): castrating female. **** REF: popular opinion, society gossip.

(7) *You had only to see the uneasy backward glance at her from his big blue eyes: just like a horse that is edging away from its master: to know how completely he was mastered.*
*SEM: skittishness. Denotatively this is a character trait but here it is tied into a larger network of signification through the symbolic code and the work of antithesis. **SYM: the repressed animal instinct. The blurb on the Penguin paperback claims that the stories 'affirm the powers of instinct and intuition . . . against the constraints of civilization'. Lawrentian texts bristle with male animals. The catalogue includes a buck rabbit, several stallions, snakes, a mountain lion, a cockerel, a stoat, pack rats, a kangaroo and a tortoise. Maleness is denoted by an animality that is repeatedly represented as thwarted and repressed. Analogy with animal life naturalizes assumptions that the discourse makes about sexual characteristics that create gender. Vitality, power, instinctive force are all ascribed to the male in the carve-up of gender-related characteristics. ***MIS: stereotypical code of sexual difference: maleness. The full force of Lou's transgression of sex role is rendered in the word 'mastered'. Master/mistress are of unequal power in setting up of gender antitheses; the former is embellished with the full force of patriarchal authority, the latter most frequently signifying submission. ****SYM: reversal of natural order, usurpation of power, and (dare I read in this text), the symbolism of castration.

(8) *She, with her odd little 'museau,' not exactly pretty, but very attractive.*
*SYM: femininity: Lou's animality is characterized by a muzzle, carrying connotations of creatures that bite or gnaw like rodents. This is set in antithetical relationship to the noble maleness of stallions. **REF: the fabled code of animal traits. ***MIS: the inferior nature of woman.

(9) *and her quaint air of playing at being well-bred, in a sort of charade game; and her queer familiarity with foreign cities and*

foreign languages; and the lurking sense of being an outsider
everywhere, like a sort of gypsy, who is at home anywhere and
nowhere: all this made up her charm and her failure. She didn't
quite belong.
*SEM: duplicity. Lou is not what she seems, her attractiveness is
only a surface, as with Jezebel, Medusa or the gipsy Carmen. Her
attractiveness is a trap, carrying connotations of destructive
power. **MIS: Woman as unknowably Other. This otherness
brings in attendance the fear of female powers which emerges
repeatedly in male texts.

(10) *Of course she was American: Louisiana family, moved down*
to Texas.
* REF: ethnic psychology (American, worldly, duplicitous). ** MIS:
woman as deceiver.

(11) *And she was moderately rich, with no close relations except her*
mother. But she had been sent to school in France when she was
twelve, and since she had finished school, she had drifted from
Paris to Palermo, Biarritz to Vienna and back via Munich to
London, then down again to Rome. Only fleeting trips to her
America.
　So what sort of American was she, after all?
　And what sort of European was she either? She didn't 'belong'
anywhere. Perhaps most of all in Rome, among artists and the
Embassy poeple.
*SEM: cosmopolitan rootlessness. Lou has neither father nor state
to guide her choice and is therefore outside the controlling forces
of patriarchy. Her role transgresses all social order. **REF:
popular opinion, society gossip, nature of 'artistic' individuals.

(12) *It was in Rome that she had met Rico. He was an Australian,*
son of a government official in Melbourne, who had been made a
baronet. So one day Rico would be Sir Henry, as he was the only
son. Meanwhile he floated around Europe on a very small
allowance – his father wasn't rich in capital – and was being an
artist.
*ACT: progress of a marriage, the meeting. **REF: artistic
temperament. ***SYM: rates of exchange, she offers moderate

riches for his moderate title in the economic barter of bourgeois marriage.

III Exchange and Bart(h)er

The question raised here, which will not be answered until the final line of the narrative is what is worth buying? In this instance the bargaining strength lies in the hands of the woman whose moderate riches are used to 'buy' first a husband, Rico; then the stallion, St Mawr, and finally a Mexican ranch, Las Chivas. The market place and sexual identity are as interdependent in this 'modern' text as they are in the nineteenth-century work 'Sarrasine'. The two women's superior purchasing power transgresses the partriarchal system by which women are commodities not traders. It is part of the narrative's insistence on a reversal of 'natural' roles, which results in the 'mastery', or attempted mastery of the men, thereby effecting their castration. Barthes has repeatedly emphasized that the social function of literary language is to transform thought into merchandise and that the author, as distinct from the writer/intellectual, participates in the economy of the bourgeois market place. In *S/Z* he lays bare the network of mercantilism that underlies Balzac's 'Sarrasine' where the mysterious provenance of Parisian gold, having no legitimizing origin, and therefore of itself empty or castrated, is shown to be a point of entry into the narrative's symbolic field of castration (*S/Z*, p.88). The woman reader who enters into the contract with this narrative will risk the reversal of this exchange: the text has castrating designs on her.

(13) *They met in Rome when they were twenty-two, and had a love affair in Capri.*
*ACT: progress of a relationship, romantic attachment, idyllic phase. **REF: popular wisdom: Capri, honeymoon isle.

(14) *Rico was handsome, elegant, but mostly he had spots of paint on his trousers and he ruined a necktie pulling it off. He behaved in a most floridly elegant fashion, fascinating to the Italians. But at the same time he was canny and shrewd and sensible as any young poser could be and, on principle, good-hearted.*

*SEM: artistic temperament revealed in exhibitionism and the desire to be on view which also suggests femininity. **REF: the man has an occupation, a profession. ***MIS: the woman, on the other hand 'drifts'.

IV Being an artist

For Rico, being an artist is a professional role which defines his place in society. Without anything to say in the medium of paint he is 'absolutely serious' about his career as a popular artist. His choice of subject matter, the fashionable portrait, is further sign of the emptiness of his role. The analogy is with the role Barthes assigns to the author in *Critical Essays*: 'The author performs a function, the writer an activity'.[14] Lou's social function, on the other hand, is defined by her marriage. As in society, so in fiction, the man is placed by his occupation, the woman by her marital status.

(15) *anxious. He was anxious for his future, and anxious for his place in the world, he was poor, and suddenly wasteful in spite of all his tension of economy, and suddenly spiteful in spite of all his ingratiating efforts, and suddenly ungrateful in spite of all his burden of gratitude, and suddenly rude in spite of all his good manners, and suddenly detestable in spite of all his suave, courtier-like amiability.*
*SEM: artistic temperament, neuroticism. **REF: psychology of the artist. Freud characterizes the artist as neurotic, oppressed by excessively powerful instinctual needs but lacking the means of satisfying them. Rico, characterized as anxious (neurotic) throughout, displays wilfully destructive tendencies, the result of repressed desire. His contradictory actions are those of the '*composite*' (*S/Z*, p.92) and their citation in conjunction with other feminine traits serves to mark him as deficient, castrated. ***MIS: the inferior status of the feminine, stylized as a deficiency in the male subject.

(16) *He was fascinated by Lou's quaint aplomb, her experiences, her 'knowledge', her 'gamine' knowingness, her aloneness, her pretty clothes that were sometimes an utter failure, and her southern 'drawl' that was sometimes so irritating. That sing-song which was*

*so American. Yet she used no Americanisms at all, except when she
lapsed into her odd spasms of acid irony, when she was very
American indeed!*

*SEM: knowingness, calculated charm, sophistication. **ACT:
progress of a relationship, infatuation. ***SYM: artifice, a snare.
Lou's attractiveness is characterized as premeditated deception.
Lou's androgyny is a mirror image of Rico's femininity. The
attraction is a narcissistic one in which Rico seeks to identify
himself with Lou and, correlatively, she with him.

(17) *And she was fascinated by Rico. They played to each other like
two butterflies at one flower. They pretended to be very poor in
Rome – he 'was' poor: and very rich in Naples. Everybody stared
their eyes out at them. And they had that love affair in Capri.*
*SEM: artistic temperament, exhibitionsim. **ACT: (1) progress of
a relationship, to become one, (2) to be recognized as a couple by
society. ***SEM: the composite, suppression of difference in
narcissistic desire.

(18) *But they reacted badly on each other's nerves. She became ill.
Her mother appeared.*
*ACT: progress of a relationship, ennui, the difficulties begin. Lou
is in a state of 'amorous panic'; sensing her own destruction she
recoils from the loss of self and regresses to a state of infantile
dependency; thus her crisis of repressed sexual identity is now
converted to a (hysterical) illness which recalls the mother to her
side.

(19) *He couldn't stand Mrs Witt, and Mrs Witt couldn't stand him.*
*ACT: progress of a relationship, enter the mother-in-law. **SYM:
contradictory responses to the mother figure who is at one and the
same moment desired but feared.

V The Mother-in-law
Of all stereotypes none is so hated as the false, or replaced
mother; in both myth and joke this figure attracts to itself all the
most despised human characteristics. If to be female in a
patriarchal system is to be a lesser being, then femininity reaches

its nadir in the shape of the menopausal female (it is repeatedly stated that Mrs Witt is fifty-one), particularly if widowhood or celibacy places her outside direct patriarchal control. She is constituted as eternally Other, or the negative pole and, as scapegoat, burdened with the most despised human attributes. In her mythical and historical configurations are included Lilith, the Great Whore of Babylon, Medusa, Jezebel, Duessa, the Wife of Bath, a multiplicity of hags and crones, and every comedian's mother-in-law. From such cultural fragments is composed Mrs Witt, embodying in her stone-like gaze Western civilization's horror of female autonomy. Semes scattered throughout the text draw on references to Medusa, both in name (*St Mawr*, p.29) and by repeated citation of the power of her 'terrible grey eyes' which have the power to pierce appearances. Clustered round her, too, are references to weaponry: she has 'weapon-like health' (p.16), her face is a 'weapon in itself', she uses a pair of long scissors, 'like one of the Fates' to cut off her groom's hair (p.52). She is figured as the castrating mother/goddess who has appropriated for herself the authority of the absent father. The text subverts the reader's expectation of a simple opposition of the sexes. It is Rachel, not Lou Witt, whose malignant activity is opposed to Rico's passivity. What is important in this opposition of the sexes is not romantic, but Oedipal love. Mrs Witt is the pivotal figure in the text's structuration of gender and both Lou and Rico are set in binary opposition to her, with Lou oscillating between castrating and castrated roles.

V Antithesis
One of Barthes' pleasures in analysis is to disrupt conventional binary structures by seeking the term which trangresses the neat disposition of difference, for in those oppositions are the key to the construction of meaning: 'Being the figure of opposition, the exasperated form of binarism, antithesis is the very spectacle of meaning'.[15] In this text the reader's expectation is that the antithesis will concern itself with the antagonistic opposition of the sexes; however, a structuration of the symbolic field through biological class is not particularly productive. Oppositions of primitive versus civilized; or neurotic opposed to instinctual; even English society's snobbery set against American classlessness; are all points of entry into the text's symbolic field. However, as the

plethora of symbolic codes that cluster round Mrs Witt signify, castrated/castrating is the most productive antithesis and the text's main hatred, despite the repeated insistence (voiced through Lou) of male failure, is of the autonomous woman. The text is locked into a love/hate dialectic with the feminine and, in particular, the maternal. The most powerful antithesis is of mother to child. In pursuit of the structuration of this opposition I shall now analyse a further short passage of the tutor text from page 22. I have marked the discontinuity by numbering from 100. ·

(100) *She wanted to buy St Mawr. She wanted him to belong to her.*
For some reason the sight of him, his power, his alive, alert
intensity, his unyieldingness, made her want to cry.
*SEM: possessiveness, the desire to own, a feature attributed most commonly to women. **MIS: woman's nature, the possessiveness of female desire. ***SYM: Lou's relationship with Rico has not bought wholeness, rather it has increased her anxiety. St Mawr is now fashioned into the image of the Other.

(101) *She never did cry: except sometimes with vexation, or to get*
her own way. As far as weeping went, her heart felt as dry as a
Christmas walnut.
*SEM: anxiety, another seme that reinforces the composite identity of Lou/Rico. **SYM: repression of desire, response to unyielding- ness of loved object, response to the rejecting mother figure. ***MIS: woman's tears as manipulation.

(102) *What was the good of tears, anyhow? You had to keep on*
holding on, in this life, never give way, and never give in. Tears
only left one weakened and ragged.

*SEM: repressed desire. **REF: popular wisdom. Here the voice of the character is again absorbed into the voice of narration. The distant anonymous 'authority' of the external focalization becomes confused with the internal focalization of the character so that at a later stage, the views of the narrator, who pretends to anonymity (the tale tells itself), can be foisted on the reader through the voice of Lou. This allows dissatisfaction with the balance of power between the sexes to be expressed as the woman's acknowledgement of her own 'utter sexual incompetence' when confronted by the 'aboriginal phallic male' (p.142). The internally focalized sexual encounters between Lou/Phoenix and Mrs Witt/Lewis (both experienced as the frustration of desire) are loaded with connotations of Western civilization's sexual disintegration that are characteristically Lawrentian. The internal focalization becomes the mouthpiece of the author, the female character a mask for the patriarchal viewpoint.

(103) *But now, as if that mysterious fire of the horse's body had split some rock in her, she went home and hid herself in her room, and just cried.*
*HER: Who or what is St Mawr? **ACT: a subconscious challenge or, in psychoanalytical terms, a paraxis which signals the return of a repressed desire in the shape of the fantastic; thus a desire which has been kept secret and hidden from the self is re-placed and dis-located by hallucinatory perception. ***SYM: the phallus. Of course the obvious symbolism arrived at (taking a lead from the examples in Lawrence's polemical writing on the subject), is woman's submission to the potency of the phallus as the life-force.

(104) *The wild, brilliant, alert head of St Mawr seemed to look at her out of another world. It was as if she had had a vision, as if the walls of her own world had suddenly melted away, leaving her in a great darkness,*
*SYM: power of the Other. This hallucinatory episode signals a return in Lou of animistic thinking, which is characterized by a denial of external reality and a desire for 'dedifferentiation', a blissful state where all difference is refused. It is signalled here by the dissolution of the melting walls.

(105) *in the midst of which the large, brilliant eyes of that horse looked at her with demonish question, while his naked ears stood up like daggers from the naked lines of his inhuman head, and his great body glowed red with power.*
*SEM: active power, an aggressive challenge. ** SYM: the phallus or, as Lacan has it, the master-signifier of desire; or is it?

VI Semes and symbols
In Barthes' analysis of both Poe's 'Valdemar' and Balzac's 'Sarrasine', much more significance attaches to the hermeneutic code on which the narrative is threaded. Even the central enigma surrounding the force and fate of the stallion is allowed to fade out of the narrative once the phallic power has been preserved. What is strikingly obvious in applying Barthes' codes to this text is the preponderance of *description* over action. Psychological states are elaborated rather than events plotted. Of course actions occur in the novella but these are illustrative of character rather than worked into plot. St Mawr, the eponymous figure, is dropped from the narrative when the symbolic role has been satisfied. The weight of semes and symbols signify the work of the unconscious that simultaneously conceals and gratifies desire.

VII Phallic symbols, male potency and the Lawrentian life force
Lawrentian texts have been read as manifestos of male supremacy, which locate the source of antagonism in the resisting female will. In his reading of this text F.R. Leavis describes the powers of Rachel Witt and St Mawr as oppositional forces, the former placed as 'the destructive negation, the spirit of rejection and disgust' (p.284), while the stallion represents 'the deep impulsions of life that are thwarted in the modern world' (p.288). Such a straightforward antithesis relies on a whole discourse of gender-defined characteristics that are embedded in the literature of Western civilizations in the guise of essential human characteristics that conflate gender and sex. To be caught up in this system is to accept the phallic, or vital active force as masculine, and as its opposite a passive, acted-upon feminine. Yet the very symbols brought into play in connection with the stallion are exactly those employed to signal Mrs Witt, specifically in the emphasis on the power of her gaze and the analogies with weaponry. The destructiveness of clever wives or mistresses is an insistent theme in the discourse of Western literature, where outraged sons, Hamlet-like, abjure the object which is simultaneously most desired and feared, the mother. In this text, St Mawr and Rachel Witt can be placed more effectively within a symbolic field when read, not as oppositional entities, but as a single *actant*, to adapt Todorov's term; that is, an interdependent combination of characters with a common function. This figure is the desired object of both Lou and Rico, a St

'Ma' as it were, or the mother restored to her full phallic potency who is both desired and feared. This transgressive coding of the symbolic field also requires a revision of the dominant role figured within the character named Lou. Lou/Rico in this structuration figures as a single actant, an unfulfilled child/lover whose desire is repeatedly deferred and neurotically displaced.

III

Methodological Implications

Opening up the symbolic field in this way suggests that the threadwork of semes and symbols might be pursued in the service of a fuller psychoanalytical study of the text's unconscious. The manner in which such a reading might be developed is indicated by the unweaving of a latent content within the symbolic codes A criticism which is centred on the symbolic could be put either to the service of a vulgar Freudian analysis of the author (in the manner of Bonaparte's analysis of Poe's 'The Black Cat') or more effectively, after Lacan, to reveal the interrelationship of reader, text and language in the displacement of desire.[16] The task of attending to this voice within the text lies within the scope of another essay in this collection. Yet my preliminary decoding suggests that the pursuit of the semes and symbols on which the construction of gender roles within this story rests would discover a repressed but radically feminist consciousness in this most phallocentric of texts. What is emerging is an acknowledgement of the power of a maternal life force, which is both revered and dreaded. Nor is a psychoanalytical reading outside a feminist one. Freudian theory has itself focused on the problematic nature of female sexuality or the acceptance of traits in male sexuality which are defined as feminine, in societies which have been categorized by the male. My re-reading was not intended to arrive either at a full psychoanalytical disclosure, nor a self-sufficient feminist interpretation, but to insinuate the reader as gendered subject between the text and the Leavisite assumption that a work of English Literature embodies truths of lived experience. This more conventional approach to reading Barthes has described as:
'The *mastery of meaning*, a veritable semiurgism, is a divine attribute, once this meaning is defined as the discharge, the emanation, the spiritual effluvium overflowing from the signified

toward the signifier: the *author* is a god (his place of origin is the signified); as for the critic, he is the priest whose task is to decipher the Writing of the god' (*S/Z*, p.174). There has been no shortage of critics both male and female willing to perform this convention-al critical office for Lawrence.

Barthes has also drawn our attention to the contractual nature of the relationship between narrator and narratee: for the Balzacian storyteller in 'Sarrasine' this is 'a night of love in exchange for a story'. In *The Second Sex* Simone de Beauvoir has called Lawrence's novels 'guidebooks for women',[17] defining his contract as that of a teacher/guide to the pupil/follower. I have been concerned to employ the methodology of Barthes' *S/Z* to refuse such one-sided, patriarchal, narrative contracts. The simple act of dividing the text into lexias forces an active role on the reader restoring pleasure to the act of reading. A text that for me represented a tedious prattle of misogynous, hectoring prejudices has been transformed to produce, at certain points of departure, as in the digression on the myth of the mother-in-law, and the discovery of a (secret) female origin for the phallic life force, the explosion of energy that Barthes names 'jouissance'. In reading as a woman I have taken my (multiple) pleasure by refusing the passive role of reader/receiver and claiming through the codes a re-visionary writer's role.

Further Reading

This essay draws on a wide range of criticism from post-structuralism, feminism and psychoanalysis. Other essays in the collection are therefore of interest both as comparisons and for a fuller account of the theoretical issues. Of particular relevance are Anne Jones's account of Kate Millett's *Sexual Politics* and Roger Poole's of Lacan. Both have good recommendations for further reading in these areas.

All Barthes' works engage the reader in new textual strategies and repay close reading. *Mythologies* (1957), trs. Annette Lavers (London, Cape, 1972), is a good place to start, in conjunction with *Barthes: Selected Writings*, ed. Susan Sontag (London, Cape, 1982), which includes key essays from major collections and extracts from longer works. *S/Z* deserves to be read in its entirety and *Roland Barthes by Roland Barthes* (1975), trs. Richard Howard (New York, Hill and Wang, 1977) contains interesting reflections on the preoccupations of *S/Z*. A useful introduction to *S/Z* and Barthes' critical essays is provided by Ann Jefferson in *Modern*

Literary Theory: A Comparative Introduction, eds. Ann Jefferson and
David Robey (London, Batsford, rev. ed., 1986) pp. 107–12. Jonathan
Culler, *Barthes* (London, Fontana, 1983) provides a fuller account of
Barthes' practice and theoretical positions; see, particularly, pp.81–9 for
an account of *S/Z*. Annette Lavers, *Roland Barthes: Structuralism and
After* (London, Methuen, 1982) is also useful for placing Barthes' work in
relation to contemporary developments in theory.

The fullest and most useful account of feminist theory to date is Toril
Moi's *Sexual/Textual Politics: Feminist Literary Theory* (London:
Methuen, 1985). This is the first general account of feminism to survey the
field and offer comparisons between the Anglo-American and French
approaches.

The following works by women writers and critics have also informed
my reading without necessarily being cited as references. They have
played their part in constituting the 'I' of the reading subject and to them
can be partially attributed the difference in my reading of *St Mawr*.

BEAUVOIR, SIMONE DE, *The Second Sex*, trs. H.M. Parshley,
   Harmondsworth, Penguin, 1972.

CARTER, ANGELA, 'The Naked Lawrence', in BARKER, PAUL, ed., *Arts in
   Society: A New Society Collection*, Glasgow, Fontana, 1977, pp. 263–8.

COWARD, ROSALIND, *Female Desire: Women's Sexuality Today*, London,
   Paladin, 1984.

ELLMANN, MARY, *Thinking About Women*, London, Virago, 1979.

FELMAN, SHOSHANA, 'Women and Madness: The Critical·Phallacy',
   Diacritics, 5, 4, 1975, pp.2–10.

FETTERLEY, JUDITH, *The Resisting Reader: A Feminist Approach to
   American Fiction*, Bloomington, Indiana UP, 1978.

GILBERT, SANDRA M. and GUBAR, SUSAN, *The Madwoman in the Attic:
   The Woman Writer and the Nineteenth Century Literary Imagination*,
   New Haven, Yale UP, 1979.

KOLODONY, ANNETTE, 'Some notes on defining a feminist literary
   criticism', in BROWN, CHERYL and OLSEN, KAREN, eds., *Feminist
   Criticism: Essays on Theory, Poetry and Prose*, Metuchen, N.J.,
   Scarecrow Press, 1978.

NIN, ANAIS, *D.H. Lawrence: An Unprofessional Study*, London, Neville
   Spearman, 1961.

OLSEN, TILLIE, *Silences*, London, Virago, 1980.

RICH, ADRIENNE, 'When we dead awaken: writing as revision', *College
   English*, 34, 1972, pp. 18–25.

SIMPSON, HILARY, *D.H. Lawrence and Feminism*, London, Croom Helm,
   1982.

SPENDER, DALE, *Man Made Language*, London, Routledge and Kegan
   Paul, 1980.

8 Deconstruction
Henry James, *In the Cage*

Douglas Tallack

I

Deconstruction typically advertises 'inter-textuality' and 'unde-cidability'. But since my deconstructive reading must reach conclusions about a *single* text, which itself has a final full-stop, the matter of openness and closure will be addressed first in terms of how a reading relates to a text and only then in the more technical terms of signification and structure.

(i) Reading a text

In *Of Grammatology* (1967), where the word 'deconstruction' makes one of its earliest appearances, Jacques Derrida describes the practice of reading:

> Within the closure, by an oblique and always perilous movement, constantly risking falling back within what is being deconstructed, it is necessary to surround the critical concepts with a careful and thorough discourse – to mark the conditions, the medium, and the limits of their effectiveness and to designate rigorously their intimate relationship to the machine whose deconstruction they permit.[1]

A daring quality, coexisting with a claustrophobic sense of not having gone anywhere different, blurs the commonsense opposition between what is inside and outside any enclosure. This problem is dramatized from the opening sentence of *In the Cage*, but in all our efforts to say what a text means (interpretation) or describe it (formalist and structuralist analysis) or, indeed, simply to read it, we situate ourselves outside the enclosure of the text, but use language to do so. For this reason I propose to follow Derrida's example in *Of Grammatology* and treat deconstruction not as an ambitious engagement with Western metaphysics but as a radical questioning of the assumptions we make in the everyday activity of reading.

A de-constructive reading, as the hyphen implies, does not destroy the work's structure because it cannot step outside that which it reads. Derrida reminds us of Henry James's advocacy of 'the house of fiction', but undermines its autonomy, when explaining that deconstruction uses 'against the edifice the instruments or stones available in the house'.[2] A text is read against its own logic or 'machine' by fastening upon the over-looked, marginal, assumed or excessive element – as much a gap in a text as a left-over bit – which cannot be accounted for in any principle of unity controlling the limits of the text; and which is necessarily repressed. It is this inevitable incompleteness of any text which provokes a deconstructive reading, and not a violent dislike of a text as Roger Poole asserts when reviewing *Of Grammatology*.[3]

Deconstruction resembles close critical reading in attending to the minutiae of texts but, crucially, it challenges the unity and coherence which criticism variously identifies. As we shall see, narrative closure, ensuring knowledge of what the concatenation of events mean, is common to a cross-section of critical readings of *In the Cage*, some taking their lead from the importance Henry James attached to establishing a certain point of view. Other readings trace a central theme based upon a hierarchical opposition in which one term is seen as primary and the other as secondary and derivative. In *The Critical Difference* Barbara Johnson explains how deconstruction responds to these claims for coherence:

> The differences *between* entities . . . are shown to be based on a
> repression of differences *within* entities, ways in which an entity differs
> from itself. But the way in which a text thus differs from itself is never
> simple: it has a certain rigorous, contradictory logic whose effects can,
> up to a certain point, be read.... 'deconstruction' . . . is an attempt to
> follow the subtle, powerful effects of differences already at work within
> the illusion of a binary opposition.[4]

This statement broadly anticipates the *how* of a deconstructive reading. By concentrating upon Derrida's deconstruction of the standard critical concepts of signification and structure, we can go some way towards understanding *why* he insists that a text cannot be enclosed. His most startling pronouncement, that *'there is nothing outside of the text'* (*Of Grammatology*, p. 158), should not be accepted lightly.

(ii) Signification

In a communication, information is conveyed by representing an object (for example) by a signified concept. Derrida contests this model, particularly its key 'logocentric' assumption that a sign is a sign of something outside language and is therefore, as he states in *Speech and Phenomena*, 'from its origin and to the core of its sense marked by this will to derivation or effacement'.[5] Derrida reinstates the derivative, effaced elements; in effect, the re- in representation which otherwise is reduced to a detour through language, delaying the moment when the object will present itself and the structure of signs will close.

Derrida endorses Saussure's statement that:

> In language there are only differences. Even more important: a difference generally implies positive terms between which the difference is set up; but in language there are only differences *without positive terms*.[6]

Meaning arises differentially, through the relations between arbitrary signs, and not through the reference of a sign to something that pre-exists it. This is a temporal as well as spatial process for Derrida: 'Every concept is necessarily and essentially inscribed in a chain or a system, within which it refers to another and to other concepts, by the systematic play of differences' ('Differance', in *Speech and Phenomena*, p. 140). A deconstructive reading reveals this endless referral or 'play' of meanings which gives any enclosure or structure its unstable quality. In using Saussure to contest the referential model of communication, in which signification is enclosed by an origin and an end, Derrida also draws attention to the way that deconstruction 'inhabits' even the structuralist model of language inspired by Saussure. Instead of the structure or system (which in structuralism replaces 'reality' or 'the self') organizing the signifying chain, signification itself is seen to transgress the very structure which supposedly contains it.

Derrida's deconstruction of communication is best exemplified in *Speech and Phenomena* (1967), in which he reads the effects of Husserl's definition of language as the immediate expression of an intention emanating from the depths of solitary mental life. In order to preserve the purity of an inner intention while allowing for communication with others, Husserl has to cross and yet respect absolutely the boundary between the inside and the outside. Where literary criticism often resorts to the idea of a special sign (the symbol or the image) to bridge the gap,[7] Husserl divides the sign into inner and outer signs, the former part of 'a language without communication' (p. 22), an authentic monologue implied in the notion of 'hearing oneself speak' (p. 79), and the latter part of a purely arbitrary system which adds nothing to the meaning but merely carries it into the world. Husserl's conclusion is familiar, even if his philosophical route may not be. It is conveyed by the everyday statement, 'I mean to say', with its assumption that, in Ann Jefferson's account, 'speech directly expresses a meaning or intention that its speaker "has in mind"' and 'is somehow seen as being transparent to that meaning in a way that writing never can be'.[8]

Not unexpectedly, Derrida's deconstruction of the opposition between speech and writing and all it implies concentrates on the route taken, the in-between of Husserl's philosophy, and especially upon the cross-over from the pre-linguistic, non-worldly sphere to the worldly sphere. Husserl represents this metaphorically as a relationship between geological strata. Though seemingly marginal to Husserl's whole philosophical project, the distinction between two types of sign and the metaphors Husserl employs in his texts is, Derrida argues, essential if the purity of both the meaning and the 'I' which intends it is to be preserved. Yet this distinction is undermined by the necessity for the inner and outer signs to have something to do with each other as communication takes place.

In an accompanying essay, 'Form and Meaning', Derrida observes signs of strain as 'the discourse on *the logic* of speech becomes caught up in the play of metaphors' (*Speech and Phenomena*, p. 111). Derrida relentlessly follows Husserl as he cautiously 'weaves' the 'geological' strata together but cannot disentangle them: 'the linguistic "stratum" is intermixed with the prelinguistic "stratum" according to the controlled system of a sort of *text*' (*Speech and Phenomena*, p. 112). Demonstrating the figural status of supposedly literal statements is another typical deconstructive move: the search for metaphor, *not* as evidence of literary merit or a particular style but of the persistence of signs where 'experience', 'reality', 'the self', 'consciousness', 'nature', 'God' and so on ought to shine through regardless of the medium that conveys them. But once the boundary between these entities and that which expresses them (language) is breached by the figurative logic that Derrida traces in Husserl, then everyday, public, 'written' signs appear where they ought not to be: in the private, unmediated instant of perception where not only literary authorship but also the self has its origin.

Signs in general are the undecidable element. Without them there could be no communication and the system would logically break down; with them, meaning, including the meaning of the self, is constructed in language and can, therefore, be deconstructed by the differential movement of language described by Saussure. Language cannot be seen as that which is added on, a mere 'supplement'. But if language is 'always already' there then *'there is nothing outside of the text'*.

(iii) Structure

Derrida's clearest exposition of inside and outside relations is his essay 'Structure, Sign, and Play in the Discourse of the Human Sciences' (1966), in which he argues that we objectify a structure 'by a process of giving it a center or referring it to a point of presence, a fixed origin'.[9] The undecidable element here, which must be repressed if the structure is to be seen as complete, is not marginal but central; indeed it is the centre or, we might say, the meaning of a text to the extent that the meaning organizes the text, however subtly. The centre, Derrida argues, is at once inside and therefore part of the structure of signs (where else and what else could it be?) and outside to the extent that it, alone, limits the structure by 'escaping structurality'. 'The center is not the center' (p. 248).

This contradiction within apparently coherent assumptions about a structure returns us to the relation between a text and a reading of it, since the most neutral and self-effacing reading of a literary work *adds* something thought to be lacking. Derrida describes this as 'the movement of *supplementarity*', with the translator confirming that 'supplement' means 'to supply a deficiency' and 'to supply something additional' (p. 260). Yet the centre is generally understood to be 'the point at which the substitution of contents, elements, or terms is no longer possible' (p. 248). As in his deconstruction of Husserl's original moment of intention, Derrida demonstrates that for a structure to be complete it must – paradoxically – have an 'extra' element. However, 'infinite substitutions' and the *'freeplay'* (p. 260) of competing interpretations, are not dependent upon the degree of ambiguity of a particular text, since ambiguity implies that the meanings are contained and somehow balance each other. Freeplay is the consequence of the lack of a centre that is definably *inside* or *outside* a structure and so able to unify it.

II

'Stories and meanings without end';[10] elliptical messages that go astray or are forgotten; insides and outsides; and a succession of puns ('wiring', 'sounder' and so on) within the general context of the postal system. But *In the Cage* rigorously encloses its own telegraphic play and it is this marked relationship between openness and closure which must be *read*, even if it takes us outside the text to James's Preface.

In *On Deconstruction*, Jonathan Culler advises that prior readings of a text can help to locate a controlling opposition. Despite notable critical disagreements over *In the Cage*, the relationship between the telegraphic theme ('play of mind', freedom, subjectivity, imagination, and signification/'meanings without end') and the – for James, unusually strong – economic theme (work, constraint, objectivity, reality, and structure) has been determined by effectively relegating the long, confusing middle of the text. The consistency amongst critics, which goes beyond the categorizing of women identified by Anne Jones (pp. 71–74 above), is most evident in Ralf Norrman's statement that 'The central thematic question . . . is how far the subjective reality of the romantic telegraphist squares with objective reality'. He is emphatic that 'the supremacy of objective reality is asserted', while Charles Samuels refers more gently to a 'comedy of misperception'. Peter Messent is sympathetic to the telegraphist's imaginative efforts, but resigned: 'The drama *has* to end.... She accepts her misunderstandings, accepts too that class and economics cannot be denied.' Tony Tanner and Walter F. Wright see the telegraphist as dramatizing the problem of the artistic rather than the deluded imagination, but when she falls short these two readings join rival ones in their recourse to the author. Here there tend to be simply differences of emphasis between, for example, Stuart Hutchinson, who runs his account of Mr Mudge's sexual power into James's artistic 'energy', and Tanner, who regards *In the Cage* as part of an 'inquiry' into the imagination.[11]

The will to know and arrive at a destination which *In the Cage* shares with all narrative is repeated in the different interpretations which, implicitly or explicitly, converge on the last meeting of the telegraphist and Mrs Jordan:

> They sat there together; they looked out, hand in hand, into the damp, dusky, shabby little room and into the future, of no such very different suggestion, at last accepted by each... and what our heroine saw and felt for in the whole business was the vivid reflection of her own dreams and delusions and her own return to reality. (p. 96)

Less obviously, this scene enforces narrative closure at the expense of the play of signs. According to the logic Derrida discerns in 'Structure, Sign and Play' some principle of closure (reality, truth, a superior consciousness) is reserved a privileged place outside the text, from where it determines the secondary status of its opposite: what is illusory, mistaken; an instance of a limited if – in some accounts – brave consciousness; and, when the Preface is consulted, an 'experiment' in the representation of a consciousness. Signifier is effectively reduced to signified, however mediated and complex this relationship may be in one of Henry James's later works.

Derrida's insistence that signs are never consumed or spent, and his scrutiny of reserved elements, which allow for closure but are not allowed for themselves, suggest a deconstructive reading. By way of situating it, three positions on the text will be 'read': Ralf Norrman's essay exemplifies the difficulty in knowing the truth about a text; Stuart Hutchinson's attempt to know the text from within by taking a character's point of view releases signifying processes that radically open up the text; and Henry James's Preface, written a few years later, is a definitive frame that draws the author into a 'supplementary' relationship with his own text. Additionally, their interconnections reveal lines of figuration which transgress all structures, including the opposition between economic reality and language and its reversal in James's Preface. This reading will necessarily shift its ground but I shall signpost changes of perspective.

☆ ☆ ☆

The girl looked straight through the cage at the eyes and lips that must so often have been so near his own – looked at them with a strange passion that, for an instant, had the result of filling out some of the gaps, supplying the missing answers, in his correspondence. Then, as she made out that the features she thus scanned and associated were totally unaware of it, that they glowed only with the colour of quite other and not at all guessable thoughts, this directly added to their splendour, gave the girl the sharpest impression she had yet received of the uplifted, the unattainable plains of heaven, and yet at the same time caused her to thrill with a sense of the high company she did somehow keep. She was with the absent through her ladyship and with her ladyship through the absent. (p. 46)

The written signs of the telegram underline Everard's literal absence and also position the telegraphist in the middle. She encounters the gaps of a language system and, naturally, looks for the positive terms which define its limits, on one occasion actually tracing 'the marks' of Everard's message with her pencil in an effort to transcend mere writing. Yet in the above passage the written signs are given meaning through the telegraphist's initial trust of facial expressions, which are then acknowledged as arbitrary and as signs of other signs. She briefly recognizes that the repetition of signs in different contexts – this being one definition of writing – adds to the interest by involving her in a matrix of relations. Then she closes the circuit by correcting an error in Lady Bradeen's telegram. Having 'leaped – cleared the top of the cage', 'our young friend fairly pitied her; she had made her in an instant so helpless, and yet not a bit haughty nor outraged. She was only mystified and scared. "Oh, you know –?" "Yes, I know!" ' (p. 48).

Ralf Norrman concentrates on this scene, also seeking closure but at the telegraphist's expense:

The dash stands for ellipsis – a blank-type ambiguity. In other words Lady Bradeen did not finish her sentence. She is just aghast at the little spying, meddling telegraphist. 'You know –' for the telegraphist means 'You know – [*the right word*]', but to Lady Bradeen we may very well imagine that it means something like 'You know – [*about my affair with Captain Everard. You know whom I usually send telegrams to. You spy into my private life and meddle in my business*]'. But the girl thinks her guess was correct. (p. 426)

Norrman resolves the opposition between the telegraphic and the economic theme by leaping a divide himself in a single-minded interpretation of the 'linguistic and semantic elements' that actually face him.[12] These include an ellipsis, a very arbitrary sign indeed. Aside from the various meanings the ellipsis has for the telegraphist, its meaning for Lady Bradeen is that this telegraphist knows about the affair but it is impossible to say definitively how much is known and whether she is 'just aghast' (Norrman) or embarrassed or distraught, or for that matter, 'mystified and scared' at the sudden loss of secrecy, or relieved because the secret has (inevitably) leaked out, but thankfully only to a nonentity who has, after all, assisted her. Norrman states that the Lady Bradeen–Lord Bradeen–Everard plot is unimportant to the plot but its internal relations, which come to light through the telegraphic activity and its replay in the conversations between the telegraphist and Mrs Jordan, point to heterogeneity in the class divisions that seem to structure the story so rigidly. We can return to this point.

Point-of-view criticism, which locates ambiguities and ironies in character–narrator–author relations, seems to end up with still more all-embracing interpretations. According to Walter F. Wright, 'the telegrams suggest a universal truth. One does not really know the full thoughts of others' (p. 175). But the persistence of an indeterminate ellipsis (it refuses to be definitively filled even with the twenty-odd words Norrman adds) foregrounds the textual status of knowledge. More than this, the opposition between signs and reality, which Norrman interprets as the telegraphist's error and Wright interprets as the unknowable, points to the difference *within* the entity of truth that Nietzsche, before Derrida, discerns in one of the most quoted aphorisms from *The Will to Power*: ' "Truth" . . . does not necessarily denote the antithesis of error, but in the most fundamental cases only the posture of various errors in relation to one another.'[13] All of this is not, it must be stressed, a cue for mere interpretive 'play', a view of post-structuralism in general to which Roger Poole gives credence (pp. 92–93 above) and which Elaine Millard regards as a positive development in Roland Barthes' writings (p. 156 above). When an undecidable point prompts the deconstructive claim that every reading is a misreading, we have to trace the logic which both allows for expressions of knowledge *in* as well as *about In the*

Cage and undermines their privileged point of view. That logic
takes us – as in the introduction – from questions of signification
towards questions of structure and from one reading of *In the Cage*
to another.

✩ ✩ ✩

Stuart Hutchinson's provocative argument that Mr Mudge's 'latent
force' puts him in the know is an example of an interpretation
which posits, but does not acknowledge, what Barbara Johnson
has called a structural 'frame of reference' (*The Critical Difference*, pp. 110–46). Consequently, any direct objection Anne Jones
might make to Hutchinson's assertion that the telegraphist needs
'a Mudge' to put her 'in her place', 'liberate her sexual self' (p. 24)
and restore order, has to be displaced into a larger (structural)
concern with the status of Mr Mudge's reality and what he knows.

It is perhaps a minor point – compared with a sexual politics
critique – but Hutchinson apparently exempts Mr Mudge's
maleness from the wordplay of the text, thereby situating him both
before and after the telegraphic theme which occupies nearly all of
the pages of *In the Cage*. Unlike Drake's, Buckley's, Cocker's or
Everard's name, Mr Mudge's name contradicts his realness: 'Now
we understand why the "h" is missing from the middle of
[Everard's] name. He can jokingly sign a telegram "Mudge", but
so lacking is he in "latent force", he could never actually *be* a
Mudge' (p. 24). 'The language of men' – to borrow a phrase from
Norman Mailer – is a rich field for the slippage of metaphor
generally, but what is specific here is the overlap between
economic and sexual language, with resulting difficulties – which
Hutchinson elides – in knowing what 'a Mudge' can '*be*'. To '*be*'
('a Mudge' or, generically, a *self-made man* or, for that matter,
any other entity) presupposes a static separation between self and
determining factors. The structural frame permits this presupposi-
tion but since the frame is located *in* the text it can hardly not be
fully read. It is in chapter 1, we recall, that Mr Mudge is removed
to a post office in Chalk Farm, from where he exhorts the
telegraphist to save three shillings a week on travel rather than
indulge in a 'play of mind'. More pointedly still, his 'daily, deadly,
flourishy' letters (p. 13) are supplanted by the telegraphic play
between Everard and Lady Bradeen. Henceforth Mr Mudge can
be defined in terms of his thrift, that is to say, his reserved,
self-sufficient quality, which Hutchinson chooses to interpret as an

essential maleness immune to any linguistic dressing. But, as Mudge himself knows, it is the context of *exchange* and *interrelation* which is the condition for saving:

> The exuberance of the aristocracy was the advantage of trade, and everything was knit together in a richness of pattern that it was good to follow with one's finger-tips. . . . The more flirtations, as he might roughly express it, the more cheese and pickles. (pp. 37 and 38)

Mr Mudge is implicated in the economic system *and* the telegraphic theme through his thrift. He changes position through saving, as Everard changes position through expenditure, and they are further involved when Everard signs himself 'Mudge'. This coincidence of marginal characters concludes a spiralling passage, in which Everard is described as a character whose identity depends on the reality attributed to 'manners' by the telegraphist, who fixes her own identity in relation to Everard, though at the end in relation to Mr Mudge. If we do no more than mention one other narrative intersection – the two episodes on a bench (chapters 15–19) – and include a relevant passage from Barthes's *S/Z*, we begin to appreciate the instability of the text's structure. We are also made aware of a certain voyeurism which – Hutchinson's interpretation notwithstanding – is persistently associated with the latency of Mr Mudge but which we as readers share:

> Like a telephone network gone haywire, the lines are simultaneously twisted and routed according to a whole new system of splicings, of which the reader is the ultimate beneficiary: over-all reception is never jammed, yet it is broken, refracted, caught up in a system of interferences: the various listeners (here we ought to be able to say *écouteur* as we say *voyeur*) seem to be located at every corner of the utterance, each waiting for an origin he reverses with a second gesture into the flux of the reading.[14]

Although Hutchinson reverses critical opinion on the story by crediting Mr Mudge with central significance, his complex identity arises not from something 'latent' and prior to signification but from his re-presentation in the text. Mr Mudge is not a figure of the frame, 'a deferred presence' or 'investment' (*Speech and Phenomena*, 151), who can return to settle matters.

A common strategy in Derrida's writing is the skewed use of everyday or localized words, such as investment but, more widely, frame, trace, supplement, hinge, and economy. The last of these bears interestingly on *In the Cage*:

> I have tried . . . to indicate what might be the establishment of a rigorous, and in a new sense 'scientific', *relating* of a 'restricted economy' – one having nothing to do with an unreserved expenditure . . . – to a 'general economy' or system that, so to speak, *takes account of* what is unreserved. ('Differance', in *Speech and Phenomena*, p. 151)

Ordinarily, economy means a structure in which one thing is exchanged for another on the basis of an external standard (gold in a money economy). However, in the text the excess released by the (economic) metaphors used to describe Mr Mudge 'breaks up any [closed or 'restricted'] economy' (*Speech and Phenomena*, p. 150) once it is put in play and not illegitimately held in reserve in the frame of the story. It deconstructs the economic *theme*, by which critics mean the use of social and economic *reality* as a 'given' explanation for textual effects, in particular for why 'the drama *has* to end', as Peter Messent puts it.

The structural frame 'put[s] by' the telegraphist as well as Mr Mudge, specifying the economic, social and familial 'pressures that reduce the girl to guessing, that determine the form of her fantasies'.[15] This basic opposition defines the logic of the whole text and controls the key transition from the frame into (and out of) the middle of the text; for instance, the telegraphist's flawed understanding of the leisure class is often attributed to the 'sacred pause', when she reads popular fiction (p. 11). Yet there is an alternative transition across the seemingly rigid social and structural divide:

> *They* never had to give change – they only had to get it. They ranged through every suggestion, every shade of fortune, which evidently included indeed lots of bad luck as well as of good, declining even toward Mr Mudge and his bland, firm thrift, and ascending, in wild signals and rocket-flights, almost to within hail of her highest standard. (p. 24)

The '*They*' are 'her gentlemen', who – Everard included – are constantly on the move, aware of the importance of 'pleasant appearances' and of 'handling, as if their pockets were private tills, loose, mixed masses of silver and gold' (p. 24). This is the first indication that the leisure class is not a homogeneous block, and when Mr Mudge is suddenly reintroduced we glimpse a social and economic system constituted by relations. To 'read' an economy relationally, as Saussure reads language, involves more than, say, Heath Moon's explanation that this is a class society being eroded by bourgeois capitalism.[16] A recourse to assumed progressive or regressive models of history is likely to ignore the necessary incompleteness of any social and economic system. The mythology of the self-made man in an 'open' society is also shored up by a surprisingly fixed link between success and innate ('latent') qualities. Whether bodily signs are read or an explanatory model, such as Protestant theology, is consulted the link derives its authority – and the 'restricted economy' its stability – from the assumed naturalness of another system of signs.

In the above passage, we observe 'change' figuring relationally not referentially. It is the routine, unimaginative side of money, dross not gold, and therefore akin to Mr Mudge's 'bland, firm thrift'. Nevertheless, gold, far from having a true property free from the mere signs of it in the gentlemen's pockets, assumes value and glamour from the everyday exchange of 'change'. The story is also about 'change' of 'fortune', 'fortune' referring doubly to, on the one hand, an excess of money and the 'wild signals and rocket-flights' that are apparently so different from the dross of money and, on the other hand, to 'luck'. We might yet be tempted to fix the meanings of words, with reference to a linguistic gold standard, and adopt one or other of the meanings of 'change' and 'fortune', except that the meaning of 'luck' is also impossible to fix. It derives its meaning from the system and puts the other words into relationship with each other. In Derrida's terminology, it is the 'unreserved' element in any economy, that which cannot be theorized. Efforts to control its indeterminism always invoke the rigid determinism of Providence, but with it the authority of yet another text.

In 'Narrative and History' J. Hillis Miller observes that fiction derives its authority from (but in turn undermines) 'assumptions about history', among them 'the notions of origin and end; . . . of unity and totality; . . . of "fate", "destiny", or "Providence"; of causality; of gradually emerging "meaning"; of representation and truth'.[17] These assumptions are prominent in *In the Cage*, which aims to begin where it ends with the telegraphist 'at last so unreservedly, so irredeemably' (p. 10) recognizing her destiny with Mr Mudge.

None the less, in the over-determined conclusion where, in Miller's words, the 'fates of the characters as well as the formal unity of the text' (p. 461) are supposedly resolved, the 'common lot' of Mrs Jordan and the telegraphist is subject to continuing discriminations. The story advances logically but, in being picked up again, releases meanings that leave the text, like Mrs Jordan's doors, neither open nor shut (p. 88). The telegraphist has a succession of relayed insights into a social and economic flux which incorporates all the characters. Mr Drake – another marginal character, like Mr Mudge and Everard – is central to the relay of information about relations *within* classes, but himself repeats the whole problematic of limits (which cannot but involve the author and any reader) by deriving knowledge from his position inside and outside doors. The word 'engaged' is much emphasized, with its contradictory associations of entanglement, speaking in advance, holding fast, and employment. The vision of a shifting, insecure world, opened up by Mr Drake, and upon which the telegraphist so intensely speculates as she gazes into the Paddington canal, 'settle[s]' her destiny (pp. 101–2). A figure of insecurity (Mr Drake) is therefore linked with the economic security associated with the very figure whose identity depends most clearly upon relations: Mr Mudge. The 'facts' of social and economic class – against which the telegraphist's 'play of mind' is measured – are themselves elements within a 'restricted' narrative economy, which can be deconstructed to reveal destiny as an effect of narrative, rather than, as is usually assumed, the reverse.

It would be presumptuous – and in some circles insulting – to leap from an awareness of 'undecidability' to some utopia of social and economic freedom. But, then, deconstruction advises against such athleticism, pointing simply to the inscription within and across any 'restricted economy' of a different (and scandalous) set of relations. Relations, even in the telegraphist's 'framed and wired confinement' (p. 9), are based upon 'recognition', another keyword in *In the Cage* and one which, rewritten as re-cognition, suggests a linguistic process of re-presentation or metaphorical transfer through which someone is treated-as. A deconstruction of *In the Cage* does not substitute for the telegraphist's closed world a classless one; it does, however, draw attention to 'the structurality' of any entity, including social and economic class. Michael Ryan (glossing Derrida) provides a rationale for sticking with the workings and unworkings of a text, even when 'extrinsic' and, quite likely, sympathetic explanations press hard. 'By text', he explains, 'we mean the tissue or web of differential relations and references that . . . envelops both linguistic processes and the historical world.'[18]

It is entirely in line with the notion of deconstruction, as Culler explains in *On Deconstruction*, that *In the Cage* should stage an acute concern with language set loose from its intention through a telegraphist, who works in an office where telegrams are dispatched but never arrive. At some expense James himself sought to stamp his authority upon the many telegrams he dispatched from Rye, where he exiled himself in 1898 and very soon afterwards wrote *In the Cage*.[19] In circumstances when 'unreserved', 'supplementary' or 'excessive' elements along the narrative line precipitate anxiety about the limits of the text the 'restricted economy' of a telegram, like the 'empty', outer signs which so interest Derrida in Husserl's philosophy, might preserve the inward meaning in transit. Still, the economy of the telegram can be undone by the desire to economize on words, as Derrida remarks:

> To write in a *telegraphic* style, for the sake of economy. But also, *from a-far*, in order to get down to what *é-loignement, Ent-fernung*, 'distance' *mean* in writing and in the voice. Telegraphics and telephonics, that's the theme.[20]

In James's *The Portrait of a Lady* (1881), telegrams are referred to as 'the art of condensation' but the transfers of information, like those effected in the metaphorical language we have inspected in *In the Cage*, allow for a certain waywardness, 'admit[ting] of so many interpretations'.[21] It is the openness to the contexts of the public world and not the lostness of telegrams in *In the Cage* which reminds us, in Derrida's words, that 'a letter does *not always* arrive at its destination, and since this belongs to its structure, it can be said that it never really arrives there'.[22]

It is important to stress that, in spite of the arbitrariness of interpretations and sense of alienation experienced by the telegraphist, movement and chance are associated with the networks and institutions of the public world. Property and propriety of meaning are not unconnected and derive their respective authority from ownership of the in-between – here the postal system – by 'the class that wired everything, even their expensive feelings' (p. 18). There is an unrecognized complicity between the ideal of a private communication transcending public divisions – such as the telegraphist imagines she has with Everard in the crowded post office – and an ordered because natural society. The destiny of characters (and all that we have seen this to imply about economic and social reality), together with the destiny of the narrative, is linked with the destination of signs. With something *textual* at stake it is not surprising that James finds it necessary to transgress the limits of his text in order to re-cognize and re-count *In the Cage*.

☆ ☆ ☆

While deconstruction emulates even New Critical close readings in its microscopic attention to details, the process of displacement, which we have traced through patterns of signification and the internal frame, deconstructs the autonomy of *In the Cage*. To omit the narratorial frame and the title (who writes the title, by the way?) and then halt the process with the 'external' frame that is James's Preface is to demonstrate but a mild form of 'intertextuality':

> [*In the Cage*] speaks for itself, I think, so frankly as scarce to suffer
> further expatiation. Its origin is written upon it large, and the idea it
> puts into play so abides in one of the commonest and most
> taken-for-granted of London impressions that some such
> experimentally-figured situation as that of 'In the Cage' must again and
> again have flowered (granted the grain of observation) in generous
> minds. It had become for me, at any rate, an old story by the time
> (1898) I cast it into this particular form. The postal-telegraph office in
> general, and above all the small local office of one's immediate
> neighbourhood, scene of the transaction of so much of one's daily
> business, haunt of one's needs and one's duties, of one's labours and
> one's patiences, almost of one's rewards and one's disappointments,
> one's joys and one's sorrows, had ever had, to my sense, so much of
> London to give out, so much of its huge perpetual story to tell, that any
> momentary wait there seemed to take place in a strong social draught,
> the stiffest possible breeze of the human comedy.[23]

The movement from natural images, through social and economic ones, and back (or on) to the universal image of 'the stiffest possible breeze of the human comedy', encloses a series of part–whole relationships: the particular narrative representation of a familiar general story; the local office and the postal network; 'one's immediate neighbourhood' and London with its 'huge perpetual story'. The passage repeats the enclosed structure of *In the Cage* but, significantly, asserts not a heavily determined narrative and economic relationship between the telegraphist's imagination and the world but an analogical one in which economic determinants are themselves enclosed by the author's imagination. There is a sharp contrast between the telegraphist's bit-by-bit relational way of knowing and the immediacy of a part–whole connection.

The mixture of natural, social and textual images in the final sentence and the slight oddity of the 'grain' that 'flowered' alert us to another disconnection in a passage which a criticism perhaps indebted to James might well describe as 'organic'. Working against the part–whole relations is an arbitrary string of terms: 'business', 'needs', 'duties', 'labours', 'patiences', 'rewards', 'disappointments', 'joys' and 'sorrows'. These are the links between the neighbourhood and the city. They are the in-between that a telegram and a text traverses, the latter perhaps on its way from writer to publisher/reader. The logic of this detour is not derived from nature, that is to say, from an authority which permits connections between the origin of an idea and its realization in a text to be described as an inevitable 'growth'. The authority is a particular (historical) economy which, through 'transaction[s]', connects 'business', 'needs', 'duties', 'labours', 'rewards', 'disappointments' and so on, and in which James, like his characters, is engaged.

The heavily figured movement between the spheres of nature and economics, through which James positions himself in relation to his text, is curtailed only in the final sentences of the Preface, but by a typically authoritative self-deprecation which only provokes further speculation:

> The great advantage for the total effect is that we feel . . . how the theme *is* being treated. That is we feel it when, in such tangled connexions, we happen to care. I shouldn't really go on as if this were the case with many readers. (p. 158)

The care and sympathy for the telegraphist which is writ large in the Preface, the text (we think of the narrator's confiding 'our young woman'), and in many interpretations of the text is reserved for the artistic imagination and the reading which understands it. Undoubtedly, there is room here for existing moralistic objections to James and the ivory tower but, again, deconstruction shifts ground to consider the coherence, the 'magnificent security' of a subjectivity that can so disentangle itself from 'connexions' that it can include the local oppositions between subjective and objective reality that structure *In the Cage*.

A rhetorical analysis of the language of the Preface suggests that the 'restricted economy' of the self is constituted, and not merely expressed, by 'unreserved elements', by the worldly, the differential and the historical; in effect by signs, as Derrida shows in *Speech and Phenomena*. In the Preface there is a revealing twist, and 'expenditure' is attributed to the 'generous' mind in contrast with the 'thrifty' telegraphist but, more importantly, the distinction between thrift and expenditure and between James's imagination and hers is given a class orientation:

> Admirable thus [the working class's] economic instinct; it is curious of nothing that it hasn't vital use for... but somehow, after all, it gives no pause to the 'artist', to the morbid imagination. That rash, that idle faculty continues to abound in questions, and to supply answers to as many of them as possible; all of which makes a great occupation for idleness. (p. 155)

This statement could fuel an argument, germane to Steve Giles's (pp. 51–53 above), that James reacts against the nineteenth-century bourgeoisie only to repeat their error of mistaking alienation for individual power by, himself, mistaking the alienation of the artist for a different order of subjectivity. However, the reified view of classes *and* of a certain kind of subjectivity, which is apparent in *In the Cage* and its Preface, is deconstructed from within (rather than by importing Lukács' master narrative) by the delineation of a counter-logic of figurative movement in and across both texts. In the Preface idleness is the still centre, the reserved position from which the position of the telegraphist can be determined. It is the gold standard in an economy of composition, which a rhetorical analysis yet shows to be as fluid as the relations of exchange in *In the Cage*. Idleness is the product of much effort and expenditure and, consequently, leaves traces of engagement, the left-over bits. So, too, gold, which James tightly links with germination and with composition in the Preface to *The Spoils of*

Poynton, only to confuse cause and effect and 'found' what Derrida has called 'dissemination': 'beyond the first step of the actual case, the case that constitutes for him his germ, his vital particle, his grain of gold, life persistently blunders and deviates' (p. 120).

In *In the Cage* the simplicity of the telegraphist and of a class – as seen from the end of a narrative which *has* to end – is caught up in the complexity of relations in a modern society. In the Preface, the very complexity of the enclosing imagination, as James describes its workings, takes on a simple because undivided quality, only to find itself enmeshed in the public world, 'that deepest abyss of all the wonderments that break out for the student of great cities' (p. 155). James's Prefaces are re-readings which, in their very precision, disclose gaps in the texts they address which ought not to be there; seek to fill those gaps; and, in so doing, leave an excess, tell-tale signs of a defensive manoeuvre.[24] Derrida's observation, of Husserl, that 'the moment of crisis is always the moment of signs' (*Speech and Phenomena*, p. 81) positions Henry James ' "in" the cage'.

III

Three issues arising from this reading of *In the Cage* tie in with the larger debate over deconstruction: the status of the author; the status of the deconstructive reading; and the politics of reading deconstructively.

To argue that James is limited by his social and economic situation is not a deconstructive reading. But to argue that it is the play of language – James's own business – which not only runs contrary to James's intentions but runs on without his knowledge *is* to read deconstructively. It is to demonstrate the manner in which a 'ground' is constituted in language for the self (characters, narrator and, by a process of displacement, author and then reader), only for that ground to be undermined by what Paul de Man calls 'the intentionality of rhetorical figures' (*Blindness and Insight*, p. 88). Derrida openly acknowledges that 'there are authors, there are intentionalities, there are conscious purposes', but endeavours to 'situate' the self in 'a system of forces which is not personal'.[25] My reading – particularly of the Preface – could be developed along the lines of de Man's claim, in *Blindness and*

Insight, that an awareness of 'the process of negative totalization' characterizes 'the work of all genuine writers' (p. 35). James's dramatization of the detour of signs points to an acute awareness that a text can *not* arrive. This insight is repressed, as are the unreserved elements in, for example, social and economic entities. These effects can be 'read' in in any text, including *The Figure in the Carpet*, *The Turn of the Screw* or James's 'late' works, which seem to anticipate the near-anarchic relativism and linguistic freeplay we may associate with deconstruction itself.[26]

Returning, in a blatant frame of my own, to the relationship between a reading and a text raises questions about the 'position' of a deconstructive reading and the relationship between theory and practice. To object that deconstruction is finally another interpretation (arrived at by a fixed method), which supersedes or fails to measure up to existing interpretations, is to credit deconstruction with a power to enclose which it decidedly lacks. If interpretation is understood as something that readers *do*, rather than as something that is *done* then a distinction is only tactically necessary. But so pervasive are logocentric ways of thinking that tactics remain crucial. There is no special deconstructive language or form, so the reading can only resist closure and its own theory by shifting ground. For example, the point of undecidability in Ralf Norrman's reading of *In the Cage* leads us to 'interpret' the logic which allows for expressions of knowledge as one of displacement; but only by *tracing* it and so joining 'the movement of *supplementarity*'. 'The enterprise of deconstruction', Derrida observes in *Of Grammatology*, 'always in a certain way falls prey to its own work' (p. 24).

Undecidable moments are, nevertheless, seductive for critics. At times, my deconstruction of the aesthetic, economic and social 'establishment' of *In the Cage* seems to celebrate a hyperbolic laissez-faire, suggesting that the division between politically radical and conservative deconstructive readings cannot be maintained absolutely. Hence Derrida's response to the question, 'How does one decide that certain terms are "undecidable"?':

> It is not a matter of decision. In certain historical and theoretical situations, some terms can appear to have this indeterminacy. In order to discover and exploit their indecidability, however, you must yourself be inscribed in a certain situation. (*Literary Review*, p. 21)

The overlap with Steve Smith's reading of *Heart of Darkness* is evident. So, too, is Derrida's relevance to the study of power relations, though he has yet to place himself in relation to contemporary Marxist critiques of ideology. What we do have, though, is a commitment to 'writing', and with it to the public and historical world where the 'differences' which structure our lives 'have been produced' (*Speech and Phenomena*, p. 141). When our seminar discussions of literature-and-life take on an 'academic' quality, it could be that we have assumed these differences and have stopped reading (deconstructively).

Further Reading

As is apparent from the collection, *Deconstruction and Criticism* (London, Routledge and Kegan Paul, 1979), the authors and leading practitioners of deconstruction – Harold Bloom, Paul de Man, Jacques Derrida, Geoffrey H. Hartman and J. Hillis Miller – differ markedly. Three important deconstructive strategies may, however, be distinguished from the following.

(i) Jacques Derrida:
Of Grammatology, trs. Gayatri Chakravorty Spivak (Baltimore, Johns Hopkins UP, 1976 (1967)), especially Part I; *Writing and Difference*, trs. Alan Bass (London, Routledge and Kegan Paul, 1978 (1967)), especially chs 1, 7 and 10; and *Positions*, trs. Alan Bass (London, Athlone, 1981 (1972)).

(ii) Paul de Man:
Blindness and Insight: Essays in the Rhetoric of Contemporary Criticism, 2nd ed., revised (London, Methuen, 1982), especially chs 1, 2, 7 and 10.

(iii) J. Hillis Miller:
Fiction and Repetition: Seven English Novels (Oxford, Blackwell, 1982); 'Narrative and history' (*English Literary History*, 41, 1974, pp. 455–73); and 'The critic as host' in *Deconstruction and Criticism* (pp. 217–53, details above). The last of these arose from a debate with M. H. Abrams which bears upon the relationship between deconstruction and prior readings. See M. H. Abrams, 'The deconstructive angel' (*Critical Inquiry*, 3, 1977, pp. 425–38). See also Denis Donoghue's 'Deconstructing deconstruction', a review of *Deconstruction and Criticism* and de Man's *Allegories of Reading* (*New York Review of Books*, 12 June 1980, pp. 37–41).

The most helpful commentaries on deconstruction are: Jonathan Culler, *On Deconstruction: Theory and Criticism after Structuralism*

(London, Routledge and Kegan Paul, 1983), especially chs 2 and 3, the latter an expert survey of deconstructive criticism in action; Christopher Norris, *Deconstruction and Criticism: Theory and Practice* (London, Methuen, 1982); and Vincent Leitch, *Deconstructive Criticism: An Advanced Introduction* (London, Hutchinson, 1983). Leitch's book – unlike Culler's and Norris's, and unlike this essay – openly acknowledges the contradictions in writing 'about' deconstruction in its style and structure. So, too, does Gayatri Chakravorty Spivak in her excellent 'Translator's Preface' to *Of Grammatology* (pp. ix–lxxxvii, details above). She also comments on the relevance of Derrida to the strand of feminist criticism discussed in Part II of Toril Moi's *Sexual/Textual Politics: Feminist Literary Theory* (London, Methuen, 1985). Barbara Johnson brilliantly effaces the distinction between theory and practice in *The Critical Difference: Essays in the Contemporary Rhetoric of Reading* (Baltimore, Johns Hopkins UP, 1980). The 'Opening Remarks' and chs 1, 6 and 7 are particularly important. Of these books, Culler's, Norris's and Moi's contain useful 'further reading' sections.

M. H. Abrams and Denis Donoghue (above) provide knowledgeable criticism of deconstruction from a traditional literary critical perspective. For the continuing – and more important – debate within the politics of criticism see the following: Fredric Jameson, 'The ideology of the text' (*Salmagundi*, 31–2, 1975–6, pp. 204–46); Edward Said, 'The problem of textuality: two exemplary positions' (*Critical Inquiry*, 4, 1978, pp. 673–714); and Michael Ryan, *Marxism and Deconstruction: A Critical Articulation* (Baltimore, Johns Hopkins UP, 1982). Ryan's introduction also merits inclusion as a useful account of deconstruction. In *After the New Criticism* (London, Methuen, 1983), especially chs 4, 5 and 8, Frank Lentricchia also contributes valuably to this debate within the format of a critical history, as does Steven Connor, in his single-author study of Dickens, by working through and comparing structuralist, post-structuralist and Marxist approaches: *Charles Dickens* (Oxford, Blackwell, 1985).

9 Marxism and Ideology
Joseph Conrad, *Heart of Darkness*

Steve Smith

I

The focus of this essay will be Pierre Macherey's *A Theory of Literary Production*,[1] first published (as *Pour une théorie de la production littéraire*) in Paris in 1966. Macherey's book marked an attempt to relate the Marxist philosophy of his contemporary Louis Althusser to the specific domain of literature. In many ways an uneven and inconsistent book, not least in that its textual readings (of Balzac, Borges and Verne) never quite represent 'applications' of its theoretical opening section (which, in any case, was the last to be written), it challenges the reader with a plethora of insights and ideas. Etienne Balibar, a regular collaborator with Macherey, recently summed it up as a 'polemic against all the variants of literary criticism . . . which depend in one way or another on hermeneutics, and for which, consequently, the concept of meaning functions as the central concept, defining the literary object or literary text as *that which must be interpreted*'.[2] 'Hermeneutics' is here used as a term covering all those critical methods which (implicitly or explicitly) attribute to the literary text, as an object of interpretation, a 'reason or hidden explanation', a stable and enduring essence which it is the task of criticism to extract and display in the critical discourse. When Macherey confronts a literary text it is not as an isolated, autonomous object, complete in itself, but as an object which exists necessarily in a complex relation to the historical conditions of its production. For him, the literary text draws its very ability to produce meaning from the particular 'literary' textualization which it performs on the reality within which it finds its raw materials. This is not to say that the text reflects or is identical to that reality; it is, rather, that the text establishes a peculiar distance between itself and its raw materials and it is this in which Macherey is interested, as we shall see in our discussion of *Heart of Darkness*.[3] It is only through an analysis of this that we can understand how, in particular cases, reality and its history leave their inevitable traces on the process of literary production.

If the manifold relations that link text and history form the final object of study, Macherey contends that this is only possible when the relation of critical to literary discourse has been properly thought through. Crucial to Macherey's theory is the contention that the categories and techniques criticism employs – and no method is without them – play as much of a determining role on the critical discourse as does the object text itself. To believe that they can be simply effaced from critical discourse (that criticism, in other words can be truly 'objective' even in principle) is to fall prey to the 'empirical fallacy' – the illusion that the text can simply be appreciated unproblematically 'as it is'.

If Macherey finds inadequate the traditional technique of the respectful commentary or appreciation of the text, he also rejects structuralism on the grounds of its a-historicity. For instance, Macherey would certainly agree with the kind of critique Bernard McGuirk acknowledges at the outset of his essay (see above, p.29). At the same time, it should be added that *A Theory of Literary Production* does share with structuralism something of the polemical, demystificatory impulse Diana Knight attributes to the work of Barthes and Genette (see above p.27), and may even be said to develop some of their insights. Macherey is merely suspicious that isolating the formal structures of a work by means of the notion of the 'model', implies a reduction of its productive processes. To recover this complexity Macherey proposes moving outside the work, not to a literary model, but to that network of socio-historical forces – whose code-word is 'history' – which he considers central to its understanding.

In this respect Macherey's practice is more readily identifiable with that of interpretation. Where Macherey departs from any strictly 'hermeneutic' model is his contention that criticism is irreducibly transformative of its object, and that, in a certain way, the knowledge it produces is, in fact, a new knowledge, which is not exactly a knowledge 'of the text'. We shall return later to this question. For now we shall merely echo Macherey's insistence that criticism cannot produce a copy of the text, and stands, rather, in a kind of double relation to the text: on the one hand, the text is a determinate, finished object – its 'words on the page' cannot be changed or replaced by criticism; on the other, the work is not self-sufficient, cannot simply detach itself from the conditions of its production. It is marked by these conditions just as the Freudian dream is explicable only in terms of factors which are strictly exterior to it, although it is not reducible to these factors. The Machereyan critique may correspondingly be separated into two stages. The first, remaining within the parameters of the text, attempts to examine the levels on which the text attains a certain coherence or unity; it is a matter, Macherey states, of 'identifying the class of truth which constitutes the work and determines its meaning' (p.78). In his analysis of Jules Verne's novels, this is identified as nineteenth-century (bourgeois) man's increasing mastery of nature as exemplified in the futuristic representation of scientific progress (in the depiction of ships, submarines, hot-air balloons and the like, and the prodigious feats they achieve). Such textual elements, however, are not taken as natural or inevitable parts of the narrative, but as the product of certain choices made by the writer. We might here refer to Diana Knight's Genettian emphasis on the text as a constructed cultural product, the outcome of a succession of choices made, consciously or unconsciously, by a writer. It is simply the kind of factors that determine these decisions that is in dispute. It is the inevitability of choice as a condition of narrative that leads Macherey to posit that what the text does say is 'entirely significant', while it sustains a necessary relation with *what it does not say*. The relation of the text to what it does not say now opens up the second stage of the Machereyan reading, wherein the critic's object now becomes the analysis of the particular historical conditions determining the play of absence and presence in particular texts. Terry Eagleton usefully summarizes the point thus:

> Criticism, then, does not site itself in the same space as the text itself, allowing it to speak or completing what it leaves unsaid. On the contrary, it installs itself in the text's very incompleteness in order to *theorize* that lack of plenitude – to explain the ideological necessity of its 'not-said'.[4]

In regarding lack or incompleteness as constitutive of narrative as such, a Machereyan analysis might go along with deconstruction, but it also seeks to go further in the attempt to theorize it in terms of a relation to *ideology*.

Of Marx's many disparate references to ideology it is such as the following that Macherey, following Althusser, finds crucial: 'Consciousness is . . . from the very beginning a social product, and remains so as long as men exist at all'; 'It is not the consciousness of men that determines their being, but, on the contrary, their social being determines their consciousness'; 'The phantoms of the human brain also are necessary sublimates of men's material life-process'.[5] Ideology, then, involves the relation through which individual subjects make sense of or rationalize the world around them. An analysis of the functioning of ideology enables us to understand 'the ways in which social relations are reproduced through ideology's ability to shape, and indeed to perform the conscious desires and beliefs of individuals'.[6] This is because 'the individual subject is always in a material relation to the object world, constructing its (and the "subject's") "reality" in specific ways'.[7] In Althusser's formulation, ideological practice refers to the complex ways in which a given relation of this type is confirmed, modified, or overturned within the everyday actions and attitudes of the individual subject. The epithet 'ideological', then, implies as much an active affirmation of (acquired) misconceptions about the nature of social reality, as a merely passive reproduction of them. Moreover, while it may be that particular ideological positions are incoherent or internally contradictory, they necessarily do not appear so at the moments of their social effectivity, that is, within social praxis, because ideology functions precisely to efface such discrepancies, inconsistencies or contradictions, presenting itself as a seamless web of obvious or commonsense tenets which underpins that praxis and gives it meaning. Marxism is able to intervene in this comfortable relation by showing how particular positions are, despite appearances, contradictory or incoherent. It is a matter of showing how particular ideological practices (and the scale and nature of the connections are necessarily simplified at this level of generality) 'reproduce and reassert that lived relation in a way that serves the . . . ends of particular social formations'.[8]

The Althusserian notion of the 'symptomatic reading' is a strategy through which the historical conditions that determine a particular ideological practice are analysed or brought to bear in such a way that the latter's spontaneous or natural appearance is dispelled. An access to history is gained via the very mechanisms through which it is repressed. History is conceived as an 'absent cause', present only in its effects as the symptomatic absences of ideology. For example, in his analysis of Verne, Macherey subjects the version of history elucidated (that of the triumphant forward-march of the bourgeoisie) to such a symptomatic reading. He shows, for example, in a complex analysis, how the consistent allusions to Robinson Crusoe, 'the generic ancestor', in *The Mysterious Island* symptomatically point towards a profound but repressed insecurity on the part of the bourgeoisie, for whom Verne wrote, concerning its own history. That the 'fantastic' representation of the future should be tied structurally to the past betrays an inability, in the final analysis, to efface its historical origins (in the struggle through which it displaced the aristocracy as the dominant class), and which, ideologically, it must suppress if it is to present itself as the 'naturally' dominant class within society.

II

Unlike the texts of Verne, Conrad's *Heart of Darkness* appears explicitly to address itself to pressing contemporary questions. The most obvious of these is the theme (perhaps the ethics of) colonialism. This text was, of course, published at the height of the infamous European 'scramble for Africa' and is indebted to the author's personal experiences in the Congo some ten years earlier. However, in mentioning such details we do not wish to argue that they constitute the cause of the text or the key to its meaning. As we have already emphasized, our object is the text itself, and the peculiarity of its textual transformation of such details. Nevertheless, given our point of departure, it is worth noting that Conrad was not himself insensitive to the political nature of his material, writing to his (conservative) publisher in 1899, 'tho' I have no doubts as to the *workmanship* I do not know whether the *subject* will commend itself to you'.[9] Furthermore, the very representation of such a situation certainly constituted a political gesture in the eyes of Conrad's socialist friend Cunninghame-Grahame, who expressed his approval of the powerful account of the excesses of the imperialist encounter. At the same time, acknowledging such a view does not involve our uncritically accepting it. Rather, our strategy in reading *Heart of Darkness* will be as follows: initially we shall construct an oppositional gesture in the way the colonial situation is represented. This will correspond to the first stage of Macherey's reading, remaining within the parameters of the text. We shall then interrogate the apparent coherence of this gesture by tracing its historical coordinates, that is, by establishing an ideological framework through which it is seen to make sense, to suggest, finally, that this may not be the whole story.

If *Heart of Darkness* appears to be some sort of critique of imperialism – as, indeed, has often been argued – it is primarily to the striking images that greet Marlow upon his arrival in Africa and some of his scathing comments on them that we must look. What Marlow calls the 'great demoralization of the land' (p.46) or 'a flabby, pretending, weak-eyed devil of a rapacious and pitiless folly' (p.43) comprise an array of outrages which clearly have a certain shock value, and present a challenge to any sense of logic or order: resources are mismanaged, the natives mercilessly exploited and, in one scene, reduced to slavery or forced labour. Against this backdrop of the tropical jungle, the combination of inefficiency and exploitation takes on an unreal, almost absurd character. Marlow's distinct and disturbing impression is that all is not well, that something profoundly natural or good is being interfered with or upset by the Western settlers. As such, these images are clear and unequivocal, and testify to Conrad's overt intention to base the novel on 'the criminality of inefficiency and pure selfishness when tackling the civilizing work in Africa' (Cox, p.23). Now, we should be aware of the ground which permits these images to be construed as a critique of colonialism and to be presented textually in such obvious, commonsensical terms. That is to say that exploitation, for example, is only such within the context of the doctrine of humanism. This term broadly refers to that body of beliefs in which the human subject is deemed to be central, and which projects his self-realization, humanity and essential equality as absolute goals. Marlow's observations fuel a critique on humanistic grounds by presenting the colonial experience as an essentially degrading one for all concerned, exploiters and exploited alike. These observations suggest an additional, distinctly *political* resonance when it is realized that it is precisely a humanist ideology that is being used by the exploiters to underwrite and explain away the reality of the situation to those back home, and perhaps to themselves, too. Marlow is not unaware of this, as his frequent references to the colonizers as philanthropists show. He mentions, for example, the 'philanthropic pretence of the whole concern' (p.54), ironically refers to the Westerners' 'philanthrophic desire of giving the criminals [the natives] something to do' (p.44) when contemplating a useless hole in the ground, and later declares: 'To tear treasure out of the bowels of the land was their desire, with no more moral purpose at the back of it than there is in burglars breaking into a safe' (p.61). At the same time, Marlow has the benefit of a fairly precise knowledge of the workings of the colonial economy, and is not afraid to enunciate it: 'a stream of manufactured goods, rubbishy cottons, beads, and brass wire sent into the depths of darkness, and in return came a precious trickle of ivory' (p.46).

Marlow's discourse, thus, frequently foregrounds that revealing incongruity between the rhetoric and the reality of colonialism. In the cases of such figures as the company employees in 'the sepulchral city' whose sin is, as much as anything, plain ignorance, through to the agents on the spot interested only in self-enrichment, the dissonance between truth and falsity is easily distinguishable. In so far as it relates to the functioning of ideology, the case of Marlow's aunt is especially interesting; in this scene Marlow calls to see her just after visiting the Company's offices. He recounts:

> It appeared, however, I was also one of the Workers, with a capital – you know. Something like an emissary of light, something like a lower sort of apostle. There had been a lot of such rot let loose in print and talk just about that time, and the excellent woman, living right in the rush of all that humbug, got carried off her feet. She talked about 'weaning the ignorant millions from their horrid ways', till, upon my word, she made me quite uncomfortable. I ventured to hint that the Company was run for profit.
> 'You forget, dear Charlie, that the labourer is worthy of his hire', she said, brightly. (pp.38–9)

The aunt is clearly some way from reconciling the Company's pursuit of profit with its humanitarian rhetoric. Indeed, the biblical allusion of the rejoinder suggests the extent to which the earlier discourse of the puritanical work ethic had been absorbed and then mobilized to serve the dominant interests of the time. When the question of profit (and, therefore, of exploitation) is broached, the aunt's reply effectively endorses the whole social structure of labour relations as some pre-ordained order without social determinants and without a history. (Significantly, the plight of the natives is not even mentioned.) That she should move so quickly on to such an abstract, general level is perhaps indicative of some discomfort with immediately felt contradictions. Furthermore, when such an absolute, timeless structure is invoked, it is all the easier to view present shortcomings or crises as purely contingent imperfections, leaving the reference point of harmony, coherence or order quite untouched. This, in fact, serves two apparently contradictory though, upon analysis, mutually supporting functions. First, it provides a way of skipping over particular social unpleasantness (and thus is thought to be true of the way things really are). And, second, it is a legitimizing but in principle inaccessible ideal enabling the subject to relinquish the need to strive for change, to tell him/herself that worldly imperfections cannot be countered by human intervention.

If we have shown (albeit briefly) how *Heart of Darkness* sketches out various subject positions it is to underline how such positions are always in a dual relation: on the one hand, to ideology (in so far as they involve imaginary (mis-) representations of the real); and, on the other, through what they necessarily exclude, to history (in that they can be made to yield the material conditions of their production). Thus far, however, we have only shown how the ideology of humanism is used against itself in Marlow's discourse to reveal its contradictions; now we must turn to the character of Marlow himself in order to examine symptomatically the ideological coordinates of his represented subject-position. This will correspond to the second stage of the Machereyan analysis.

Marlow's status as a traditional ocean-going seafarer is marked through much of the text. From the ignominy of having a woman procure him the job: 'Then – would you believe it? – I tried the women. I, Charlie Marlow, set the women to work to get a job. Heavens!' (p.34), through the rigours of a 'two-hundred-mile tramp' (p.47), and the 'monkey tricks' he is forced to perform on the 'tin-pot steamer' amongst 'men with whom I had no point of contact' (p.40), Marlow consistently refers to his sense of displacement. This appears to constitute an affront to his very status and identity, as both the force of 'I, Charlie Marlow . . .'

and the following suggest:

> I sweated and shivered over that business considerably, I can tell you.
> After all, *for a seaman*, to scrape the bottom of the thing that's
> supposed to float all the time under his care is the unpardonable sin.
> (p.67, my emphasis)

Despite the fact that the prospect of going to Africa certainly captures his imagination, we should bear in mind that Marlow's initial decision is forced upon him by his failure to find work on the sea. Once in Africa he is then rather peremptorily thrust into the chaotic bustle of contemporary commerce, being sucked into the Company infighting through his being associated with what is referred to as 'the gang of virtue' (p.55). It is in terms, moreover, of Marlow's total unfamiliarity with his surroundings that we should read his sense of disorientation; the larger-than-life descriptions it produces ('Going up that river was like travelling back to the earliest beginnings of the world' (p.66)) and the insistence upon the 'unearthly' character of the up-river journey. After landing at the first station, he stares uncomprehending at the boiler 'wallowing in the grass', the railway truck 'on its back with its wheels in the air', the 'objectless blasting' (p.42) and the negroes with the appearance of 'bundles of acute-angles' (p.45). For all his knowledge of the underlying economic structures, this nevertheless appears inexplicable, excessive, more than a mere by-product of the (albeit unequal) exchange of worthless trinkets for the 'precious trickle of ivory'.

But if this sense of disorientation is clearly marked, we must attempt to account for it in terms of historical factors which, we shall argue, can be located within the text itself. We must begin by viewing Marlow as constructed astride two worlds: that of the serene existence of the sea-captain on the bridge, aloof from the social world implied by his cargo, related to the world beyond his ship 'by a slightly disdainful ignorance' (p.30); and, secondly, that of the hectic environment of colonialist trade where, as the captain of the fresh-water steamer, he is anything but isolated from the world around him. Marlow can thus be considered in relation to a whole mode of production that predates the frenzied colonialist penetration of the African continent and which is now threatened, or profoundly transformed, by its arrival. But Marlow's insertion into this new era of colonialism does not imply concomitant acceptance of the ideology which accompanies and justifies it. The narrative of *Heart of Darkness* plays out a historically significant struggle of how one mode of production and its ideology is overlaid on an older, previously established one. This does not take place as a simple replacement, but is effected in an uneven, fragmented and conflictual fashion. Marlow's disquiet is an intimation of these very forces (over which he has no direct control) and thus the space for a critique or, at least, a certain demystification, is opened up. However, in this case it actually represents something of a throw-back to a previous era, deriving its force, that is, from a reactionary rather than a progressive position. From the Marxist viewpoint this denies Marlow any effective grasp of the real (primarily economic) conditions that determine the course of the changing world around him. It is here that we may see how the text is related to history in an essentially negative way. The text does not *reflect* reality; rather we can trace the effects of that reality in what is *not* reflected, in what the text cannot say. It is, moreover, for this reason that the threat posed to the whole colonialist enterprise by the frailty of its ideology presents no particular discomfort to Marlow, for the values he embraces are not predominantly its values; indeed, as we showed above, the inadequacies of the humanist ideology of colonialism bear the full brunt of his sharply ironic tongue. What *is* threatening, however, is the degradation wrought by the colonial experience on what, for him, is the age-old and utterly reassuring relationship between man and nature, or, as he experiences it, between man and the sea. Throughout his narrative Marlow betrays a marked penchant for a stable, ordered world, which functions smoothly and, as it were, naturally. In this light colonialism, in its more excessive forms (the useless holes in the ground, the broken sewerage pipes, the dehumanizing of the natives and so on), presents itself as distinctly threatening. In the midst of such disorder, Marlow strives to highlight and revive the 'natural' and 'real'. Hence, 'The voice of the surf now and then was a positive pleasure, like the speech of a brother. It was something natural, that had its reason, that had a meaning' (p.40). But at one crucial point Marlow's idea(l) of the natural betrays its dependence on an essentially economic order: 'The simple old sailor, with his talk of chains and *purchases*, made me forget the jungle and the pilgrims in a delicious sensation of having come upon something unmistakably *real*' (p.71, my emphasis).

The effects of this position on Marlow's conception of the situations in which he is involved make themselves felt on various aspects of the narrative. Among these is an inability to think historically. That is to say that there is a tendency to regard the material world not as the ongoing product of human activity (as Marx said 'all social life is essentially practical')[10] but as merely a modulation of timeless structures, of a pre-given pattern. It does not mean that he ignores or is unaware of the past. The problem lies, rather, in its relation to the present. For example, at the outset of the text, as the five men contemplate sunset over the Thames, he alludes to the Roman occupation of Britain as a historical parallel to the contemporary European 'occupation' of Africa:

> And this also . . . has been one of the dark places of the earth. . . . I was thinking of very old times, when the Romans first came here, nineteen hundred years ago – the other day . . . Sand-banks, marshes, forests, savages, – precious little to eat fit for a civilized man, nothing but Thames water to drink. (pp. 29, 30)

This is especially striking in the wake of the primary narrator's exaltation of the triumphs of 'the great knights-errant of the sea' (p.29). We are here close to some kind of critique of the assumptions underlying colonialism and its educating ideals. It is potentially subversive in so far as its suggestion of cultural relativism robs that ideology of its moral imperative to wean those 'ignorant millions from their horrid ways'. The same may be said of Marlow's later remarks about 'your [the 'Civilizers'] remote kinship with this wild and passionate uproar' (p.69) and his attempts to see the whites as the blacks see them produce an almost comic inversion of an ethnocentric cliché: 'This was simple prudence, white men being so much alike at a distance that he could not tell who I might be' (p.43).

However, while all this does imply that the now hegemonic Westerners also have a history and were once themselves 'savages', the contemporary political resonance of Marlow's point is somewhat overtaken by his mythic emphasis on the cyclicality of history. Though the two separate invasions are empirically quite distinct, such, perhaps, that they can hardly be unproblematically compared, this difference is effaced or, at least, less sharply focused, when they are both regarded as subject to the same timeless law or structure. Such a reduction to a timeless pattern constitutes the kind of dehistoricizing gesture that is echoed in other aspects of the text as a whole: notably, the generic motif of the journey or quest – an age-old narrative structure – which links the narrative to, among others, the 'timeless' classics of Homer, Virgil and Dante. In this connection we may also cite the complete absence of place-names, which has the effect of despecifying what, as we have already noted, are clear historical references, and also the tendency to what Fredric Jameson has called 'aestheticization', the 'impressionistic strategy of modernism whose function is to derealize the content and make it available for consumption on some purely aesthetic level'.[11] It is in this light that we may understand why Marlow's interest in the well-dressed accountant is not so much in the severe contradictions to which he unwittingly points as in his appearance and his 'wonderfully odd' expressions (p.45). Marlow also has the propensity to refer those 'surface' phenomena which, for determined reasons, he fails to understand, to universal categories; thus his dislike of lies is put down resignedly to 'temperament, I suppose' (p.57), and left at that. This attitude, in fact, echoes his aunt's earlier reaction to his own 'hint' about colonialism which Marlow had scorned in the following revealing terms: 'It's queer how out of touch with truth women are. They live in a world of their own, and there had never been anything like it, and never can be. It is too beautiful altogether' (p.39). Once more Marlow's universalizing tendencies are to the fore, causing him completely to overlook cultural or historical determinants on 'how women are'. For him, then, reality (and he is anxious to uncover its nature) is governed by universal forces which are not always immediately obvious, but are there all the same. They are given in advance of history, language or experience, for they ultimately depend on none of these things:

> The mind of man is capable of anything – because everything is in it.
> . . . What was there after all? Joy, fear, sorrow, devotion, valour, rage – who can tell? – but truth – truth stripped of its cloak of time. (p.69)

At the same time, the assured stability of Marlow's world-view is, as we have argued, under threat from the new forces of colonialist expansion (to such an extent, perhaps, that 'the mind of man' proves not entirely 'capable of anything'). It is increasingly apparent to him that the deep structure of reality is not, as he would wish or imagine it, governed by some reassuring transcendent category but is becoming infringed upon or overtaken by the very worldly, historical phenomena of (colonialist) capitalism and the unsavoury forces (of self-interest, destruction, irrationality) it appears to conjure up with it. Not now the sublime 'idea' which can be 'bowed down before' that the serenity of nightfall on the Thames suggests in the opening pages. It is in this light that we should now turn to a symptomatic analysis (in keeping with the second stage of our study) of Marlow's obsessive and apparently mysterious attraction for Kurtz.

In a way, Kurtz and Marlow have in common a position outside the dominant material and ideological practices of colonialist capitalism: Marlow, as we have noted, comes from an earlier maritime mode of production while Kurtz is a Company man of the new 'gang of virtue' who came to Africa, as Marlow has it, 'equipped with moral ideas of some sort' (p.62). As Hunt Hawkins has recently shown,[12] the European trading companies were, at this time, becoming aware of the need to assuage public opinion, outraged by the tales of excess that had lately leaked out about trading practices in Africa, and this had directly precipitated the philanthropic image they were then adopting. Marlow, with customary scepticism, is initially curious to know how such ideas would fare in the cut-throat atmosphere of the jungle; 'I was curious to see whether this man . . . would climb to the top after all and how he would set about his work when there' (p.62). Kurtz's 'idealism' is later confirmed when Marlow is given for safe keeping a document Kurtz had been commissioned to write for the 'International Society for the Suppression of Savage Customs'. Marlow picks out the opening sentence which argues that 'we whites, from the point of development we had arrived at, "must necessarily appear to them [savages] in the nature of supernatural beings – we approach them with the might as of a deity. . . . By the simple exercise of our will we can exert a power for good practically unbounded"' (pp. 86–7). This strikes Marlow as 'ominous'. A little closer examination suggests that it is, indeed, ominous; while, on the one hand, it might be read in the context of the educating liberal ideal, on the other, it implies something altogether less savoury in that it also suggests a judgement of a *political* nature has been made. For there is no reference here to the absolutes normally entailed by liberal thinking, the moral superiority of the white, for example. Rather, the white man's supremacy is construed as a direct consequence of a contingent historical situation (specifically, the Westerners' technological prowess). The basis for the ability to achieve a 'power for good' is, then, due not to some innate quality of either race but to the very possession of the means to exercise power at all. In such circumstances this ability is, undeniably, 'practically unbounded'.

This provides the first indication of Kurtz's 'lack of restraint', his resistance to the very forces of (Western) civilization, its values, morality, attitudes – in short its dominant ideology. Similarly, he takes the colonialist economy for the exploitative practice it is – and takes it to its practical limit. Like Marlow, Kurtz has a knowledge of how the exploitative system works, and of how to play it efficiently to his own advantage: ' "You show them you have in you something that is really profitable, and then there will be no limits to the recognition of your ability," he would say. "Of course, you must take care of the motives – right motives – always" ' (p.110). Kurtz carries out his work transgressing the normal restraining ideological protocols that the Company employs both to control its own agents and to keep up its image at home. The truth is, as Kurtz realizes, that these controls are not only practically unenforceable but, more importantly, are as arbitrary and flawed as the ideology they serve to uphold (and which, in fact upholds them). Thus, Kurtz constitutes a threat to the Company's operations that overrides his financial worth; although he is by far the Company's most successful agent, his methods are deemed to be 'unsound': for all his fabulous output, the manager tells Marlow, 'Mr Kurtz has done more harm than good to the Company' (p.102). Kurtz's 'madness', then, is a refusal to set the kind of *a priori* limits on his conduct, ambitions or values that appear to be forced upon him by his position within the colonial economy. Consequent on this refusal, these are pushed as far as circumstances will allow. The result is a kind of rampant individualism – hence, 'You should have heard him say, "My ivory." Oh yes, I heard him . . . everything belonged to him . . . The thing was to know what he belonged to . . .' (p.85). Kurtz becomes that god prefigured in the report: 'He had taken a high seat amongst the devils of the land – I mean, literally. . . . His ascendancy was extraordinary . . . the chiefs came every day to see him' (pp. 85, 97). That Marlow intimates that there is more to Kurtz than what his fellow Company employees make of him is clear. However, because of our distrust of metaphysical solutions, which merely bypass the historical, we cannot simply accept his judgement that 'powers of darkness' had 'claimed him for their own' (p.85), and must look to his own discourse for more historically specific reasons for the phenomenon of Kurtz. To do this we must now relate our discussion of Marlow's position vis-à-vis colonialism to his position vis-à-vis Kurtz, for their coincidence as constituents of the same text is not, of course, accidental.

We have already related Marlow's discomfort to traces of a wider historical displacement that leaves him struggling for some fixed coordinates that are not simply one more facet of the corrupting power of capitalism in the colonies. His alienation from his surroundings initiates a struggle that forces him increasingly into himself, as the only viable reference point for his experience: 'No, it is impossible . . . to convey the life-sensation of any given epoch of one's existence . . . we live, as we dream – alone' (p.57). At the same time, his rejection of the ideology of humanism precipitates an increasing disregard for humanity, and its replacement by the kind of scientistic, distanced approach to his surroundings prefigured in the curious scene with the Company doctor. Hence his ambivalent attitude to his helmsman, whose body he disposes of without the least ceremony, shocking his fellow-travellers with his coldness: 'Perhaps you will think it passing strange, this regret for a savage . . . Well, don't you see, he had done something, he had steered; for months I had him by my back – a help – an instrument. It was a kind of partnership' (p.87). This is echoed in his attitude to Kurtz as well: 'Oh, I wasn't touched. I was fascinated' (p.111), he states of the dying Kurtz whom he had earlier described as an 'impressively bald' 'specimen' (p.84). This distancing extends, at one point, even to himself: 'I felt I was becoming scientifically interesting' (p.49). In the face of this loss of any collective sense, Kurtz represents or, rather, promises a kind of substitute solidity: the promise of new reference points originating in the privatized individual, in the force of will itself. As Marlow earlier stated, 'principles won't do . . . No; you want a deliberate belief' (p.69).

Faced with what he describes as a 'choice' of nightmares (p.105), Marlow appears to side with Kurtz. On the down-river trip he feels himself to be the only one left of 'unsound method' and, on his return to Brussels, is disgusted at the barren lives of those he sees in the streets 'with no hope . . . and no desire' (p.113), their individuality crushed by the de-individualizing and de-naturalizing conditions of urban life. In addition, he perpetrates two telling lies, one to Kurtz's fiancée, and the other, less directly, by tearing off the PS to Kurtz's report ('Exterminate all the brutes') before offering it to the Company man and then giving it to Kurtz's cousin 'for publication' (p.115). This latter incident, which has attracted less critical attention than the former, is perhaps the more important of the two untruths (which clash so spectacularly with Marlow's earlier comments on the topic), because without its 'valuable' PS Kurtz's work is free to be disseminated as one more support to the colonialist ideology which, as we have seen, is rejected by both Marlow and Kurtz. That Marlow, through his own part in underwriting and perpetrating the colonialist myth, shows himself to have little respect for the truth here is revealing. It suggests that for him truth is only such in so far as it affects him – otherwise he is totally indifferent to it. Marlow's salvation, if indeed it is a salvation, is a supremely personal one: 'Droll thing life is . . . The most you can hope from it is some knowledge of yourself' (p.112). Wider issues do not come into it.

Marlow's position at the close of *Heart of Darkness* is, then, one of a sublime aloofness from the mundane but unpalatable realities of history and politics. This comes, as we have seen, of a rejection of liberalism, a loss of confidence in any sense of community and in collective answers to acutely felt contemporary problems, engendered by the growing resources and demands of capital. But this is not to say that it is Kurtz who is to be the new Messiah; Marlow finally refuses any enthusiastic acceptance of the 'answers' he offers. For Marlow considers that Kurtz, despite his imposing attractions, lacks 'restraint', is, like the helmsman, 'a tree swayed by the wind' (p.88). Kurtz's rejection of contemporary mores involves a loss of control too, because his is essentially a negative, even nihilistic gesture. Consequently, Marlow intuits a gap, a hollow, and one that for all his alienation, he feels he cannot share: 'there was something wanting in him – some small matter which, when the pressing need arose, could not be found under his magnificant eloquence' (p.97). While Kurtz's gestures are outward-looking – he is trader, journalist, poet, musician, painter, lover, and leader of a whole tribe that Marlow finds quite impenetrable – Marlow is distanced, ironic, restrained, uninvolved. While Kurtz takes on the world, Marlow's primary urge is one of withdrawal. Moreover, it is he who, lives to tell the tale, while Kurtz is expunged by a tropical disease – a necessary risk in taking on a wilderness. One might say that it is in the very act of narration that Marlow finds his solace, when narration is considered a secondary, fallen replacement for experience, an exercise where no risk is taken, where the ideological sense-making mechanism is (seemingly) most free of the restrictions imposed on it by reality. Significantly, perhaps, Marlow imagines Kurtz not 'as doing . . . but as discoursing' (p. 83). *Heart of Darkness*, a narrative in which nothing happens but a narration, is told to an audience consisting of a lawyer, an accountant, a director of companies and the primary narrator, each of whom has 'two good addresses' (p.84) and is unlikely, in any material way, ever to be affected by the contents of the narration. All of this brings to mind modernism (and its respectful criticism); for it is here that we find a literature that, taking its raw materials from the world and human experience of it, finds its primary impulse in the desire to escape or recuperate those realities under the aegis of something essentially unworldly, that is to say, of the hermetic world of the 'work of art'. For Marxist criticism, language, as the vehicle of meanings generated by and in history, cannot be so easily isolated from its social setting. It is precisely this historicity of language that permits us to establish the 'literary' text as the object of a different kind of analysis from that which it would itself appear to sanction.

III

In this way the Machereyan reading furnishes a method of recovering that relation which inextricably links the Conrad text to the colonialist problematic, without reducing the former to the latter as a Lukácsian reading would tend to do. The text is no longer considered a unified whole; rather, it establishes an internal distance from its raw materials – in this case the whole colonialist issue – and it is through this that it is then constituted as an 'autonomous' object. It is in this sense, moreover, that the 'symptomatic reading' is not a 'hermeneutic' reading of the type elucidated by Balibar in our introduction. The goal of the reading undertaken above can in no way be given in advance of the actual reading. It is not exactly the 'meaning' of the text, a stable, coherent meaning latent in the text that we sought to uncover, but a relation which, being historically dependent, must include those particular factors which have conditioned this reading (not least the constraints of the 'text-book' form, of an 'introduction', etc.). Such a denial of the autonomy of meaning puts into question precisely that self-identical intelligibility of meaning that interpretive methods assume.

At the same time, despite the emphasis Macherey places on the multiple relation that links text to history, such an approach does run the risk of prioritizing the value of 'history' such that this then becomes the absolute meaning of the text. The risk is that the text is simply inserted into a history which is no more than a finished complex of events and relations, and fundamentally unaffected by the text's encounter with it. In such a schema the method becomes as typologizing and undynamic as any formalist 'reading'. While we would not want to claim to have overcome this difficulty, we have attempted above to counter it (at least rhetorically) by emphasizing that we can only bring history to bear on the text in so far as the text itself alludes (both positively and negatively, by inclusion or exclusion) to factors 'external' to it, and not the other way around. It is in this context, moreover, that we may refer once more to the notion of history as 'absent cause', available only to us in a textual, or what amounts to the same, in an ideological form. History, paradoxically, becomes both the cause and the effects of these forms. It is this contention that assures the Machereyan reading of a certain openness or unpredictability; it is not a matter of analysing the text with a view to simply extracting from it a history now divested of its ideological trappings, but of examining the specific interaction of text, ideology and history without presupposing that any one of these elements can be isolated as such.

The question of epistemological guarantees, of the 'truth-value' of a discourse, has dominated much Althusser criticism and is not irrelevant to Macherey's critical practice either. For now, we shall limit ourselves to the contention that, in the absence of the possibility of the absolute grounding of readings of literary texts in some trans-historical concept of truth, evaluation becomes a question of how adequately (or, indeed, convincingly) a critical text accounts for a literary text (bearing in mind always that criticism actually constructs the text as an object of knowledge). Once this is realized, we may understand the history of criticism, to quote Macherey in another connection, as 'a conflict of tendencies',[13] a dialectical struggle of interrelated theories, practices, institutions, critics and critical schools, always subject to historical change resulting from factors both internal and external to it. Macherey's work since *A Theory of Literary Production* has increasingly emphasized the institutional nature of literary criticism as an important arena of ideological struggle, in which the study of literature is regarded not so much as the disinterested scholarly pursuit of a knowledge condemned forever to be 'elsewhere' – in books, in libraries, in a dead past, within the rigid confines of the Academy itself – but a social arena in which ideological forces play an irreducible part in shaping the terms of the debate. Understanding these forces enables us to see how the apparently discrete activity of reading involves a necessarily socio-political component. Macherey would argue that this question has only ever been properly addressed within a Marxist framework.

Further Reading

Terry Eagleton's 'Pierre Macherey and Marxist literary criticism' (in G.H.R. Parkinson, ed., *Marx and Marxisms*, Cambridge, CUP, 1982), is a fuller exposition of Macherey's book than has been possible above. James H. Kavanagh's 'Marxism's Althusser: toward a politics of literary theory' (*Diacritics*, 12, 1, 1982, pp. 25–45) is a comprehensive though difficult overview of wider issues and debates. John Frow's 'Structuralist Marxism' (*Southern Review*, 2, 1983, pp. 208–17) covers Macherey's use of Althusser clearly and sympathetically. Alex Callinicos's *Althusser's Marxism* (London, Verso, 1976) is a concise, general introduction.

Macherey's post-1966 work on literature, marking his shift in interest from the production to the consumption of literary texts, includes the following: 'The problem of reflection', trs. Susan Sniader Lanser (*Sub-Stance*, 15, 1976, pp. 6–20), and with Etienne Balibar, 'Literature as an ideological form: some Marxist propositions', trs. Ian McLeod, John Whitehead and Ann Wordsworth (*Oxford Literary Review*, 3, 1978, pp.

4–12). Two interviews with Macherey are available in English: in *Red Letters* (5, 1977, pp. 3–9), trs. and ed. Colin Mercer and Jean Radford, and (with Balibar) in *Diacritics* (12,1, 1982, pp. 46–51), trs. James H. Kavanagh.

Other recent work in the field includes Fredric Jameson's *The Political Unconscious: Narrative as a Socially Symbolic Act* (London, Methuen, 1981), which draws heavily on both Althusser and Lukács and includes an important chapter on Conrad. Catherine Belsey's *Critical Practice* (London, Methuen, 1980) includes a Machereyan reading of a Sherlock Holmes story, while Tony Bennett's *Formalism and Marxism* (London, Methuen, 1979) deals challengingly with the thorny question of Marxism, aesthetics and formalism. Both these books contain useful bibliographies.

NOTES

Chapter 1 pp. 9–28

1 Gérard Genette, *Narrative Discourse: An Essay in Method*, trs. Jane E. Lewin, Oxford, Blackwell, 1980 ('Discours du récit', in *Figures III*, Paris, Seuil, 1972). Page references will be given after quotations in the text.

2 Terry Eagleton, *Literary Theory: An Introduction*, Oxford, Blackwell, 1983, pp. 108–9.

3 For a brief account of Saussure see Ann Jefferson and David Robey, eds., *Modern Literary Theory: A Comparative Introduction*, London, Batsford, rev. ed., 1986, pp. 47–51.

4 See, for example, 'Dominici, or the triumph of literature', in *Mythologies*, trs. Annette Lavers, London, Granada, 1973, pp. 43–6; *Critique et vérité*, Paris, Seuil, 1966, especially pp. 27–35; and *Le Grain de la voix: Entretiens 1962–1980*, Paris, Seuil, 1981, p. 44.

5 Gérard Genette, 'Frontiers of narrative', in *Figures of Literary Discourse*, trs. Alan Sheridan, Oxford, Blackwell, 1982 (pp. 127–44), p. 127. The translation has been slightly modified.

6 See the conclusion to Genette's three chapters on time (pp. 157–60). The idea of playing with time (or making a game out of it), is derived from a quotation from Proust.

7 Joseph Conrad, *Heart of Darkness*, ed. Paul O'Prey, Harmondsworth, Penguin, 1983 (1902), pp. 115–21. All page references to *Heart of Darkness* will be included after quotations in the text.

8 For his discussion of *Heart of Darkness* see *The Great Tradition*, Harmondsworth, Penguin, 1972 (1948), pp. 201–9.

9 Letter of 31 May 1902, quoted by H.M. Daleski, *Joseph Conrad: The Way of Dispossession*, London, Faber, 1977, p. 73.

10 Here, as elsewhere in this chapter, I have not given page references for explanations of Genette's terminology. These are easy to locate through the index to *Narrative Discourse*.

11 By Leavis, for example, op. cit., pp. 209–10, and by Allon White: 'Conrad's fantasy woman is an embarrassing mixture of Mata Hari and the Eternal Eve', 'Joseph Conrad and the rhetoric of enigma', in *The Uses of Obscurity: The Fiction of Early Modernism*, London, Routledge and Kegan Paul, 1981 (pp. 108–29), p. 128. White's reading of *Heart of Darkness* complements my own in so far as it also takes as its starting point the 'blatant obscurity' of the text.

12 Tony Tanner, ' "Gnawed Bones" and "Artless Tales" – eating and narrative in Conrad', in Norman Sherry, ed., *Joseph Conrad: A Commemoration*, London, 1976 (pp. 17–36), p. 31.

13 All italicizings of Conrad's text, here and elsewhere, are my own.

14 Quoted by Norman Sherry, *Conrad and his World*, London, Thames and Hudson, 1972, p. 97. Compare Marlow's comment: 'with solid pavement under your feet, surrounded by kind neighbours ready to cheer you or to fall on you, stepping delicately between the butcher and the policeman, in the holy terror of scandal and gallows and lunatic asylums – how can you imagine what particular region of the first ages a man's untrammelled feet may take him into by way of solitude?' (p. 85).

15 Eagleton, op. cit., p. 106.

Chapter 2 pp. 29–48

1 Raman Selden, *A Reader's Guide to Contemporary Literary Theory*, London, Harvester, 1985, pp. 67–8.

2 Henry James, *Selected Literary Criticism*, ed. Morris Shapira, London, Heinemann, 1963, p. 58.

3 As with much structuralist theory, it is Saussurean linguistics which provides both base and model. Ann Jefferson summarizes the point succinctly: 'since language is a self-sufficient system, meaning is not determined by the subjective intentions and wishes of its speakers: it is not the speaker who directly imparts meaning to his utterances, but the linguistic system as a whole which produces it. Transposed onto literature, this at once excludes both the author and reality as points of departure for interpretation. A structuralist approach will dispense with these linchpins of traditional literary history and criticism in order to reveal the signifying systems at work in literature. Taking its cue from structural linguistics, it will concentrate on the signifiers at the expense of the signifieds. It will be concerned with the way in which meaning is produced rather than with meaning itself. Genette speaks of this change in emphasis as a restoration of equilibrium in literary studies: "Literature had been regarded as a message without a code for such a long time, that it became necessary to regard it momentarily as 'a code without a message' . . . The 'structuralist method' consists in an analysis of the 'immanent structures' of a work in contrast with what Wellek and Warren call the extrinsic approach". Ann Jefferson and David Robey, eds., *Modern Literary Theory. A Comparative Introduction*, London, Batsford, 1982, p. 87.

4 Cf. Diana Knight's discussion of the term 'diegesis', pp. 16–20, above.

5 Jonathan Culler, *Structuralist Poetics: Structuralism, Linguistics and the Study of Literature*, London, Routledge & Kegan Paul, 1975, p. 230. Hereafter *SP*.

6 Particular and extreme instances of such theory are discussed by Ann Jefferson in her study of the French *nouveau roman*. She makes the point that even in the Jean Ricardou-defined 'era of the grammatical person', Alain Robbe-Grillet is able to admit that 'Man is present on

every page, in every line, in every word'. Jefferson elaborates: 'Robbe–Grillet is claiming that the existence of human beings in his fiction takes the form not of individuality and objective representation, but of anonymity and point of view'. *The Nouveau Roman and the Poetics of Fiction*, Cambridge, CUP, 1980, pp. 58–9.

7 Roland Barthes, *Image, Music, Text*, trs. Stephen Heath, London, Fontana, 1977, pp. 79–124. Hereafter *IMT*.

8 *The Compact Edition of the Oxford English Dictionary*, 1979, p. 2086.

9 A.J. Greimas, *Sémantique structurale*, Paris, Larousse, 1966, pp. 129 ff., cited and discussed by Barthes, *IMT*, pp. 106–7.

10 Roland Barthes, *S/Z*, trs. Richard Miller, New York, Hill and Wang, 1974, p. 92.

11 *In the Cage*, in Henry James, *In the Cage and Other Stories*, ed. S. Gorley Putt, Harmondsworth, Penguin, 1983. All references are to this edition and are contained in parentheses, with both chapter and page number, in the text.

12 Roland Barthes, 'The reality effect', in *French Literary Theory Today*, ed. Tzvetan Todorov, trs. R. Carter, Cambridge, CUP, 1982, p. 16.

13 Ann Jefferson, *op. cit.* p. 59, quoting from Alain Robbe-Grillet, *Pour un nouveau roman*, 1963, p. 28.

14 The term *mise en abyme*, first used by André Gide in his *Journal* of 1893, describes a process of internal repetition, of framing within frame, deployed in both literature and the plastic arts (as in the heraldic depiction of one coat-of-arms within another). The term has become a commonplace of structuralist analysis. It is most rigorously defined and illustrated by Jean Ricardou in 'Le récit abymé' in *Le Nouveau roman*, Seuil, Paris, 1973, pp. 47–75.

15 I deliberately echo Roland Barthes' essay 'The Death of the Author', *IMT*, pp. 142–8.

16 Jacques Lacan, 'The insistence of the letter in the unconscious', trs. Jan Miel, *Yale French Studies*, 36–7, 1966, p. 136.

17 Diana Knight's definition. See footnote 4.

Chapter 3 pp. 49–66

1 See the introduction and conclusion to Terry Eagleton, *Literary Theory: An Introduction*, Oxford, Blackwell, 1983, and Tony Bennett, *Formalism and Marxism*, London, Methuen, 1979.

2 The essay was first published as 'Erzählen oder Beschreiben? Zur Diskussion über Naturalismus und Formalismus', *Internationale Literatur*, 11, 1936, pp. 100–18, and 12, 1936, pp. 108–23. It is normally reprinted without the final section, which discusses problems in Soviet literature, and my references are to the reprint in Peter Bürger (ed.), *Seminar: Literature- und Kunstsoziologie*, Frankfurt am Main, Suhrkamp, 1978, pp. 72–115. Translations from the essay are my own,

and any divergences between my account of 'Narrate or Describe?' and the published version in Georg Lukács, *Writer and Critic and Other Essays*, trs. and ed. Arthur Kahn, London, Merlin, 1978, pp. 110–48, merely reflect the inadequacies of the Merlin translation.

3 Fredric Jameson, *Marxism and Form: Twentieth-Century Dialectical Theories of Literature*, Princeton UP, 1971, p. 196.

4 Peter Bürger, *Vermittlung-Rezeption-Funktion: Ästhetische Theorie und Methodologie der Literaturwissenschaft*, Frankfurt am Main, Suhrkamp, p. 35.

5 For further discussion see David Pike, *German Writers in Soviet Exile, 1933–1945*, Chapel Hill, North Carolina UP, 1982, pp. 261–75.

6 Karl Marx, 'Preface', *A Contribution to the Critique of Political Economy*, trs. S.W. Ryazanskaya, ed. Maurice Dobb, Moscow, Progress Publishers, 1970, p. 21.

7 For a useful introduction to Marxian theory see Peter Singer, *Marx*, Oxford, OUP, 1980.

8 Lukács's valorization of drama and his aesthetic theorizing in general are heavily influenced by Hegel, even at this stage in his career. Further discussion of his views on drama and the epic at this time may be found in Georg Lukács, *The Historical Novel*, trs. Hannah and Stanley Mitchell, Harmondsworth, Penguin, 1981, pp. 103–79. For a brief but succinct account of Hegel's theory of drama see Steve Giles, *The Problem of Action in Modern European Drama*, Stuttgart, Heinz, 1981, pp. 11–18.

9 The Merlin translation renders *Weltanschauung* as 'ideology', despite the fact that the standard German term for ideology is *Ideologie*. I have preferred to leave *Weltanschauung* untranslated given the specific connotations Lukács attributes to it.

10 In the 'world of Prose',

> the universal principles which have to guide human action are no longer part and parcel of a whole people's *heart* and attitude of *mind* but already appear objectively and independently as a just and legal order, firmly established on its own account, as a prosaic arrangement of things, as a political constitution, and as moral and other prescriptions; the result is that man's substantive obligations enter as a necessity external to him, not immanent in himself, and compelling him to recognize their validity.

(G.W.F. Hegel, *Aesthetics: Lectures on Fine Art*, trs. T.M. Knox, Oxford, Clarendon, 1975, Volume II, p. 1046).

For further discussion see Hegel, op. cit., Volume I, pp. 193–4 and Volume II, pp. 1046–52, and Jameson, op. cit., pp. 352–4.

11 All references will be to D. H. Lawrence, *St Mawr, The Virgin and the Gipsy*, Harmondsworth, Penguin, 1984.

12 The only notable exceptions are analepses on pp. 15, 116–19, 148–60.

13 For further examples of free indirect discourse see pp. 37 (Mrs Witt), 43 (Rico), 141–4 (Phoenix).
14 For further examples of scenic presentation see pp. 19–20, 24, 54–8, 61–4, 67–70, 88–92, 110–15, 126–31, 162–5.
15 For further discussion see Jameson, op. cit., pp. 165–9 and 196–202.
16 My application of rhetorical categories is based on Jacques Dubois et al., *Allgemeine Rhetorik*, München, Fink, 1974. *St Mawr* is particularly notable for its use of pleonasm (pp. 14, 16, 18, 26, 39, 45, 77, 80, 82–3, 94, 97, 107, 153, 157, 164) and polysyndeton (11, 12, 101, 133, 153–4, 164).
17 See D.H. Lawrence, *Fantasia of the Unconscious*, London, Heinemann, 1961, pp. 9–10.
18 For illustrations of Lawrence's political views see ibid., pp. 5, 73, 91, 179.
19 See *St Mawr*, pp. 94, 98, 122.
20 Lawrence, *Fantasia of the Unconscious*, p. 83.
21 For further discussion see Fredric Jameson, *The Political Unconscious: Narrative as a Socially Symbolic Act*, London, Methuen, 1981, pp. 9–102.
22 It could also be argued that in Balzac's case, his insights into the mechanisms of capitalist society derive from an ideological commitment to the *ancien régime* that distances him from the dominant tendencies of the age and thereby releases a critical perspective, and that Balzac was a specialist rather than a non-specialist writer. This would further weaken Lukács's account of the relationship between textual strategies and the writer's societal position.
23 This is not to say that Hegel's aesthetic categories have no epistemological value: for further discussion see Giles, op. cit., passim.

Chapter 4 pp. 67–87

1 Kate Millett, *Sexual Politics*, London, Virago, 1977, pp. 26 and 23. Subsequent page references will be given after quotations in the text.
2 Ann Oakley, *Sex, Gender and Society*, London, Temple Smith, 1972, pp. 156–7. Subsequent page references will be given after quotations in the text.
3 Elaine Showalter, 'Feminist criticism in the wilderness' in Elizabeth Abel, ed., *Writing and Sexual Difference*, Brighton, Harvester, 1982, p. 14.
4 Cheri Register, 'American feminist literary criticism: a bibliographical introduction', in Josephine Donovan, ed., *Feminist Literary Criticism: Explorations in Theory*, Lexington, Kentucky UP, 1975, p. 3.
5 Stuart Hutchinson, 'James's *In the Cage*: a new interpretation', *Studies in Short Fiction*, 19, 1982, p. 24.
6 Heath Moon, 'More royalist than the king: the governess, the

telegraphist, and Mrs. Gracedew', *Criticism*, 24, 1982, p. 34.

7 Walter Wright, *The Madness of Art: A Study of Henry James*, Lincoln, Nebraska UP, 1962, p. 175.

8 Charles T. Samuels, *The Ambiguity of Henry James*, Urbana, Illinois UP, 1971, p. 154.

9 Leon Edel, 'Introduction' to *The Complete Tales of Henry James, Volume 10, 1898–1899*, ed. Leon Edel, London, Hart-Davis, 1964, p. 10. Subsequent page references will be given after quotations in the text.

10 E. Duncan Aswell (quoted in Heath Moon, op. cit., p. 31).

11 Ralf Norrman, 'The intercepted telegram plot in Henry James's "In the Cage" ', *Notes and Queries*, 222, 1977, p. 425. Subsequent page references will be given after quotations in the text.

12 L. C. Knights, *Explorations: Essays in Criticism, Mainly in the Literature of the Seventeenth Century*, London, Chatto and Windus, 1963, p. 165.

13 Henry James, *In the Cage*, collected in *In the Cage and Other Stories*, ed. S. Gorley Putt, Harmondsworth, Penguin, 1983, p. 51. Subsequent page references will be given after quotations in the text.

14 Judith Fetterley, *The Resisting Reader: A Feminist Approach to American Fiction*, Bloomington, Indiana UP, 1978, p. 116. Subsequent page references will be given after quotations in the text.

15 Patricia Stubbs, *Women and Fiction: Feminism and the Novel, 1880–1920*, London, Methuen, 1981, p. 156. Subsequent page references will be given after quotations in the text.

16 See, for example, Seymour Chatman's *The Late Style of Henry James*, Oxford, Blackwell, 1972.

17 Henry James, *The Art of the Novel: Critical Prefaces*, ed. R. P. Blackmur, New York, Scribner's, 1962, p. 155. Subsequent page references will be given after quotations in the text.

18 Françoise Basch, *Relative Creatures: Victorian Women in Society and the Novel, 1837–1867*, trs. A. Rudolph, London, Allen Lane, 1974, p. 270.

19 Alfred Habegger, *Gender, Fantasy and Realism in American Literature*, New York, Columbia UP, 1982, p. 361.

20 Philip Rahv, 'Paleface and Redskin' in *Image and Idea: Twenty Essays on Literary Themes*, Norfolk, Conn., New Directions, 1957, p. 1.

21 Ruth Bernard Yeazell, 'Podsnappery and Sexuality', *Critical Inquiry*, 9, 1982, p. 344.

22 Juliet Mitchell, *Women's Estate*, Harmondsworth, Penguin, 1973, p. 59.

23 Michèle Barrett, *Women's Oppression Today: Problems in Marxist Feminist Analysis*, London, Verso, 1980, p. 12.

24 Cora Kaplan, 'Radical feminism and literature: rethinking Millett's sexual politics' in Mary S. Evans, ed., *The Woman Question: Readings on the Subordination of Women*, London, Fontana, 1982, p. 395.

Chapter 5 pp. 89–113

1 Elizabeth Wright, 'Modern Psychoanalytic Criticism', in *Modern Literary Theory: A Comparative Introduction*, eds. A. Jefferson and David Robey, London, Batsford, rev. ed., 1986, p. 145.
2 Jacques Lacan, *Ecrits*, trs. Alan Sheridan, London, Tavistock, 1977, pp. 57–8.
3 Sigmund Freud, *The Interpretation of Dreams*, trs. James Strachey, London, Allen & Unwin, 1954, p. 314. Subsequent page references will be given after quotations in the text.
4 Sigmund Freud, *The Psychopathology of Everyday Life*, ed. A. A. Brill, London, Collins, 1958, p. 4.
5 D.H. Lawrence, *St Mawr* and *The Virgin and the Gypsy*, Harmondsworth, Penguin, 1984, pp. 19 and 21. Subsequent page references will be given after quotations in the text.
6 See R.S. Crane, 'The Houyhnhnms, the Yahoos and the history of ideas', conveniently reprinted in *Penguin Critical Anthologies: Jonathan Swift*, ed. Denis Donoghue, Harmondsworth, Penguin, 1971, pp. 363–85.
7 Søren Kierkegaard, *Letters and Documents*, trs. Henrik Rosenmeier, Princeton, N.J., Princeton UP, 1978, pp. 268–9.
8 D. H. Lawrence, *The First Lady Chatterley*, Harmondsworth, Penguin, 1973, pp. 24–39.
9 Sigmund Freud, *Beyond the Pleasure Principle*, in vol. 11, *On Metapsychology*, in the Pelican Freud Library, Harmondsworth, Penguin, 1984, p. 316. Subsequent references will be given after quotations in the text.
10 Anthony Wilden's commentary in *The Language of the Self*, to Jacques Lacan's 'The function of language in psychoanalysis', Baltimore, Johns Hopkins UP, 1968, p. 174. Subsequent references will be given after quotations in the text.
11 I am grateful to Professor David Smail for some of the ideas and connections in the preceding two paragraphs. See his recent *Illusion and Reality: The Meaning of Anxiety*, London, Dent, 1984.

Chapter 6 pp. 115–34

1 See Katerina Clark and Michael Holquist, *Mikhail Bakhtin*, Cambridge, Mass., Harvard U P, 1984, and Nina Perlina, 'Bakhtin-Medvedev-Voloshinov: an apple of discourse', *University of Ottawa Quarterly*, 53, 1, 1983, pp. 35–47.

2   V.N. Voloshinov, *Marxism and the Philosophy of Language*, trs. L. Matejka and I.R. Titunik, New York, Seminar Press, 1973, p. 24.

3   V.N. Voloshinov, *Freudianism: A Marxist Critique*, trs. I.R. Titunik, New York, Academic Press, 1976, p. 79.

4   See footnote 19.

5   Clark and Holquist, op. cit., p. 275.

6   M.M. Bakhtin, *The Dialogic Imagination*, trs. Caryl Emerson and Michael Holquist, Austin, Texas U P, 1981, p. 170.

7   Ibid., p. 250.

8   Ibid., p. 284.

9   Ibid., p. 293.

10   Ibid., p. 299.

11   Ibid., p. 366.

12   The similarities here to Georg Lukács' ideas on typicality are significant. The two critics are briefly compared in Eva Corredar's 'Lukács and Bakhtin: a dialogue on fiction', *University of Ottawa Quarterly*, 53, 1, 1983, pp. 97–107.

13   Bakhtin, *Dialogical Imagination*, p. 300.

14   Bakhtin, *Problems of Dostoevsky's Poetics*, trs. Caryl Emerson, Manchester, Manchester U P, 1984, p. 32.

15   Bakhtin, *Dialogical Imagination*, p. 371.

16   See Ken Hirschkop, 'A response to the forum on Mikhail Bakhtin', *Critical Inquiry*, 11, 4, June 1985, pp. 672–8, and Gary Saul Morson's reply in the same issue, pp. 679–86.

17   Joseph Conrad, *Heart of Darkness*, ed. Paul O'Prey, Harmondsworth, Penguin, 1983 (1902), p. 27. Subsequent page references will be given after quotations in the text.

18   Edward Said, *The World, The Text, The Critic*, London, Faber and Faber, 1984, p. 102.

19   Bakhtin's critique of Freudian psychology emphasizes the social rather than the individual. For Freud's intra-psychic split between conscious and unconscious he substitutes an opposition between levels of discourse and their availability to the individual. The official and available discourse aims at unity and coherence, a singleness of meaning. The other repressed languages make their presence felt implicitly, in being the not-spoken which, within the system of language, allows the spoken to mean, by dialogizing the 'official' language, and causing slippage, confusion and proliferation of meanings. This is another and intriguing way of looking at Freud's recognition of the role of language in our knowledge of the unconscious, and Julia Kristeva has developed the relation between Bakhtin and Lacan's extensions of Freud through the idea of the expressions of self through the other of language and the structuring of the unconscious as a language (see *Desire in Language: A Semiotic*

Approach to Literature and Art, trs. T. Gora, A. Jardine and L.S. Roudiez, Oxford, Basil Blackwell, 1980). Where Freud threw into question the idea of a single unified self or psyche in which meaning resided, Bakhtin questions the separateness and definability of the psyche itself, seeing it as possessing 'extra-territorial status...as a social entity that penetrates inside the organism of the individual person' (quoted in Morson, op. cit., p. 683).

The self, then, is just as radically decentred as in recent theories of deconstruction, but in place of the endless and corrosive scepticism about the probability of Meaning in the singular, Bakhtin insists on the historical and social determinations of meanings in the plural.

20 See Dell Hymes, ed., *Reinventing Anthropology*, New York, Vintage, 1972, and Kevin Dwyer, 'On the dialogic of fieldwork', *Dialectical Anthropology*, 2, 1977, pp. 143–51.

21 See, for instance, the treatment of this episode in Peter Brooks, *Reading For The Plot*, Oxford, Clarendon, 1984, and Peter J. Glassman, *Joseph Conrad and the Literature of Personality*, New York, Columbia U P, 1976.

22 See Linda Hutcheon, 'The carnivalesque and contemporary narrative: popular culture and the erotic' and M.-Pierette Maleuzynsky, 'Mikhail Bakhtin and contemporary narrative theory', *University of Ottawa Quarterly*, 53, 1, 1983.

23 Fredric Jameson, *The Political Unconscious: Narrative As A Socially Symbolic Act*, London, Methuen, 1981, pp. 221–2.

Chapter 7 pp. 135–57

1 F. R. Leavis, *D.H. Lawrence: Novelist*, Harmondsworth, Penguin Books, 1973, p. 17. All page references will be given after quotations in the text.

2 Roland Barthes, *S/Z*, trs. Richard Miller, London, Cape, 1975. All page references will be given after quotations in the text.

3 Elaine Showalter, 'Towards a feminist poetics', in *Women Writing and Writing about Women*, ed. Mary Jacobus, London, Croom Helm, 1984, p. 39. All page references will be given after quotations in the text.

4 Kate Millett, *Sexual Politics*, Garden City, N.Y., Doubleday & Co., 1970, pp. 237–93.

5 Jonathan Culler, *On Deconstruction: Theory and Criticism after Structuralism*, London, Routledge and Kegan Paul, 1983. All page references will be given after quotations in the text.

6 Evelyn J. Hines, ed., *A Woman Speaks*, Chicago, Swallow Press, 1975. p. 152.

7 Judith Fetterley, *The Resisting Reader: A Feminist Approach to American Fiction*, Bloomington, Indiana U P, 1978.

8 D.H. Lawrence, *St Mawr* and *The Virgin and the Gypsy*, Harmondsworth, Penguin Books, 1984. The fragments of text I analyse are on pp. 11–12 and p. 22. All other page references will be given after quotations in the text.
9 Roland Barthes, 'Textual analysis of Poe's "Valdemar" ', in *Untying the Text: A Post-Structuralist Reader*, ed. Robert Young, London, Routledge and Kegan Paul, 1981, p. 139.
10 David H. Farmer, *The Oxford Dictionary of Saints*, Oxford, Clarendon Press, 1978, p. 274.
11 Juliet Mitchell, *Women: the Longest Revolution. Essays in Feminism, Literature and Psychoanalysis*, London, Virago Press, 1984, p. 64, quoting Aristotle: 'woman is as it were, an impotent male, for it is through a certain incapacity that the female is female'.
12 Lawrence, under a pseudonym, had written a history text book in which the essentially unchanging nature of human beings is the dominant theme. See Lawrence H. Davidson, *Movements in European History*, Oxford U P, 1918.
13 Mary Daly, *Pure Lust*, Boston, Beacon Press, 1984, p. 112.
14 Roland Barthes, 'Authors and Writers', in his *Collected Essays*, trs. Richard Howard, Evanston, Northwestern U P, 1972, p. 144.
15 *Roland Barthes by Roland Barthes*, trs. Richard Howard, New York, Hill and Wang, 1977, p. 138.
16 For a general introduction to psychoanalytical criticism see Elizabeth Wright, *Psychoanalytic Criticism: Theory in Practice*, London, Methuen, 1984. In particular see pp. 39–45, for an account of Marie Bonaparte's methodology, and pp. 113–22 for an account of Lacan.
17 Simone de Beauvoir, *The Second Sex*, trs. H.M. Parshley, Harmondsworth, Penguin Books, 1972, p. 253.

Chapter 8 pp. 159–80

1 Jacques Derrida, *Of Grammatology*, trs. Gayatri Chakravorty Spivak, Baltimore, Johns Hopkins UP, 1976, p. 14. All page references will be given after quotations in the text.
2 Derrida, *Margins of Philosophy*, trs. Alan Bass, Brighton, Harvester, 1982, p. 135.
3 Roger Poole, review of *Of Grammatology, Notes and Queries*, April 1979, p. 189.
4 Barbara Johnson, *The Critical Difference: Essays in the Contemporary Rhetoric of Reading*, Baltimore, Johns Hopkins UP, 1980, pp. x–xi. All page references will be given after quotations in the text.
5 Derrida, *Speech and Phenomena and Other Essays on Husserl's Theory of Signs*, trs. David B. Allison, Evanston, Northwestern UP, 1973, p. 51. All page references will be given after quotations in the text, including references to the two essays contained in *Speech and*

Phenomena: 'Form and Meaning: A Note on the Phenomenology of Language' and 'Differance'.

6 Ferdinand de Saussure, *Course in General Linguistics*, trs. Wade Baskin, eds. Charles Bally and Albert Sechehaye in collaboration with Albert Riedlinger, Glasgow, Fontana, 1974, p. 120. Quoted by Derrida in *Speech and Phenomena*, p. 140.

7 See Paul de Man, 'Intentional structure of the romantic image', in Harold Bloom, ed., *Romanticism and Consciousness: Essays in Criticism*, New York, Norton, 1970, pp. 65–77; and de Man, 'The rhetoric of intentionality', in his *Blindness and Insight: Essays in the Rhetoric of Contemporary Criticism*, 2nd ed., revised, London, Methuen, 1983, pp. 187–228. All page references to *Blindness and Insight* will be given after quotations in the text.

8 Ann Jefferson, 'Structuralism and post-structuralism', in Ann Jefferson and David Robey, eds., *Modern Literary Theory: A Comparative Introduction*, London, Batsford, rev. ed., 1986, p. 113.

9 Derrida, 'Structure, sign and play in the discourse of the human sciences', in Richard Macksey and Eugenio Donato, eds. and trs., *The Structuralist Controversy: The Languages of Criticism and the Sciences of Man*, Baltimore, Johns Hopkins UP, 1970, p. 247. All page references will be given after quotations in the text.

10 Henry James, *In the Cage* (1898), collected in *In the Cage and Other Stories*, ed. S. Gorley Putt, Harmondsworth, Penguin, 1983, p. 23. All page references will be given after quotations in the text.

11 Ralf Norrman, 'The intercepted telegram plot in Henry James's "In the Cage" ', *Notes and Queries*, 222, 1977, pp. 425 and 427; Charles T. Samuels, *The Ambiguity of Henry James*, Urbana, Illinois UP, 1971, p. 151; Peter Messent, 'Introduction' to Henry James, *Selected Tales*, eds. Peter Messent and Tom Paulin, London, Dent, 1982, pp. xix and xx; Tony Tanner, *The Reign of Wonder: Naivety and Reality in American Literature*, Cambridge, CUP, 1977, pp. 310–19; Walter F. Wright, *The Madness of Art: A Study of Henry James*, Lincoln, Nebraska UP, 1962, pp. 173–5; and Stuart Hutchinson, 'James's *In the Cage*: a new interpretation', *Studies in Short Fiction*, 19, 1982, pp. 19–25. All page references to Norrman, Wright and Hutchinson will be given after quotations in the text.

12 De Man, 'Genesis and genealogy in Nietzsche's *The Birth of Tragedy*', *Diacritics*, 2, 4, 1972, p. 44. For de Man, analysing 'semantic structures' is a necessary, first, formalist step in resisting a loose use of 'context'.

13 Friedrich Nietzsche, *The Will to Power*, trs. Walter Kaufmann and R. J. Hollingdale, ed. Kaufmann, New York, Vintage, 1968, p. 290.

14 Roland Barthes, *S/Z*, trs. Richard Miller, New York, Hill and Wang, 1974, p. 132.

15 L. C. Knights, *Explorations: Essays in Criticism, Mainly in the Literature of the Seventeenth Century*, London, Chatto and Windus, 1963, p. 164.

16 Heath Moon, 'More royalist than the king: the governess, the telegraphist, and Mrs. Gracedew', *Criticism*, 24, 1982, pp. 16–35.

17 J. Hillis Miller, 'Narrative and history', *English Literary History*, 41, 1974, pp. 459–60. All page references will be given after quotations in the text.

18 Michael Ryan, *Marxism and Deconstruction: A Critical Articulation*, Baltimore, Johns Hopkins UP, 1982, p. 39. Fredric Jameson keeps some distance, at least, from deconstruction but can none the less refer to class as 'a *differential* concept . . . at once a way of relating to and of refusing others'. *Marxism and Form: Twentieth-Century Dialectical Theories of Literature*, Princeton, N.J., Princeton UP, 1974, p. 380.

19 See Leon Edel, 'Introduction' to *The Complete Tales of Henry James: 1898–1899*, vol. 10, London, Rupert Hart-Davis, 1964, pp. 9–10.

20 Derrida, 'Living On. BORDER LINES', trs. James Hulbert, in Harold Bloom, Paul de Man, Jacques Derrida, Geoffrey H. Hartman, J. Hillis Miller, *Deconstruction and Criticism*, London, Routledge and Kegan Paul, 1979, p. 77.

21 Henry James, *The Portrait of a Lady*, Harmondsworth, Penguin, 1976, p. 13.

22 Derrida, 'The purveyor of truth', trs. Willis Domingo, James Hulbert, Moshe Ron and Marie-Rose Logan, *Yale French Studies*, 52, 1975–6, p. 107.

23 Henry James, *The Art of the Novel: Critical Prefaces*, ed, R. P. Blackmur, New York, Scribner's, 1962, p. 154. All page references will be given after quotations in the text.

24 See John Carlos Rowe, *The Theoretical Dimensions of Henry James*, London, Methuen, 1985, ch. 7.

25 James Kearns and Ken Newton, 'An interview with Jacques Derrida', *The Literary Review*, 14, 18 April – 1 May 1980, p. 21. All page references will be given after quotations in the text.

26 See Shoshana Felman, 'Turning the screw of interpretation', *Yale French Studies*, 55–6, 1977, pp. 94–207.

Chapter 9 pp. 181–200

1 Pierre Macherey, *A Theory of Literary Production*, trs. Geoffrey Wall, London, Routledge and Kegan Paul, 1978. Subsequent page references will be given after quotations in the text.

2 Etienne Balibar and Pierre Macherey, 'Interview', *Diacritics*, 12, 1, 1982, p. 49.

3 Joseph Conrad, *Heart of Darkness*, ed. Paul O'Prey, Penguin,

Harmondsworth, 1983 (1902). Subsequent page references will be given after quotations in the text.

4 Terry Eagleton, 'Pierre Macherey and Marxist literary criticism', in G.H.R. Parkinson, ed., *Marx and Marxisms*, Cambridge, CUP, 1982, p. 150.

5 T.B. Bottomore and M. Rubel, eds., Karl Marx, *Selected Writings in Sociology and Social Philosophy*, Harmondsworth, Penguin, 1963, pp. 86, 67, 90.

6 Alex Callinicos, *Marxism and Philosophy*, Oxford, Clarendon Press, 1983, p. 127. This is Callinicos' summary of Althusser's influential essay, 'Ideology, and ideological state apparatuses', now reprinted in the latter's *Essays on Ideology*, trs. Ben Brewster, London, Verso, 1984.

7 James H. Kavanagh, 'Marxism's Althusser: toward a politics of literary theory', *Diacritics*, 12, 1, 1982, p. 27.

8 ibid. p. 26.

9 Quoted in C.B. Cox, ed., *Conrad: Heart of Darkness, Nostromo, Under Western Eyes*, London, Macmillan, 1981, p. 23.

10 Marx, op. cit., p. 84.

11 Fredric Jameson, *The Political Unconscious: Narrative as a Socially Symbolic Act*, London, Methuen, 1981, p. 214.

12 Hunt Hawkins, 'Conrad's critique of imperialism in *Heart of Darkness*', *PMLA*, 94, 1979, pp. 286–99.

13 Pierre Macherey, 'L'histoire de la philosophie considérée comme une lutte de tendances', *La Pensée*, 185, 1979, pp. 3–25.

Index

1. Concepts

actant theory, 30–7 *passim*, 40–48 *passim*, 154–5
aesthetics,
  in Genette, 14, 27
  in Lukács, 59–60, 65, 204n, 205n
  in Marxist criticism, 49, 192, 200
ambiguity, 113, 164
anachrony, 18
analepsis, 18, 20, 21, 26, 204
antithesis, 143, 145, 146, 151–4 *passim*
aporia, 93–4, 113
  see also undecidability
author/writer, 5, 6–7
  in Bakhtin, 120–1, 122, 123, 124
  in Barthes, 43, 137, 144, 148, 149, 153, 155–6, 203n
  in Derrida, 163, 164–5, 172, 175–8 *passim*
  in Freud, 96
  in Lacan, 93
  in Lukács, 51–3 *passim*, 54, 61–2, 63, 64, 205n
  in Millett, 71, 75, 78, 85
  in structuralism, 202n

capitalism,
  in feminism, 86
  in Lukács, 50, 52–3, 60, 62, 63, 65, 66, 205n
carnivalization, 116, 121, 122, 129, 130, 131, 209n
castration complex, 98
centrifugal forces, 119, 131
centripetal forces, 119
character, *see* structuralism: character theory
chiasmus, 103
chronotope, 119
class-system,
  in Bakhtin, 121
  in criticism of Henry James, 164, 171
  in deconstruction, 172, 176–7
  in Jameson, 47, 212n
  in Lukács, 50, 56
  in structuralism, 36, 38, 46, 47
closure, 159, 160, 164, 165, 175, 177, 178
codes, 134–57 *passim*

actional/proairetic, 135, 144–5
cultural/referential, 135, 141, 142, 144, 145
hermeneutic, 47, 135, 137, 141, 154
of irony, 145
of misogyny, 142
semic, 33, 135, 138, 142, 143, 151, 154, 155
symbolic, 135, 145, 152, 155
colonialism, 130, 132
  in dialogics, 130
  in Marxist criticism, 185–97 *passim*
condensation, 90, 91
connotation, 35
content,
  in Bakhtin, 118
  in Lacan, 105, 106, 155
  in Marxist criticism, 49, 192

deconstruction, 2, 139, 159–80 *passim*, 183–4, 209, 212
  and dialogics, 209n
  and feminism, 71, 74, 180
  and Marxism, 179, 180, 183–4
  and structuralism, 46–7, 161
denotation, 35
description,
  in Barthes, 154
  in Lukács, 50, 51–2, 53, 55–6, 60–5 *passim*
diachrony, 40, 117
dialogics, 115–34 *passim*
  and deconstruction, 209n
  and formalism, 116–8 *passim*, 133
  and Marxism, 115–7 *passim*, 132–31, 208–9n
dialogue, *see* dialogics
diegesis, 16–8, 19–20, 21, 25, 26, 31, 44, 45, 202
différance, 46
displacement,
  in deconstruction, 174, 177, 178
  in Freud, 90
  in history, 195
  in Lacan, 105, 155
dissemination, 46, 177
divagations, 141
drama, 50, 55
dream, 101
  rhetoric of, 89–92 *passim*